BARBARA PYM
Writing a Life

by
Orphia Jane Allen

The Scarecrow Press, Inc.
Metuchen, N.J., & London
1994

British Library Cataloguing-in-Publication data available

Library of Congress Cataloging-in-Publication Data

Allen, Orphia Jane, 1937-
    Barbara Pym : writing a life / by Orphia Jane Allen.
        p.   cm.
    Includes bibliographical references (p.)
    ISBN 0-8108-2875-8 (acid-free)
    1. Pym, Barbara.   2. Women novelists, English—20th cen-
tury—Biography.   I. Title.
PR6066.Y58Z54   1994
823'.914—dc20
    [B]   94-18867

For

Orphia Campbell Corpening
Rachel Emma Corpening Allen

Do you suppose that
when grandma dies
more of her stays than goes?
—Paula Gunn Allen

CONTENTS

PERMISSION ACKNOWLEDGMENTS

PENGUIN USA

From AN ACADEMIC QUESTION by Barbara Pym, Hazel Holt, & Hilary Walton, Ed. Copyright © 1968 by Hilary Walton; note copyright © 1986 by Hazel Holt. Used by permission of the publisher, Dutton, an imprint of New American Library, a division of Penguin Books USA Inc.

From CIVIL TO STRANGERS: AND OTHER WRITINGS by Barbara Pym, Edited by Hazel Holt. Copyright © 1987 by Hilary Walton and Hazel Holt. Used by permission of the publisher, Dutton, an imprint of New American Library, a division of Penguin Books USA Inc.

From CRAMPTON HODNET by Barbara Pym, Hilary Walton, & Hazel Holt, Ed. Copyright © 1985 by Hilary Walton. Used by permission of the publisher, Dutton, an imprint of New American Library, a division of Penguin Books USA Inc.

From EXCELLENT WOMEN by Barbara Pym. Copyright 1952, 1978 by Barbara Pym. Used by permission of the publisher, Dutton, an imprint of New American Library, a division of Penguin Books USA Inc.

From A FEW GREEN LEAVES by Barbara Pym. Copyright © 1980 by Hilary Walton. Used by permission of the publisher, Dutton, an imprint of New American Library, a division of Penguin Books USA Inc.

From A GLASS OF BLESSINGS by Barbara Pym. Copyright © 1958 by Barbara Pym, renewed 1980 by Hilary Walton. Used by

ACKNOWLEDGMENTS

A book such as this cannot be written without a good deal of effort by scholars who, early on, recognize a writer's merit and call her to the attention of their colleagues and the public. In this respect, I am especially grateful from the early stages of this project to Janice Rossen, Jane Nardin, and Charles Burkhart, for it was their work that enriched my own appreciation of Barbara Pym.

In addition to those who initially inspired my study of Pym, there are others whose work I have synthesized and built upon in putting this book together; to them I express my gratitude. I am especially grateful to previous Pym bibliographers, Dale Salwak, Lorna Peterson, Judy Berndt, and Mary H. Myers.

I am also grateful to the many who have supported my work on this project. Thanks are due especially to New Mexico State University Library staff for helping me assemble the necessary materials: to Helen Barber, librarian; to Jeanne Howard, head of Collection Management; and to Interlibrary Loan staff Vita Montano, Esther Gil, Jivonna Stewart, Maria Luisa Serna, Katrina D'Andrea, and Maria Elena Lurie. Thanks go to Nancy King Bender and Diane Hendrix for research assistance, and to Nancy Rump for technical assistance. I thank, too, my granddaughter Kori Orphia Mooney for her help. And to my husband, Joseph H. Forsyth, I am grateful for his continued dialogue and his encouragement.

In the early stages of my research on Barbara Pym, I was assisted by a mini–grant (RC-89–002) from the New Mexico State University College of Arts and Sciences Research Center.

Grateful acknowledgment is made to the following for permission to quote from copyrighted materials:

To Penguin Books USA Inc., Macmillan London, and the Estate of Barbara Pym, permission to quote from *An Academic Question, Civil to Strangers, Crampton Hodnet, A Few Green*

Leaves, Quartet in Autumn, The Sweet Dove Died, An Unsuitable Attachment, and *A Very Private Eye: An Autobiography in Diaries and Letters.*

To Penguin Books USA Inc., Jonathan Cape, and the Estate of Barbara Pym, permission to quote from *Excellent Women, A Glass of Blessings, Jane and Prudence, Less Than Angels, No Fond Return of Love,* and *Some Tame Gazelle.*

To St. Martin's Press Inc. and Macmillan Press Ltd., permission to quote from *The World of Barbara Pym* by Janice Rossen.

To St. Martin's Press Inc. and Harvester Wheatsheaf, permission to quote from *Independent Women: The Function of Gender in the Novels of Barbara Pym* by Janice Rossen.

To the University of Iowa Press and Macmillan Press Ltd., permission to quote from *The Life and Work of Barbara Pym* by Dale Salwak (copyright © 1987 by Dale Salwak).

To West End Press, permission to quote from "Grandma's Dying Poem," *Skins and Bones: Poems 1979–87,* by Paula Gunn Allen.

LIST OF ABBREVIATIONS

Quotations from Pym's novels and from *A Very Private Eye: An Autobiography in Diaries and Letters* are from the Dutton editions, with citations abbreviated as follows:

AQ	*An Academic Question*
CH	*Crampton Hodnet*
CS	*Civil to Strangers*
EW	*Excellent Women*
FGL	*A Few Green Leaves*
GB	*A Glass of Blessings*
JP	*Jane and Prudence*
LTA	*Less Than Angels*
NFRL	*No Fond Return of Love*
QA	*Quartet in Autumn*
SDD	*The Sweet Dove Died*
STG	*Some Tame Gazelle*
UA	*An Unsuitable Attachment*
VPE	*A Very Private Eye: An Autobiography in Diaries and Letters*

INTRODUCTION

Barbara Pym died on January 11, 1980. In the decade since her death a substantial body of criticism has grown up around her novels, and she has come to be recognized as a leading post-World War II British novelist (Cotsell 2). Today there exist some sixteen books about Pym and her work, more than seventy articles in scholarly journals and collections, and hundreds of reviews of her novels.

This book is about Pym and her novels and about the critical response to her work. It includes biographical information, interpretations of the novels, a summary of the critical issues that have come to bear on her work, and a comprehensive bibliography, all designed to encourage the teaching of her novels in college and university courses and to assist scholars in further critical study of the novels and of Pym's contribution to English literature. For readers newly acquainted with Pym, this study offers background information on her life and an overview of the novels that will help to place her work in context and contribute to a deeper appreciation of her novels.

Pym's work is important for literary and historical reasons. Robert Emmet Long sees her as a "writer of first-rate talents, and one of the most original comic novelists to have written in England in the last thirty years" (*Barbara Pym* 211–12). Robert Liddell, a friend from her early years at Oxford, writes that the novels of Pym's early period "show how a large section of the community actually *lived*—and one day they will have an historical as well as a literary interest" (*Mind at Ease* 33). Robert Smith, author of the first critical essay on Pym's work, notes her "acute observation of a limited social scene" that makes the novels a "valuable record of their time, perhaps more valuable than anything an anthropological research team . . . could produce" ("How Pleasant to Know Miss Pym" 67).

Adding to their literary and historical value, Pym's novels are

timely in their treatment of feminist topics. Pym might never have
agreed that she was a feminist; her novels, however, have a special
relevance for women. Pym writes from a woman's point of view,
revealing life as it feels to women, and she does this without
evoking hostility in unsympathetic readers. Philip Larkin writes
that her "novels may look like 'women's books,' but no man can
read them and be quite the same again" ("World of Barbara
Pym" 260). Pym's humor makes the trivia and sometimes tragedy
of women's lives palatable to a wide range of readers. Just as
important is her genius for portraying the subtly ironic truth of
women's experience, the experience that keeps us saying one
thing and thinking another, all the time aware that both what we
say and what we think are true.

Pym was keenly aware of the contradictions implicit in the
social narrative by which many women live, the myth of romantic
love and deification of motherhood that says, in short, that a
woman's life must be validated by a husband. She knew that
validation didn't (and still doesn't) necessarily come with a
marriage certificate, but that sooner or later each woman must
validate her own life and that validation may come with or without
marriage. A reading of Pym's novels and *A Very Private Eye: An
Autobiography in Diaries and Letters,* compiled and published
posthumously by Hazel Holt, her literary executor, and Hilary
Pym, her sister, reveals that a part of Barbara Pym must have
wanted desperately to fall in love, get married, and live happily
ever after. She fell in love a number of times. She never married.
One can only speculate why. Perhaps her own integrity, her
inability to play the roles the men she loved expected her to play,
and their inability to accept her as she was were some of the
reasons for her remaining unmarried. At any rate, in her mid-
twenties she was describing herself as a spinster (VPE 67–71).
Some Tame Gazelle, her first published novel, started in 1934 but
not published until 1950, an acknowledged but playful autobiographical projection thirty years into the future of herself and
Hilary, portrays the two sisters as spinsters living together in a
country village. This uncanny prediction of the course her life was
to take indicates that Pym may have chosen, either consciously or
unconsciously, the role of spinsterhood in the face of conflicting
desires and social expectations. This conflict provides a tension
that recurs throughout her novels, contributing to a polyphonic

narrative style that enriches Pym's comic irony and is an important element of the signature of a Pym novel. Men and women throughout the novels seem at cross purposes in their relationships. Her women are compellingly attracted to men and influenced by myths of romantic love and happy marriages. The men they would love, however, are indifferent to love; their main concern is how women might be of use to them—typing, knitting, cooking, washing up after them.

Carolyn G. Heilbrun, in introducing *Writing a Woman's Life,* lists four ways of writing a woman's life:

> the woman herself may tell it, in what she chooses to call an autobiography; she may tell it in what she chooses to call fiction; a biographer, woman or man, may write the woman's life in what is called a biography; or *the woman may write her own life in advance of living it, unconsciously and without recognizing or naming the process.* (11; emphasis added)

Heilbrun goes on to suggest that, at times, "highly gifted women" may fail to lead "the conventional life, to find the conventional way early," signifying not that they have been "dealt a poor hand of cards," but rather that they may have formed their lives "in the service of a talent felt, but unrecognized and unnamed" (52–53). Pym, I believe, felt her talent early. And I believe that to some extent her unrequited-love relationships may have resulted from her unconscious urge to live the unconventional life in the service of her art. *Some Tame Gazelle* may indeed have been an unconscious writing of her own life as a spinster in the sense that Heilbrun describes.[1]

Each of Pym's novels is self-contained. Yet to read the novels in the context of her life can heighten the reading experience. An awareness of the facts of her life and seeing how she brings her

---

[1]Laura Doan, in her Introduction to *Old Maids to Radical Spinsters: Unmarried Women in the Twentieth-Century Novel,* defines the spinster as one whose "primary commitment in life is not to partnership but to independence and autonomy" (5). In "Pym's Singular Interest: The Self as Spinster," Doan cites Pym's letters and diary entries as indicating that Pym may consciously have chosen to remain a spinster, noting that "[f]or Pym, the act of writing and the process of self-definition are inextricably connected." Pym's focus on single women in her novels suggests that through her writing she sought "personal reconciliation" with her "unmarried state" and resolution of "her ambivalence toward marriage and sexuality" (141).

novelist's technique to that life to transmute the issues that
concerned her most contribute to a deeper appreciation of the
novels. Pym's novels exemplify the type of fictional self-writing
that Molly Hite cites as involving "more, rather than less, artistry
and artifice than the writing of other kinds of fiction" (xv).

Pym's Oxford education gave her a strong sense of the English
literary tradition, and her use of allusion throughout the novels
indicates that she was keenly aware of her own responsibility as
an author within the greater context of the canon. Her writing is, to
a large extent, in the novel of manners tradition, a fact that results
in frequent comparison with Jane Austen and considerable critical
argument on the topic. Her subtle wit and irony engage the reader
in the common round of English drawing room comedy, infusing
with energy and thus validating the trivia of women's lives.
Moreover, Pym's genius at transmuting autobiographical elements into fiction can be especially instructive as the reader marks
her use of literary techniques to charge everyday experience with
feeling, to transform life into fiction.

Each part of this four-part study is designed to be read and used
independently. Together the parts are intended to distill an
essence of Pym that will encourage further study. Part 1 briefly
introduces all thirteen of Pym's published novels, as well as
fragments collected in *Civil to Strangers and Other Writings,* in
the order in which they were written, relating some of the events
in her life—including the public reception of her work—to some
of the topics of the novels. Part 2 is a study of the ten novels that
Pym herself prepared for publication. Here the focus is on some of
the autobiographical elements in the novels that derive from
Pym's deeper concerns about issues surrounding romantic love,
the church, and literature. Attention is given to some of the
techniques Pym used in transmuting these issues into fiction and
to the evolution of theme as she proceeded to write her life. Part 3
is a bibliographic review essay that summarizes the scholarly
literature elicited by the novels and suggests areas for further
study. Finally, Part 4 is a comprehensive bibliography of primary
and secondary sources.

PART ONE—BARBARA PYM: HER LIFE AND WORK

During her sixty-seven years, Barbara Pym wrote and saw through publication eight novels and several short stories. Subsequently Hazel Holt, her literary executor, and Hilary Pym, her sister, arranged for the publication of several novels (two of which Pym prepared and clearly intended for publication), several of her short stories, and a radio talk.

Pym's reliance upon the common round of her own experience for much of the material of her novels compels those who study her work to read her novels in the context of her life. Further, reading the novels in the order in which she wrote them, with some knowledge of their public reception, contributes to a better understanding of the life of an important English novelist and a genuine appreciation of the fiction she created.

Barbara Mary Crampton Pym was born on June 2, 1913, in Oswestry, Shropshire, the first of two children born to Frederick Crampton and Irena Spenser Pym. A sister, Hilary, was born in 1916. Frederick Crampton Pym and Irena Spenser Thomas married when he was thirty-two and she was twenty-five. Irena was the youngest of ten chidren; her father, Edward Thomas of Oswestry, was an ironmonger. Frederick, the illegitimate son of Phoebe Pym, a domestic servant, set up practice as a solicitor in Oswestry after his marriage to Irena (VPE 1–2).[1]

Barbara and Hilary had a relatively comfortable childhood—Hilary describes it as "happy, unclouded" (VPE 2). When Barbara was a young child, the Pyms moved to Morda Lodge, a large redbrick Edwardian house on the outskirts of Oswestry. There they had the help of two maids, one who filled the role of nanny. The family attended Church of England services in Oswestry where Irena was assistant organist, Frederick sang bass in the choir, and Barbara and Hilary attended children's services.

The family was on "social terms with the vicar, curates, and organists," and entertaining curates at supper was "a long established tradition" (VPE 3). Thus Pym's treatment of the Church of England in her novels derives in part from the integral role of the church in her own life from early childhood.

EARLY YEARS AND THE JUVENILIA

Barbara Pym's literary career started early. According to Hilary, Barbara's "first (publicly recognized) creative work" was an operetta, "The Magic Diamond," performed at Morda Lodge in 1922 by Barbara, Hilary, and several of their cousins (VPE 3). In the operetta, which starred Barbara as Princess Rosebud and her cousin Neville Selway as Prince George, Princess Rosebud comes to the rescue of the Prince, offering to save him from the wizard's curse. Already, as Constance Malloy has noted, Barbara had "reversed the fairytale in which the man comes to the woman's rescue" ("Quest for a Career" 195).

When she was twelve, Barbara went away to boarding school at Liverpool College, Huyton, where she read widely, wrote poems and parodies, and chaired the Literary Society. When she was sixteen, Barbara wrote a novel titled "Young Men in Fancy Dress," inspired by her reading of Aldous Huxley's *Crome Yellow*. In this, "her first completed novel manuscript" (Wyatt-Brown, "Ellipsis, Eccentricity and Evasion in the Diaries of Barbara Pym" 35), Pym tells the story of Denis Feverel, a "young would-be writer," and begins to establish "her own style and fictional world by a process of parody of a fictional influence and a self-deprecating humour" (Cotsell, 11–12).

THE OXFORD YEARS AND THE EARLY NOVELS
(1931–1941)

In 1931, at age eighteen, Barbara went to Oxford to read English at St. Hilda's. Her close association with Oxford and her Oxford friends had a profound influence on her career as a novelist, providing the material of several of her novels and an inspiration that lasted throughout her life. Friends met at Oxford, including Robert Liddell and Henry Harvey, remained friends. The theme of unrequited love and her concern with the plight of the unmarried woman, issues that occupied her life as well as her novels, originated in her experiences in the years from 1931 to 1939.

The image of Pym portrayed in her letters and diaries of the 1930s seems not unusual for a young woman attending Oxford at that time. She had an active social life and was concerned with clothes and how she looked in them. She frequently mentions her fur coat and the outfits she wore: "I was dressed all in grey with a blue and white check blouse," or, playfully,

> I was wearing a brown check skirt, yellow short sleeved jersey—yellow suede coat—brown hat and Viyella scarf—flesh coloured fishnet stockings, brown and white ghillie shoes (blue celanese trollies—pink suspender belt—pink kestos—white vest)—brown gloves—umbrella. (VPE 21)

She also notes what others wear, describing Henry Harvey at one point with "his nice herring-boney grey tweed overcoat—also the pathetic green scarf and little brown leather gloves—lined with lambs-wool" (VPE 19).

Hilary tells us that Barbara was tall and good-looking, extrovertish, and entertaining. She had many admirers and attended an endless round of social functions. At Oxford, she decorated her room with checked gingham and embroidered her cushions with the name "Sandra," a name she chose to reflect "the more dashing aspects of her character." Hilary speculates that the name may have been a shortening of Cassandra or of Alexandra with its "overtones of Russian and Central European aristocracy" (VPE 9).

The diaries and letters of the period from 1931 to 1939 reflect a vivacious but somewhat naïve sentimentality that led Barbara to become romantically involved with several men. Her diary entries for 1932 indicate a close association with Rupert Gleadow, a fellow student. By 1933, her interest had focused on Henry Harvey, and she had become friends with Robert (Jock) Liddell and John Barnicot, friends of Harvey's; all three are important figures in her first published novel, *Some Tame Gazelle*. Barbara fell in love with Henry Harvey, and his ambivalence toward her affections had a lasting influence on her life and her fiction. Her passion for finding out about people by looking them up in references such as *Who's Who, Crockford,* and street directories, even going so far as to tail them, is evident in her early interest in Harvey's affairs. At one point in her diaries she writes of arranging to be at a particular location where she knows Harvey will pass by on his way to lecture. Another time she writes of following him to Balliol (VPE 34). This characteristic is expressed in her novels when she writes of doing " 'research into the lives of ordinary people' " and is portrayed in the sleuthing of Dulcie in *No Fond Return of Love* (VPE 10). In 1934 Harvey accepted an appointment at the University of Helsingfors, and by 1937 her dream of romance with him was dissolved by his marriage to Elsie Godenhjelm.

But there were other men who caught her attention during the 1930s. One was Harry Harker, a student at Oxford; another, Friedbert Gluck, whom she met on a National Union of Students tour of Germany in 1934. Pym's relationship with Friedbert continued for several years and involved an exchange of letters and visits to Germany in 1935 and 1937 (VPE 10). Her diary entries for 1934 reflect that she is at the same time seeing Harry Harker, who asked her to marry him (Holt, *Lot to Ask* 27), and is infatuated with both Harvey and Gluck (VPE 40–42). In addition, Holt tells of a relationship with Brian Mitchell, the brother of an Oxford friend, with whom Pym went on holiday in Scotland and who in 1935 took her "several times to meet his parents." Mitchell proposed to her, but "she was not in love with him" and refused to marry "simply 'to be married' " (*Lot to Ask* 58–59).

Another male figure who becomes the object of Pym's affections during her Oxford years and who appears in her fiction is Julian Amery, or "Jay," whom she met when she was twenty-four and he was eighteen. She saw him several times at Oxford and met his mother in Mayfair in 1939. A diary entry for July 1939 reflects the complexity of her feelings for Jay (VPE 92). Her attachment to him is reflected in the novels and short stories, mostly unpublished, that Pym wrote in the late 1930s.[2]

But her love affairs were not the only real-life subjects that made their way into Pym's novels. Her love of the homely, the everyday, the "trivial round" shows up in these early years. Not only did she concern herself with the minutiae of clothes and lipsticks, but she sewed many of her own clothes and frequently mentions her knitting.

An integral part of her life was the literature—the works of "the greater English poets"—that she read during these years and that made its way into her novels in numerous quotations and allusions. Her readings range from the diaries of Anthony à Wood to a rereading of Aldous Huxley's *Point Counterpoint.* She wishes that her "diary were as interesting and instructive" as Wood's diary (VPE 61)—a wish implied by Tom Dagnall in her final novel, *A Few Green Leaves.* The rereading of *Point Counterpoint* she compares with her first reading at age sixteen, when she found it "disjointed, muddled and boring." In 1933 she finds Huxley "the most interesting modern novelist" (VPE 24). Among the readings mentioned in the diaries for the Oxford years are Burton's *Anatomy of Melancholy;* Ivy Compton-Burnett's *More Women than Men;* Ronald Knox's *The Belief of Catholics;* the poems of Young and Betjeman; Byron's *Don Juan;* Keble's *The Christian Year;* and *Moll Flanders,* all reflecting her wide range of interests, and some of them furnishing lines and allusions for her novels. In December 1933, she writes, "I would love to be able to write a book like *Moll Flanders* which I'm reading slowly and thoroughly" (VPE 32).

After taking a second in English at St. Hilda's in 1934, Pym returned to Morda Lodge, where she lived with her parents and concentrated on her writing. In the autumn of 1938 she spent a few weeks in Katowice, Poland, where she had taken a job as a governess in the home of Dr. Michael Albert. Political circumstances caused her to return to England, however, where she joined Hilary in a flat in London. Hilary had by then completed a secretarial course and taken a secretarial job with the British Broadcasting Corp. (BBC). Barbara continued to write, noting in a letter to Elsie Godenhjelm Harvey a sense of happiness and well-being and the feeling that she could not be happy unless she were writing (VPE 86). During the years from 1939 to 1941 she lived again in Oswestry with her parents, writing, reading, and doing volunteer work in support of the war effort. Among other duties, she worked in the local YMCA soldiers' camp and at a first-aid post near her home and helped her mother care for several children evacuated from Birkenhead (Malloy, "Quest for a Career" 6).

In these years after coming down from Oxford, Pym expresses a strong sense of self in her letters and diaries. She is no longer the naïve young girl of the early diaries but a writer who can describe herself at twenty-six, as she does in a letter to Robert Liddell and Henry and Elsie Harvey, as a "so dull spinster which is like the old brown horse walking with a slow majestic dignity" (VPE 68). The light, humorous tone of this letter and Pym's ability, reflected in several letters of this period, to stand back and view herself from a distance point to her growing maturity and her strong sense of self. By this time her diaries reflect a greater objectivity, a tendency to look outward at the world and to penetrate with a novelist's eye the minute goings on around her. By 1941, still unpublished but with several novels written, Barbara was certain she was a writer.

Pym worked on at least eight separate novels during the years from 1934 to 1941: *Some Tame Gazelle, Civil to Strangers, Gervase and Flora, Crampton Hodnet,* a "Home Front" or "War" novel, a "Spy" novel, "Beatrice Wyatt; or, The Lumber Room," and "Something to Remember." All of these fictions reflect her experiences at Oxford and during the early years of the war before she went to work with the Censorship in Bristol in October 1941. Only one, *Some Tame Gazelle,* was published during her lifetime. *Civil to Strangers, Gervase and Flora, Crampton Hodnet,* the "Home Front" or "War" novel, and *So Very Secret* (the "Spy" novel) were edited by Holt and published posthumously. "Beatrice Wyatt" exists only in rough draft among Pym's papers at the Bodleian Library, Oxford. "Something to Remember," adapted as a radio play and aired by the BBC in 1950, also exists with drafts of the other novels in the papers at the Bodleian (VPE 184).

Pym started writing *Some Tame Gazelle* in 1934. In her diary for September 1 she writes: "Sometime in July I began writing a story about Hilary and me as spinsters of fiftyish. Henry, Jock and all of us appeared in it." Her diary indicates she is writing it " 'for Henry' "—"an excuse for revealing some of my present feelings about Henry" (VPE 44). She referred to *Some Tame Gazelle* as "my novel of real people" (VPE 45), and parallels can be drawn between her friends at Oxford and most of the characters. Belinda Bede is Barbara; her sister Harriet is Hilary. The Archdeacon Henry Hoccleve is Henry Harvey, and his wife Agatha is Alison

West-Watson, who at Oxford attracted Henry Harvey's attention. Harvey's close friends John Barnicot and Robert Liddell are represented in the novel by John Akenside and Dr. Nicholas Parnell. In *Some Tame Gazelle,* Parnell, like Robert Liddell in real life, is a librarian. Another Oxford friend, Honor Tracy, is portrayed in the novel as Edith Liversidge. And Barbara's friends Judith Packenham and Count Robert Weiss are portrayed as Lady Clara Boulding and Ricardo Bianco (VPE 11).

Pym completed *Some Tame Gazelle* in 1935 and sent it to Chatto and then to Gollancz. Both publishers rejected it. She then sent it to Jonathan Cape who, in August 1936, suggested some minor alterations. Pym made the changes, but Cape rejected the novel, writing that he personally liked the novel but feared that if he offered to publish it, the publishing house would ''be unable to give it all the care and attention . . . necessary if it is to be successfully launched.'' Distressed by the rejection, Pym set the novel aside until after the war when she revised it again and again sent it to Jonathan Cape, who published it in 1950 (VPE 11).

Some Tame Gazelle is set in a country village and follows six months in the lives of two fiftyish spinster sisters, Belinda and Harriet Bede. Belinda chastely dotes on the married Archdeacon Henry Hoccleve, whom she has loved for thirty years. Harriet dotes on young curates. Their comfortable and commonplace spinsterly way of life is threatened by the appearance of two outsiders in the village, Mr. Nathaniel Mold, who proposes to Harriet, and Bishop Theo Grote, who proposes to Belinda. Rebuffed by the spinster sisters, who prefer their already comfortable lives to the questionable futures offered by two insensitive, infantile males, the intruders go away—Mold back to his library, Grote engaged to Connie Aspinall, another village spinster. The sisters are left happy, their lives unchanged. A third intruder in the novel is Olivia Berridge, a young Agatha Hoccleve, who lures Harriet's young curate, Father Donne, into marriage. But all ends well; Father Donne is replaced by another curate, a pale young Italian even more in need of Harriet's motherly cooking and knitting than Father Donne had been. Life goes on.

One remarkable feature of this novel is that it is somewhat prophetic. It establishes a paradigm for Pym's work while at the same time anticipating the very turns her own life was to take. It is almost as if in writing the novel Pym determined the course of her

own life. First, *Some Tame Gazelle* establishes the pattern that
Pym would follow as a novelist. It exudes, line after line and
episode after episode, a dry humor and a sense of irony that must
have been an integral part of her own life. The basic discontinuity
between what society tells women they can and should expect in
life and what they indeed find in life—the age-old conflict
between illusion and reality—provides tension and humor
throughout the novel. Thus Belinda comes to realize that she loves
Henry Hoccleve even more than his wife, Agatha, does, yet she
realizes that her feeling "may be the stronger for not having
married him" (STG 161). In Belinda's moment of revelation she
comes to understand that Agatha, like Olivia Berridge in the case
of Father Donne, was most likely the aggressor and had probably
proposed to Henry. *Some Tame Gazelle* deals with the commonplace, the daily life of women, their relationships with men of
dubious maturity, and their more satisfactory relationships with
one another. The use of literary allusion and quotation and the
themes of unrequited love and of the contentiousness and ineptitude of the clergy Pym introduces in this, her first novel. One finds
here, too, a touch of satire on the language of anthropologists.
Pym plays on these same motifs in the novels that follow.

These very themes were central to Pym's own life. Her
unrequited love for Henry Harvey was only the first in a line of
somewhat similar experiences. And the resolution of the sisters
Bede, who are, contrary to what society would expect, comfortable in their unmarried state, indicates that by the time *Some Tame
Gazelle* was published, Pym may have realized that the unmarried
state was for her the preferred one. Almost uncanny is her seeming
prediction that she and Hilary would live together, which they did
for most of their lives—and toward the end in the country village
of Finstock—and that her relationship with Henry Harvey would
continue into old age. She and Harvey remained friends throughout her life.

Pym wrote *Civil to Strangers* in 1936, but it was not published
until 1987 when, along with other unpublished manuscripts, it
was edited by Hazel Holt and published in Great Britain by
Macmillan and in the United States by Dutton in a collection titled
Civil to Strangers and Other Writings. Originally titled "Adam
and Cassandra," the novel contains, as few of Pym's novels do, a
foreign interest, this time Budapest, where Pym visited in 1935

with a group from the National Union of Students (CS 8). *Civil to Strangers* does not reflect Pym's mature style, and she seems to have abandoned the novel without revising it for publication (Rossen, "Pym Papers" 158). It is interesting, however, in its contrasts with and anticipation of her subsequent work. Its primary theme is the marriage game. Set in the village of Up Callow in Shropshire, its main characters are Cassandra and Adam Marsh-Gibbon, one of the few somewhat happily married couples to be found in Pym's novels. Cassandra, the virtuous, mothering wife, cares diligently for her self-centered poet-novelist husband. But to overcome his indifference to her, she fosters the attention of the intruder in the village, the Hungarian businessman Stefan Tilos. After a too-coincidental round of events that unites Cassandra and Adam in Budapest, "City of Love," the novel ends happily with all the single men and women finding their appropriate mates. In this novel, Pym continues to poke fun at the clergy, as she did in *Some Tame Gazelle*. The inept rector, Rockingham Wilmot, is more interested in cricket than in leading his flock and believes that his young curate, Mr. Paladin, should marry for safety, to protect himself from the spinsters in his parish. And who can doubt that the infantile and indifferent Adam, carefully tended by Cassandra, reflects some of Pym's own experiences with the ambivalent Henry Harvey. The novel is full of the typical Pym "trivia"; it is humorous, ironic—all Pym trademarks. But its ending is too straight; it lacks the irony and ambiguity characteristic of the later novels.

Gervase and Flora, written in 1937–1938, "began as a series of letters to Henry Harvey" (CS 173). It is a tongue-in-cheek story of twenty-four-year-old Gervase Harringay, lecturer in English at Philadelphia College in Helsingfors, Finland, who has just come down from Oxford with a First in English, and his somewhat indifferent relationships with two women: Flora Palfrey, a young Englishwoman who loves him and whose "passion had thrived on its diet of a cooling and pretty constant neglect" (CS 180), and Ingeborg Lindblom, a young Finnish woman of "negative personality" (CS 186), daughter of Gervase's landlady, who offers a room at special rates because Gervase can talk English to the daughter. The plot is a thinly veiled treatment of Pym's relationship with Harvey and of his relationship with and marriage to Elsie Godenhjelm, whom he met and married while a lecturer in

Helsingfors. The novel entertains with comic irony. Pym pokes
fun at English snobbery in the household of Gervase's Aunt Emily
Moberley, an Englishwoman in Finland who speaks of the Finns
as foreign. Gervase's indifference to Flora, particularly when he
tells Ingeborg that Flora "can just as easily fall in love with
somebody else—it's her nature" (CS 203), reflects Pym's remarkable talent for distancing herself from her own unrequited
love experiences and anticipates themes that appear repeatedly in
her later novels. The novel, published posthumously in *Civil to
Strangers and Other Writings,* is somewhat uneven, no doubt
because Pym never seriously considered it for publication. It may
have been useful to her in coming to terms with her relationship
with Harvey—"*So endete eine grosse Liebe,*" she writes in her
diary under an entry indicating Harvey's marriage to Elsie on
December 12, 1937 (VPE 62)—and in accepting her "dear sister"
Elsie.

Pym wrote *Crampton Hodnet,* her "North-Oxford" novel, in
1939 after the outbreak of World War II (VPE 100). This novel,
which it is doubtful Pym intended for publication in view of her
reuse of parts of it in later novels, was edited by Holt and
published in Great Britain by Macmillan and in the United States
by Dutton in 1985. It is perhaps Pym's funniest novel, though for
obvious reasons it lacks the depth of development found in her
later work. Besides being highly entertaining it is useful in that it
shows Pym developing her skill with humor and irony, and it
includes prototypes of characters who appear in the more mature
novels.

Crampton Hodnet, set mostly in the drawing rooms of North
Oxford, is a study of the illusions of romantic love purveyed by
characters speaking words that meet social expectations while
they mask the speakers' own feelings. The novel, its classical
balance similar to that of *Some Tame Gazelle,* begins and ends in
October at tea for new undergraduates in the Victorian Gothic
drawing room of Miss Doggett, attended by her companion Miss
Morrow, both characters redrawn with significant change in the
later novel *Jane and Prudence.* Three love affairs provide the
action. One is the extramarital affair of the Oxford don Francis
Cleveland with his student Barbara Bird, an affair that thrives on
miscommunication. Francis pursues the affair because he feels
superfluous at home; Barbara, a cold fish as Francis comes to

discover, seeks only a platonic relationship and believes that a happy marriage consists of two people reading poetry together. Tragedy—divorce and remarriage with associated discomforts— is averted when Barbara deserts Francis in a Dover hotel, and Francis, having caught a cold in the rain, rushes home to the comfort of his books and the motherly services of his wife, Margaret, who likes nothing better than looking after an invalid. A second love affair is that of Francis's daughter, Anthea, and Simon Beddoes. Simon's political ambition takes precedence over Anthea; he finds another, more useful love, and Anthea must look for another Oxford undergraduate. The third affair is that of the thirty-five-year-old curate, Stephen Latimer, whose need to save himself "from the advances of designing women" (CH 21) and the consequences of seeming indiscretion provoke him to lie to the vicar's wife about his reasons for missing Evensong and leads him to the decision that "for his own safety and peace of mind" (CH 63) he should propose to Miss Morrow, even before he knows her first name. When she rejects him, he hastily arranges to marry Pamela Pimlico, whom he meets on vacation in Paris.

In *Crampton Hodnet,* Pym writes from her own experience. The Oxford setting and drawing room scenes obviously derive from her years at Oxford, and several of the novel's characters seem to reflect aspects of Pym's own life. Anthea Cleveland's unrequited infatuation with the politically ambitious Simon Beddoes is based in part on Pym's romantic attachment to Julian Amery.[3] Barbara Bird's name, her interest in literature, and her romantic fantasy about Francis Cleveland may also reflect some of Pym's experiences.[4] Certainly the ironic voice of Miss Morrow, whose humorous observations include "falling in love is never ordinary to the people who indulge in it. Indeed, it is perhaps the only thing that is being done all over the world every day that is still unique" (CH 203), is frequently the voice of Pym herself.

Observations such as this one by Miss Morrow provide a subversive chorus throughout the novel, furnishing a large part of Pym's characteristic humor. Another of Pym's characteristic techniques for achieving humor in this early novel is the use of caricature. Thus Miss Doggett is marked by her absurd hats whose decorative birds nod in concert with her interference in the affairs of others, and Jane Wardell's trademark is the gardening shoes she forgets to change before appearing at social functions. Much of the humor, as well as the plot, in *Crampton Hodnet* derives from the miscommunication between characters who say what they are expected to say when they think otherwise, thus precipitating untenable action and absurd situations. It is thus that Francis Cleveland announces his love to Barbara Bird in the British Museum over Milton's commonplace book and then prompts her to admit she loves him, too. With their love declared he must "do something" about it. This something, arranged against the background of his awareness that life with Barbara would be less comfortable than his present marriage but that Barbara was probably domesticated and that "it was natural for women to do housework," includes a romantic boat ride that ends with both of them doused in the river, and their departure for Paris aborted on a rainy night in Dover. All of this Francis arranges because he feels it is what Barbara expects, while Barbara laments—but only to herself—that "it should come to this!" (CH 102) and almost wishes "she had never seen Francis Cleveland" (CH 104). Throughout the novel, cynical interjections by characters thinking one thought while they voice another provide a subtext that contradicts the cozy atmosphere of the North Oxford sitting room with its warm fire, tea, and cakes.

Pym's comic technique, used effectively in *Some Tame Gazelle,* seems almost overdone in this thinly developed novel. No doubt sensing the weaknesses in *Crampton Hodnet,* Pym never revised it for publication but freely used material from it for her later work.[5] In *Jane and Prudence,* she uses Miss Doggett and Miss Morrow, though somewhat subdued, as key characters; she projects Jane Wardell's inattention to dress in the character of Jane Cleveland; and she brings Francis Cleveland back as a vicar. In *An Academic Question,* she returns to academic satire, while the theme of the disparity between romantic fantasy and life appears repeatedly throughout her novels.

The remaining two published novels of her early period, the "Home Front" novel and *So Very Secret,* Pym wrote in 1940 and 1941. Edited and trimmed by Hazel Holt for publication in *Civil to Strangers and Other Writings,* they are among the least developed of Pym's work. Nevertheless, they offer insights into her developing maturity. Both depend heavily on her experiences in the early war years while she lived at home in Oswestry doing volunteer work at a YMCA canteen and assisting with evacuees.

The "Home Front" novel is set in a village reminiscent of the village setting of *Some Tame Gazelle* and recounts the reactions of several households to the September 1, 1939, announcement of Germany's invasion of Poland. Agnes Liversidge compares with Edith Liversidge of *Some Tame Gazelle* in her brusque treatment of her live-in relative Connie Aspinall—the same character appears in both novels—and with Miss Doggett of *Crampton Hodnet,* interfering not in love affairs but in overseeing the installation of blackout curtains. Into each household come refugees who pose a series of inconveniences. At the vicarage, the refugee children have head lice and wet their beds. In one instance an evacuee teacher, Miss Stoat, is obnoxious enough to drive the invalid Mrs. Wyatt from her bed to independence. The vicar's daughter, Flora Palfrey, believes herself in love with the politically hopeful Edward Wraye "since there was really nobody else to be in love with" (CS 253). Flora gets her reward when Edward, who has been obviously bored with her and has avoided her for some months, chooses to pay her a farewell visit on his departure for the front. Edward brings her his photograph and explains that he couldn't go without saying good-bye, and Flora discovers that "he was not as *tall* as she had always thought him" and "had a spot on his forehead" and a manner that "was really rather *affected*" (CS 256).

The spy novel, *So Very Secret,* whose fiftyish sisters Cassandra Swan and Harriet Jekyll recall the Bede sisters of *Some Tame Gazelle,* consists of an extended chase that sends Cassandra in pursuit of Harriet. All ends well, but not before Cassandra is chloroformed at a tea in Oxford, misses one train, overrides her destination on another train, steals a bicycle, and rides frantically to escape her enemy. She then ends up on a bed in the Great Champing and District Hospital where she finds herself used as a patient for a group of Red Cross ladies "watching a demonstration of hospital bed-making and sheet changing" (CS 309).

Both the "Home Front" novel and *So Very Secret* are entertaining and of interest to Pym fans and scholars because they show Pym's work in progress. They lack development, however, and fail to exhibit the quality of fiction that Pym was capable of creating even at this early stage in her career. The remaining two novels Pym worked on during this early period, "Beatrice Wyatt; or, The Lumber Room" and "Something to Remember," are of interest because they, too, offer insight into the development of her creative process.

"Beatrice Wyatt," written in 1938, is about a romance between an older woman and a younger man, perhaps another reflection of Pym's relationship with Julian Amery.[6] This novel, which exists only in rough draft, contains allusions to the "International Situation," most likely reflecting her growing concern with world events. It may also indicate a growing dissatisfaction with living in Oswestry and her emotional predicament after Harvey's marriage to Elsie Godenhjelm.[7] "Beatrice Wyatt" has been cited by Wyatt-Brown as indicating Pym's awareness of her own creative process as well as providing a metaphor for that process. In the novel, the heroine, Beatrice Wyatt, compares "the memory of a past love" to "a storage room or attic, 'a kind of lumber room—full of old pictures.' " The picture, or memory, having been stored away for a long period, can then be taken out and viewed somewhat painlessly. Similarly Pym stored her memories of "[u]npleasant experiences with men" without close introspection. She denied her feelings by storing them away or repressing them in the lumber room of her mind—in the process having some of them "destroyed altogether." With the passing of time, Pym was able to use the material in her novels with "honesty, irony, and detachment" ("Ellipsis, Eccentricity and Evasion in the Diaries of Barbara Pym" 45–46).[8] Pym herself says in "Finding a Voice," a radio talk broadcast in 1978, that "memory is a great tranformer of pain into amusement" (CS 383).

"Something to Remember," begun in 1940 and adapted as a radio play for a 1950 BBC broadcast, is about a "woman in love with a glamorous young M. P. who jilts her" (Long, *Barbara Pym* 11). This novel, one of three of Pym's novels that Rossen cites as having been modeled on *Jane Eyre* (the other two are *Excellent Women* and *The Sweet Dove Died*), is about Deborah Wilde, "a Jane Eyre governess figure" who renounces love for the Rev. Bernard Hoad who has jilted her for another woman. Deborah consoles herself by "cherishing" Bernard's "Christmas gift of the *Oxford Book of English Verse*" ("On Not Being Jane Eyre" 140–42). Pym described this fragment of fiction as a "novel about Julian" (Long, *Barbara Pym* 11). It may also be an attempt to deal with her unrequited love for Henry Harvey. The fact that the heroine turns to the *Oxford Book of English Verse* may reflect Pym's early

recognition, perhaps not wholly conscious, of the role that literature
and her own writing would play in her life.

THE WAR YEARS

In spite of Pym's failure to publish her novels before the war,
there is evidence of a strong belief in herself as a writer. Her diary
and letters reflect that she felt her writing style was influenced by
the style of Ivy Compton-Burnett (VPE 100), that she was
concerned about her writing process, especially her inclination to
procrastinate, and that she felt the need to accomplish something
each day—"preferably a few pages of writing" (VPE 102). In
April 1940, she wrote that she seemed "to have decided already
the sort of novels" she wanted to write—those dealing with the
trivialities associated with a woman's life—and suggested that
she might write a novel dealing with the protagonist's development "in matters of emotional restraint" (VPE 103). Her diary
entry on July 4, 1941, reflects that she submitted a short story
titled "Goodbye, Balkan Capital" to *Penguin New Writing*
without success (VPE 106).

Pym's interest in the form—and the audience—of her diary
surfaces from time to time. In one instance, she jokingly refers to
the "Gentle Reader in the Bodleian." In February 1941, she
writes of a diary she has kept for recording special events such as
"past loves like Jay or when something momentous happens, like
the invasion of Holland and Belgium," whereas everyday events
are recorded "in a neat little book which has a set space for every
day" (VPE 104). In July of 1941, after reading Katherine
Mansfield's scrapbook, she considers doing more with her own
diary, including in it bits of stories and ideas, a practice she
subsequently assumes. Pym's interest in her diary and in the
autobiographical writings of others extends throughout her life
and is reflected frequently in allusions in her novels, not to speak
of the autobiographical nature of the novels themselves.

But Pym's writing slows significantly in 1941 when, after
registering for war service, she takes a job in the Censorship in
Bristol. In December 1941, she moved into a house—The Coppice—in Bristol with Hilary. Other members of the household
included Honor Wyatt and her two children. Honor at the time was

involved, amicably, in divorce proceedings with Gordon Glover, who visited The Coppice to see the children. Pym fell in love with Glover in the fall of 1942 after, as her diaries for the following year reflect, he declared his love for her. But the affair lasted only a few months, leaving her depressed and lonely. In March 1943, she enlisted in the Women's Royal Naval Service (WRNS), perhaps hoping to assuage her grief, and in July 1943, she began her training at the Nore Training Depot, after which she was promoted to Third Officer and assigned to naval censorship (VPE 97).

Pym's life in the WRNS was socially active and included fleeting alliances with several men. She was keenly aware of the artificialities of the social life, noting in her diary after a Christmas party in 1944 that she felt "Jane Eyre-ish and socially unsuccessful" (VPE 175). Though she wrote no novels during her years in the WRNS, her diary reflects that she was thinking seriously about writing, for she notes ideas for stories and poems, particularly about Naples where she was assigned in 1944.

AFTER THE WAR: 1946–1961

In June 1945, Barbara Pym returned to Oswestry to care for her ailing mother, who died that November. Discharged from the WRNS, Pym took a job with the International African Institute in early 1946. This job was to play an integral role in forming her career as a writer, both in her choice of subject matter and in her technique as a novelist. Pym worked for Daryll Forde, eventually serving as assistant editor to him on the Institute's journal, *Africa.* Forde was professor of anthropology at University College, London, and director of the Institute. In addition to her editorial work on *Africa,* she assisted Forde in editing a series of ethnographic and linguistic surveys of Africa as well as editing monographs published by the Institute. As Hazel Holt, who worked with Pym at the International African Institute from 1950 to 1974 and eventually became her literary executor, points out, the anthropologists at the institute were of great interest to her. She wrote about them in her novels, and she learned from them, incorporating some of their research techniques in the crafting of her novels.[9]

When Pym returned home from the WRNS, she set to work revising *Some Tame Gazelle* and in 1949 sent it back to Jonathan Cape, who accepted the book and published it in 1950.[10] Holt tells us that it "had a general critical success" and that a critic in *The Guardian* called it " 'Delightfully amusing . . . but no more to be described than a delicious taste or smell' " (VPE 184). A *Times Literary Supplement* reviewer writes that the novel contains "an excellent parody of a 'literary' sermon, . . . flows cheerfully on with little wit and much incident, and many readers will compare it unfavourably with the earlier novels of Mrs. Thirkel" ("Women of Character" 417). Others, including Pamela Hansford Johnson, Antonia White, and John Betjeman, welcomed the book (Burkhart, *Pleasure of Miss Pym* 15).

In 1949, Pym attended a course of Professor Daryll Forde's lectures at University College, London, and shortly afterward wrote a radio comedy about anthropologists called "Parrots' Eggs," whose title referred to the "custom of sending five parrot's eggs to a Nigerian Chief when his suicide was required" (Holt, "The Novelist in the Field" 28). "Parrots' Eggs" was not accepted for airing, but Pym used material from it years later in *Less Than Angels* (Heberlein, *Communities of Imaginative Participation* 199). This early radio play and Pym's brief, playful attention to the language of anthropology expressed through Theodore Grote, the bishop of Mbawawa, in *Some Tame Gazelle* indicate that her work with the International African Institute was already influencing her writing.

In addition to "Parrots' Eggs" and her novels, Pym's writing during the late 1940s and the 1950s included several radio plays and a number of short stories. In 1949, she wrote a radio monologue, "How I Distempered a Room," which she submitted unsuccessfully for the BBC *Woman's Hour* (Heberlein, *Communities of Imaginative Participation* 256n22). She also adapted "Something to Remember" for the BBC, which broadcast it in 1950, starring Grizelda Hervey as the heroine Edith Gossett (Holt, *A Lot to Ask* 145). In 1950, she adapted Maura Laverty's *Never No More* for the BBC, and in 1955 she wrote a radio play "called variously 'The Vicarage' and 'The Rectory.' " The latter was accepted for *London Column,* but the series was terminated before the play could be aired (Heberlein, *Communities of Imaginative Participation* 22). During these years Pym wrote more than twenty short stories. One of the stories, "The Jumble Sale," was published by *Woman and Beauty* in 1949, but she was unable to market the other stories. Holt writes that although Pym "attempted to conform to the magazine fiction formula, her stories were too delicate and too allusive to be successful" with that market (*Lot to Ask* 145). Heberlein attributes their failure to weak plotting, stereotypical characters, and stilted dialogue, yet she notes that "the narrative prose is as smooth and transparent as in her best fiction" (*Communities of Imaginative Participation* 22).[11]

Pym was more successful as a novelist. During the eleven years following the publication of *Some Tame Gazelle,* she wrote and published five novels, all with Jonathan Cape.

The first of these novels was *Excellent Women,* published in 1952. This time Pym takes as her protagonist and first-person narrator the thirtyish self-deprecating spinster Mildred Lathbury. Mildred does volunteer work mornings for the Society for the Care of Aged Gentlewomen and spends the rest of her time visiting and helping in various ways at the rectory, settling disputes among her acquaintances and serving tea at moments of crisis.

Excellent Women follows the classically circular format that Pym used in *Some Tame Gazelle* and *Crampton Hodnet.* It takes place in a "shabby" London suburb on the " 'wrong' side of Victoria Station" (EW 7). The intruders this time are Rockingham and Helena Napier, a married couple verging on divorce who move into the empty flat beneath Mildred, and Allegra Gray, the attractive widow of a clergyman who moves into the empty flat in the vicarage and threatens the comfortable household of Father Julian Malory and his spinster sister, Winifred. In the course of the narrative, Mildred performs a variety of services for the Malorys, the Napiers, and Everard Bone, an anthropologist and dabbling archaeologist, a group that presents her with three potential suitors. Most dashing is handsome Rocky Napier, whose wife's infidelity and his own legendary powers with Wren officers have led to the brink of divorce. Second is Everard Bone, object of Helena Napier's affections, who needs a proofreader and indexer. Third is Julian Malory, thought to believe in the celibacy of the clergy, whose awakening to the true nature of Allegra Gray brings him finally to appreciate Mildred's potential. The novel begins in the winter as Helena Napier moves into the flat beneath Mildred and they consult over the inconvenience of their shared bathroom. The penultimate chapter, a year later, sees a new couple moving into the flat—the Napiers, reunited, have moved to a country cottage—and again there is consultation over a cleaning schedule and toilet tissue supply for the bathroom. But one senses that Mildred, unlike Harriet and Belinda Bede, may have grown during the year and that her life may have changed. Mildred has at least come to view more realistically the nature of her observation and involvement with others, realizing that she did ''love contriving things'' and did seem to get involved in others' lives, but perhaps it was because she ''really enjoyed other people's lives more'' than her own (EW 222). Mildred's new neighbors, Charlotte Boniface and Mabel Edgar, promise a clean bathroom, a change from Helena's sloppy housekeeping. As the novel ends, ambiguously, Mildred weighs the needs of Julian Malory and Everard Bone, the former needing protection from women who might live in his house, the latter, someone to cook his meat, proofread his galleys, and index his books.

Pym's humor, pervasive but more subtle than in her earlier works, makes *Excellent Women* one of her more polished and entertaining novels. Her humor surfaces in the ironic self-deprecation of Mildred Lathbury and in the caricatures of Everard Bone's mother and Miss Clovis. The former is ''tall with a long nose'' (EW 147); her fear of '' '[t]he Dominion of the Birds' '' leads her to '' 'eat as many birds as possible' '' (EW 149). The sensible, excellent Miss Clovis, with '' 'hair like a dog' '' (EW 190), brings couples together and assists with their separation all '' '[f]or the sake of anthropology' '' (EW 164).

Like all of Pym's novels, *Excellent Women* draws heavily on her own experience. At the time she wrote *Excellent Women,* Pym was living with Hilary, who had separated from her husband in 1946, in a flat in Pimlico—the environment described in the novel (VPE 184). Pym's Church of England background is important to *Excellent Women,* as it was in *Some Tame Gazelle.* She uses literary quotations and allusion to enhance and counterpoint the verbal expressions of her characters. And where the subject of anthropology and Africa plays a minor part in *Some Tame Gazelle,* in *Excellent Women* Pym extends the use of her experiences with the anthropologists at the International African Institute. She pokes gentle fun at Everard Bone, Helena Napier, and Esther Clovis in their roles as anthropologists. She describes a meeting of the Learned Society, where Mildred and naval officer Rocky Napier observe the observers and comment on their primitive eating habits, their " 'depressingly scientific' " books that nobody reads (EW 88), and the ceremonial nature of the reading of a paper, activities that Pym implies are comparable to Anglican gatherings and services at St. Mary's and St. Ermin's. The "premises of the Learned Society," as Mildred points out to Helena, "were not very far from St. Ermin's" (EW 87). To emphasize the parallels, Pym juxtaposes a chapter in which Mildred attends services at St. Ermin's where Archdeacon Hoccleve gives his Judgment Day sermon with a chapter in which Helena and Everard read their anthropological paper before the Learned Society.

Jane and Prudence, Pym's third published novel, came out in 1953. This novel, which involves some of the same characters and events she had used years earlier in *Crampton Hodnet,* seems, because of the continued focus on the plight of the spinster, almost a companion novel to *Excellent Women.* Pym's rewriting of scenes and characters from *Crampton Hodnet* suggests that by the early 1950s she no longer intended to prepare the earlier novel for publication.[12] Her introduction of characters from *Crampton Hodnet* is especially telling, for it was not unlike Pym to carry over characters in her novels. In *Excellent Women,* for example, Archdeacon Hoccleve preaches his Judgment Day Sermon, heard at length in *Some Tame Gazelle,* at St. Ermins. And in *Jane and Prudence,* Miss Doggett reveals that Mildred Lathbury from *Excellent Women* did indeed marry Everard Bone. In both instances the archdeacon and Mildred are still in character; they are the same characters we met when they were first introduced.

This is not the case with the characters carried over from *Crampton Hodnet* to *Jane and Prudence.* The most notable carryovers are the Cleveland family and Miss Doggett and her companion, Miss Morrow. In *Crampton Hodnet,* Francis Cleveland is an Oxford don who because he feels superfluous at home becomes involved with his student Barbara Bird. His wife, Margaret, is a comfortable, efficient housewife. Daughter Flora is preoccupied by an unrequited romance with the politically ambitious Simon Beddoes. In *Jane and Prudence,* Cleveland, whose first name is now Nicholas, is a complacent vicar. His inept wife, Jane, has difficulty dressing appropriately—as does Jane Wardell, the vicar's wife in *Crampton Hodnet.* Jane Cleveland cannot cook and blunders through one social encounter after another. Her consuming interest in the novel—she compares herself to Pandarus and to Emma Woodhouse—is to find a husband for her friend Prudence. Flora helps to keep her mother on schedule when entertaining, cooks meals for the family, and, akin to the Flora of *Crampton Hodnet,* has a consuming interest in young men, settling on an Oxford geography major. Miss Doggett is equally domineering in both novels, interfering in the lives of others and controlling Miss Morrow's existence. In *Jane and Prudence,* Miss Doggett and Miss Morrow are distant relatives; in *Crampton Hodnet,* they are unrelated. Miss Morrow is significantly different in the later novel. Although she aspires in both novels to look attractive, and both novels contain scenes showing her concern with makeup and dress, in *Crampton Hodnet* her perception of and indulgence of Miss Doggett's foibles and her honesty in her relationship with Mr. Latimer enlist the reader's sympathy. In *Jane and Prudence,* Miss Morrow is perceptive and shrewd, shrewd enough to snare Fabian Driver for her husband as a guard against becoming a distressed gentlewoman. Another character carried over with significant change is Barbara Bird, whose shyness and naïveté are transformed into a novelist who brags of having " 'just finished my seventeenth' " (JP 118–19). She bores Jane with discourse on what the critics have said about her latest novel, asks the poet at the literary society meeting they are attending to speak up, and rudely seizes a plate of sandwiches during refreshment time.

Another major carryover from *Crampton Hodnet* is a kitchen scene involving in both novels Miss Doggett's penchant for interference. In the early novel, Miss Doggett visits the Clevelands to reveal Nicholas's infidelity to Margaret and is shown, to Miss Doggett's dismay, into the kitchen where the family is topping and tailing gooseberries. *Jane and Prudence* contains a somewhat similar scene in which Miss Doggett, who has just discovered that Miss Morrow has been seeing Fabian Driver and desperately needs to tell someone, arrives at the Cleveland home and is taken into the kitchen. The table is cluttered with the paraphernalia for bottling plums, and the rest of the room is "festooned with enormous green leaves [Nicholas's tobacco harvest] which hung down from everywhere that things could hang down from" so that she felt "as if she were in some Amazonian jungle and that poisonous snakes and insects might drop on to her" (JP 182–83). What's more, she must reveal her findings in the presence of Nicholas himself, dressed not in clerical collar but in an altogether inappropriate flowered apron.

Pym's humor is more subtle in *Jane and Prudence* than in *Crampton Hodnet,* and her characters and scenes more carefully drawn. In *Jane and Prudence* she explores further the theme of the spinster's plight in ways that closely link it with *Excellent Women.* The spinsters in *Jane and Prudence* are Prudence Bates and Jesse Morrow; both pursue the widowed Fabian Driver, a sort of male counterpart to the widow Allegra Gray of *Excellent Women.* Jesse wins, as Miss Glaze points out, because Miss Morrow " 'may have stooped to ways that Miss Bates wouldn't have dreamed of' " (JP 209). Jesse also gets what she deserves, a handsome man, perhaps security against being a distressed gentlewoman, and a husband of questionable fidelity. Prudence, who "had got into the way of preferring unsatisfactory love affairs to any others" (JP 9), is free to add even more men to the "shrine of her past loves" (JP 215). Women's options are limited, Pym seems to be saying as she adds to those already portrayed in *Excellent Women.* They can, like Helena Napier and Jesse Morrow, marry a handsome man and suffer his unfaithfulness. They can, like Jane Cleveland, marry, forsaking their own interests— Jane's early promise had resulted in a book of essays on seventeenth-century poets—to become inept wives to kindly gentlemen like Nicholas. They can marry, as Mildred Lathbury does, and spend their lives making themselves useful to scholarly husbands by proofreading and indexing their work. Or like Prudence and Eleanor Hitchens, they can remain single. Yet for single women there are alternatives: Prudence's string of unsatisfactory affairs as opposed to Eleanor's comfortable spinster's life with "weekend golf, concerts and theatres with women friends, in the best seats and with a good supper afterwards" (JP 200).

Pym's interest in the spinster's lot during the 1950s when she was writing *Excellent Women* and *Jane and Prudence* no doubt reflects her concern with her own unmarried state. The rakish Fabian Driver, enhanced by fiction in *Jane and Prudence,* whose wife Constance's " 'death came as a great shock to him—he had almost forgotten her existence' " (JP 28) and whose housekeeper Mrs. Arkright cooks him a "casserole of hearts" (JP 33), was modeled on Gordon Glover, whose unrequited love had caused Pym significant grief (VPE 187). Prudence Bates may reflect Pym's coming to terms with her own unmarried state, and the office environment where Prudence works draws to some extent on Pym's office environment with the International African Institute (Holt, "Novelist in the Field" 25). Jane Cleveland, Holt writes, is a "loving celebration of Irena Pym," and Prudence "is only a slightly distorted mirror image of Barbara herself" (*Lot to Ask* 165).

Pym's next novel, *Less Than Angels,* first published in 1955, transforms her experience with anthropologists at the International African Institute into a major theme that expresses her concern with her role and technique as a novelist. Catherine Oliphant, the protagonist of *Less Than Angels,* is unmarried and thirtyish, a writer of romance fiction and articles for women's magazines. Her live-in lover, Tom Mallow, is a detribalized middle-class Englishman and anthropologist writing his Ph.D. thesis on the role of the mother's brother in an African tribe. Through her association with Tom, Catherine becomes an observer of the observers, as Pym explores more fully a theme she introduced in *Excellent Women* when Mildred Lathbury and Rockingham Napier attend Helena and Everard's paper-reading before the Learned Society. The central conflict of the novel concerns the disposition of funding for research grants for young anthropologists. Professor Felix Mainwaring thinks he has persuaded the elderly widow Minnie Foresight to endow his fund for research grants. Mrs. Foresight has only a vague idea about what anthropologists do:

> They went out to remote places and studied the customs and languages of the peoples living there. Then they came back and wrote books and articles about what they had observed and taught others how to do the same thing. It was as simple as that. And it was a very good thing that these languages and customs should be known, firstly because they were interesting in themselves and in danger of being forgotten, and secondly because it was helpful to missionaries and

government officials to know as much as possible about the
people they sought to evangelize or govern. (LTA 15)

Unfortunately for Felix and his young anthropologists, Mrs.
Foresight is unable to distinguish between their mission and the
needs of the two-faced Father Gemini and gives her money to
Gemini instead.

The striving after research grant money to finance excursions
into the field corrupts the young anthropologists competing for
the money. Their interest is in making the right impression and
ingratiating themselves with the right people. This involves
making sure the professors know their names, choosing the
appropriate drink—Tio Pepe, Amontillado, or a nonalcoholic
cordial—taking Miss Clovis, whose zeal for anthropology is as
intense as it was in *Excellent Women,* out to lunch, and coming up
with a suitably pretentious plan for fieldwork. Their youthful
optimism contrasts with the attitudes of their seniors. Professor
Mainwaring wonders "whether the whole business of going out
into the field to study a primitive tribe isn't vastly overrated"
(LTA 218). Alaric Lydgate, "invalided out of the Colonial
Service" and socially inept (LTA 57), keeps his trunks of field
notes in his attic, safe from Tom Mallow who might have found
something useful in them, unsorted, a constant reproach. Never
having written an original piece himself, he writes vitriolic
reviews of other anthropologists' work.

Women play an adjunct role among Pym's anthropologists. The
one mature woman anthropologist in the novel is Gertrude
Lydgate, who collaborates with Father Gemini in linguistic
research. But this collaboration includes helping him order a meal
in a cafeteria, where he drags his feet and sulks like a petulant
child. Her collaboration ceases when she discovers that Gemini
has obtained the research grant money that Minnie Foresight
originally had promised to Felix Mainwaring, and for a moment
she considers withholding her " 'material on the Gana verb' "
without which Gemini's project would " 'fall to pieces.' " But
with counsel from Miss Clovis that she is " 'too great a scholar to
be able to carry it through,' " she agrees that science is " 'greater
than any of us and through it we must somehow rise above our
petty squabbles' " (LTA 226). Miss Clovis, as "a kind of
caretaker in the new research centre" (LTA 13), is mother to all

the anthropologists, who send her offprints of their articles in learned journals, "prompted by a sort of undefined fear, as a primitive tribesman might leave propitiatory gifts of food before a deity or ancestral shrine in the hope of receiving some benefit" (LTA 63). Not much when it comes to making tea, she is, however, adept at organization and knows how to act in a crisis. A matchmaker, she strives to bring kindred souls together in the interests of anthropology and even suggests that nineteen-year-old Deirdre might sleep with Alaric Lydgate as a means of securing Tom's access to Lydgate's field notes. She is indispensable to Felix Mainwaring, helping him influence Minnie Foresight and seeing him through the process of selecting the research grant recipient; it is she who breaks the news to the candidates that there is no grant money because Father Gemini has stolen it. The young women anthropologists, though ostensibly receiving a comparable education and themselves competing for research grants, are viewed in terms of their usefulness to the male anthropologists. Tom Mallow, shifting his affections from Catherine, who is busy with her own work and doesn't have time to type his thesis, to Deirdre Swan, still unsure about her dedication to anthropology, considers asking Deirdre if she can type. Professor Mainwaring explains Deirdre's presence at the research center to Minnie Foresight, pointing out that women can be a great help in the field, that " '[m]any workers have found a wife a most useful asset, particularly if she has had the right kind of education" (LTA 124). Even Vanessa Eaves, a fellowship contestant, attempts to ingratiate herself with Felix Mainwaring with melting glances and the assurance that a woman can be a great help to a man in his work.

Pym's satire on anthropologists takes a comic look at their foibles and turns their practices on themselves and on the English society that they have largely ignored in their detached quest after "primitive" civilizations in Africa. At the same time, she questions the detachment of anthropological studies, setting the role of anthropologist against Catherine Oliphant's role as romance writer. At one point in the novel, Catherine observes a seemingly aimless crowd of people in the foyer of a large restaurant:

> They wandered, bewildered, rudderless, in need not only of
> someone to tell them which of the many separate cafes

would supply their immediate material wants, but of a guide
to the deeper or higher things of life. While a glance at the
menus displayed or a word with an attendant would supply
the former, who was to fulfil [sic] the latter? The anthropologist, laying bare the structure of society, or the writer of
romantic fiction, covering it up? (LTA 194–95)

The solution, Pym seems to suggest, lies somewhere between,
perhaps in the detached observation of the comic novelist.

Pym's next novel, *A Glass of Blessings,* published in 1958, was
written in 1955 and 1956, a time when Pym was intensely
interested in the work of Dennis Welch and during her early years
of friendship with Robert Smith. Welch's treatment of the commonplace and his autobiographical focus in his writing may have
helped to strengthen her resolve about the type of novels she was
writing.[13] Pym met Smith, an Oxford graduate and associate
professor of history at the University of Lagos, Nigeria, in about
1950 (VPE 354). With him she shared an interest in Anglicanism
and churches. Her diaries for 1955 and 1956 indicate their close
association, including church attendance, visiting a Proust exhibi-
tion, and walking along the river past a furniture repository,
giving rise to the possibility that Roberts may have been in some
respects a model for Piers in *A Glass of Blessings* (VPE 193–97).

In *A Glass of Blessings,* Pym's attention turns again to
women's predicaments, but this time her focus is more on
marriage than on spinsterhood. For this novel she uses a first-
person narrator/protagonist as she did in *Excellent Women.* The
protagonist, thirty-three-year-old Wilmet Forsyth, is an Emma-
character whose self-centered desire to be properly useful to
others renders her incapable of perceiving their needs. Wilmet,
who is childless, lives with her largely indifferent civil-servant
husband, Rodney, and her mother-in-law, Sybil. She perceives
herself as someone who always takes trouble with her clothes,
thereby achieving "some kind of distinction" (GB 9) and as
having "a talent for arranging flowers" (GB 11). Determined to
be useful, Wilmet plans to "take more part in the life of St.
Luke's" and "to try to befriend Piers Longridge," the seemingly
aimless brother of her friend Rowena Talbot (GB 18). Wilmet's
double and constant reminder of her uselessness is Mary Beamish,
about Wilmet's own age, a frequent blood donor "so very much

immersed in good works, so *splendid* . . . but small and rather dowdily dressed'' (GB 19). Wilmet's idleness causes her to toy with the possibility of an affair with Piers, and her insensitivity blinds her to his disinterest in her and to his homosexual interest in Keith, with whom he shares a flat. Only as the novel ends does Wilmet come to see how little she actually knows about herself and those around her. In spite of her curiosity and desire to be useful, Wilmet finds that Mary and Marius Ransome, the parish curate, Piers and Keith, and Sybil and her anthropologist friend, Professor Root, had all found one another, were ''all doing things without, as it were, consulting'' her (GB 230). And as if this knowledge were not enough, Wilmet discovers that her husband, who she thought ''would never look at another woman,'' had indeed dallied with his co-worker Prudence Bates (GB 250). In the end, Wilmet comes to see that she is indeed lacking in self-knowledge, that she has as much as Mary Beamish, and that her own life should ''be a glass of blessings too'' (GB 256).

A *Glass of Blessings* contains Pym's most favorable treatment of marriage and just possibly more marriages than any of her other novels. Here, marriage is not necessarily a happy state, though it is tolerable, and to some a comfort in old age. The two primary marriages of the novel are those of Wilmet and Rodney and of Rowena and Harry. Both marriages are somewhat colorless; both husbands have fantasies of romance with women other than their wives. Where Wilmet is unable to perceive Rodney's romantic fantasy, Rowena is aware and seems to understand Harry's need to fantasize. The marriages, however, provide stability, and the reciprocal relationship between the partners makes them, in Piers's words, ''colleagues in the grim business of getting through life'' (GB 227). Somewhat similar is the relationship between Piers and Keith. Without Keith, Piers's life, reflected in the description of his room before Keith moved in, was chaos. The relationship with Keith brings structure and order to both their lives. Marius Ransome marries Mary Beamish, perhaps for her money but also for comfort, and perhaps as assurance that he won't be further tempted to go over to Rome. The marriage of Sybil and Professor Root, who will comfort one another in old age, forces Wilmet and Rodney to search for a place of their own, a search that brings them closer than they had been in years.

In *No Fond Return of Love,* written in the years from 1957 to

1960, Pym returns, but with less success, to the love theme of *Some Tame Gazelle.* In *Some Tame Gazelle,* Harriet and Belinda Bede are driven by their need for someone to love. Similarly, in the later novel, Dulcie Mainwaring and Viola Dace, thirtyish spinsters, are controlled by their need for a love object. In this case, that object is the blond, leonine-headed scholar of English literature, Aylwin Forbes. Dulcie and Viola meet quite by chance at a learned society conference where Aylwin is presenting a paper on the problems of an editor. Dulcie's fiancé has broken off with her, and Viola already suffers from unrequited love for Aylwin. Although Viola has done some research of her own on an eighteenth-century writer and pretends to have written articles and started on a novel, both women live on the fringes of the academic world, indexing and proofreading for the more gifted males of the profession.

But *No Fond Return of Love* strains the belief of the reader with its detectivelike chase, based to some extent on Pym's own tendency to investigate the lives of people who interested her.[14] In the novel, Dulcie, with Viola as sidekick, sets out in pursuit of Aylwin, whom she knows is one of those " 'people from whom one asks no return of love. . . . Just to be allowed to love them is enough' " (NFRL 75). Mildly infatuated with Aylwin after he faints while giving his presentation, Dulcie engages in a remarkable search to learn more about him. Her acquaintance with Viola is perpetuated by a chance encounter at Temple Station that results in a meal at Viola's apartment and ends with Viola moving into a room in her house. Dulcie looks up Aylwin's address in the telephone directory and manages to walk past his house on the way home from the meal with Viola. A chance encounter, in a cloakroom of the library of a learned institution, with a woman who had been at the conference yields the information that Aylwin has a brother who is a vicar. Reference to *Crockford* provides Dulcie with the brother's name (Neville) and parish affiliation (St. Ivels); in *Who's Who,* she discovers Aylwin's birthdate, the name of his wife (Marjorie), Marjorie's father's name (Williton), a list of Aylwin's publications, and the information that his recreations were " 'conversation and wine' " (NFRL 53). Armed with this information, Dulcie manages to walk past the Williton house during a jumble sale, which provides the opportunity to go inside and come face to face with Mrs. Williton and Marjorie. Another excursion, ostensibly to deliver Christmas gifts to her Aunt Hermione and Uncle Bertram, brings her in proximity with St. Ivels, where she discovers by chance from the church housekeeper that Neville is in trouble.

Neville's trouble adds impetus to the mystery. A dinner party for Aylwin and Dulcie's ex-fiancé, designed to yield information about Neville's trouble, reveals only that home for Aylwin is somewhere in the West Country and that indeed the Reverend Neville Forbes is somewhat troublesome. The vagueness of this information necessitates a visit to services at St. Ivels to see Neville in person. Neville has fled to the West Country and his mother, but the housekeeper provides the information Dulcie and Viola need. Neville's trouble is with an infatuated parishioner, Miss Spicer, and the specifics of the West Country include the mother's proprietorship of the Eagle House Hotel at Taviscombe. Dulcie and Viola visit Taviscombe where they spend the night at the Eagle House in conjunction not only with Neville but with Mrs. Williton, Marjorie, and Aylwin. Quite by chance, Dulcie finds herself crouching behind a bookcase, eavesdropping as Mrs. Williton, Marjorie, and Aylwin settle on the dissolution of Aylwin and Marjorie's marriage. Dulcie also discovers in a confrontation with fifty-year-old Aylwin that he has designs on her nineteen-year-old niece Laurel. After these revelations, the cast, with the exception of old Mrs. Forbes, return to London. Neville returns to his church, now safe since Miss Spicer has moved to another parish. Marjorie goes off with a man she meets in the dining car of the train returning from Taviscombe. Viola will marry Bill Sedge, brother of Aunt Hermione and Uncle Bertram's cook, whom she met quite by chance the evening of the reconnaissance excursion to St. Ivels. And Aylwin, after Laurel turns down his proposal, decides to leave young girls alone and find a suitable mate, one who can help him with his work. Comparing his shift in affection to that of Edmund in *Mansfield Park,* Aylwin turns his attention to Dulcie.

Jonathan Cape published *No Fond Return of Love* in 1961. Up to this point, all of Pym's novels had been generally well-received. Holt writes that they "were praised by the critics, enjoyed a modest financial success and delighted an evergrowing circle of admirers and enthusiasts." *Excellent Women,* she notes,

"was a Book Society Choice and was subsequently serialized in
the BBC's *Woman's Hour*" (VPE 184).

Times Literary Supplement reviews of each of the novels
subsequent to *Some Tame Gazelle* are generally positive. *Excellent Women* elicits the praise that "Miss Pym is really very funny
about the tenants of the flat below," that she "wears her religion
without much self-consciousness," and that this novel shows a
definite advance on her first novel, *Some Tame Gazelle*" ("Divided Loyalties" 217). *Jane and Prudence* was not as well-
received as *Excellent Women.* The reviewer notes that "Pym
writes well," but adds that this novel "is really very small beer
indeed to have come from a brewery in which Oxford, a taste for
Jane Austen, and an observant eye have all played their parts"
("Family Failings" 625). The *Times Literary Supplement* reviewer found Pym's characters and events in *Less Than Angels*
"perhaps on the fanciful side of reality" and her "crisp dialogue
. . . agreeably dry" ("Trouble Brewing" 685). *A Glass of
Blessings* is criticized because the "self" that is the object of a
novel's quest "should be fairly interesting"; Wilmet's self is
questionable since she has too much money and too little in her
head ("Ways of Women" 281). *No Fond Return of Love* is cited
for the "good deal of quiet amusement" it provides. Its reviewer
notes that "Miss Pym's observation of genteel milieus is subtle
and penetrating," and that her theme "is entertainingly treated
and confirms her place as a witty chronicler of the shy and
delicate" ("Milieus of Love" 108).

Other reviews elicited by the first publication of these early
novels attest to their positive reception, at times comparing Pym
with Jane Austen. Antonia White, writing in *The New Statesman
and Nation,* 1 July 1950, writes that "Miss Pym, working in *petit
point* makes each stitch with perfect precision" and that she "will
almost certainly be compared to Jane Austen and very possibly to
Trollope" (21). A *Church Times* reviewer, 16 May 1952, praises
Pym's sympathetic treatment of Mildred Lathbury, noting that
Excellent Women "reveals flashes of insight into female character
worthy of Jane Austen" (11). M. Bellasis, reviewing *Jane and
Prudence* in the *Tablet,* finds the book "topical" and "out of
date" but notes its "[s]harp-eyed observation, gently-acid humour, and an agreeable undercurrent of seventeenth-century
poetry" (24 Oct. 1953: 405). *A Glass of Blessings* also elicited

comparison with Austen when a *British Book News* reviewer
"mentioned 'the flavour of a latter day Jane Austen,' the sharp
observation, and the 'sparkling, feminine malice' " (Heberlein,
Communities of Imaginative Participation 53). *No Fond Return of
Love* evoked comparison with both Austen and Ivy Compton-
Burnett (Heberlein, *Communities of Imaginative Participa-
tion* 58). A *Catholic World* review of *Less Than Angels,* the first of
Pym's novels to be published by an American publisher—
Vanguard in 1957—calls it a "mild and witty book," noting that
"[v]ivid scene succeeds vivid little scene" (Sept. 1957: 473). Dan
Wickenden, writing for the *New York Herald Tribune,* credits
Pym with "a nice sense of the ridiculous." He concludes his
review with comparisons: "She introduces sudden death as
casually as E. M. Forster, and from Jane Austen by way of Angela
Thirkell she inherits a faculty for extracting comedy from the
fatuities of the dull or foolish or pompous" (5 May 1957: 3).
Similar praise of *Less Than Angels* comes from Aileen Pippett in
the *New York Times Book Review,* 31 March 1957, who writes that
Pym "makes no attempt to wring our withers," yet she "sheds
gleams of sympathetic understanding on familiar complications, a
sigh for supposed lost simplicities. The total effect is curiously
memorable" ("Observers Observed" 33).

Pym's early novels caught the attention of important people in
the literary world. Ivy Compton-Burnett, Elizabeth Taylor, and
Lord David Cecil all wrote to her in the early 1950s to express
their pleasure in reading her books. Lord David Cecil praised her
"sense of reality and sense of comedy." "[T]he people in your
books," he wrote, "are living and credible and likeable. I find this
rare in modern fiction."[15] In 1961, on the publication of *No Fond
Return of Love,* Philip Larkin wrote to Pym offering to review her
next novel, thus beginning a correspondence and friendship that
was to continue throughout her life (VPE 201). Sadly, it would be
sixteen years before Pym would publish another novel. Yet Philip
Larkin would figure significantly in its publication.

THE WILDERNESS YEARS: 1961–1977

In the meantime, Pym set to work on her next novel, *An
Unsuitable Attachment,* written in the early Sixties but not

published until 1982, two years after her death. The ending of *No Fond Return of Love* is ambiguous. As the novel closes, Aylwin has designs on Dulcie, not because he wants to return *her* love, but because he sees her as a suitable mate, someone to help him with his work, to proof his books and make his indexes. That Dulcie will return *his* love is somewhat doubtful. *Some Tame Gazelle* stresses women's need for someone to love and men's failure to respond. *No Fond Return of Love* explores the theme further to suggest some of the reasons men fail to respond to women's needs. *An Unsuitable Attachment* continues to explore the theme of love, requited and unrequited, raising in its title the question of what indeed constitutes a *suitable* attachment. At the same time, Pym develops in the character of Rupert Stonebird a more favorable picture of a male character than she has hitherto portrayed.[16]

One of the strongest characters in *An Unsuitable Attachment* is Rupert Stonebird, an anthropologist whose observations of women open and close the novel. The main theme of the novel is the human need for attachment, and Rupert, aware that "men and women may observe each other as warily as wild animals hidden in long grass" (UA 13), waivers between a possible attachment with two women. One is Penelope Grandison, whose name he usually cannot remember but whose awkward moments of dress and action can on occasion—for example, when he notices that her silver lame cocktail dress has "split at the back" (UA 131)—evoke in him a pity akin to love. The other is Ianthe Broome, a canon's daughter, who dresses and behaves with propriety and seems "almost too good to be true" (UA 153). Rupert elicits sympathy because he is a "quiet sort of person" who dislikes "pushing himself forward" (UA 34). He seems sincerely to want to communicate, yet he is helpless to make the contact he needs to form a suitable attachment.

Ianthe Broome, the novel's protagonist, falls not for Rupert, who would seem most suitable, but for the unsuitable John Challow, who lacks finesse, wears too-pointed shoes, can't keep his finances straight, and is five years younger than Ianthe. It is this attachment that evokes a chorus of "unsuitable" from the other characters in the novel and for which one might assume the novel gets its name.

But the novel is filled with unsuitable attachments. The clergyman Mark Ainger and his wife, Sophia, are so unsuitably attached, in large part because Mark is perpetually detached, that Sophia develops an unsuitable attachment for her cat Faustina. Several of the characters, including Ianthe, and particularly her librarian colleague Mervyn Cantrell, experience questionable attachments to their mothers. Mervyn, attached to Ianthe's Pembroke table and Hepplewhite chairs, proposes to her with the understanding that the arrangement was pending so long as his mother lived. Edwin Pettigrew, the veterinarian, and his sister Daisy are attached to cats instead of people. And Ianthe's aunt and uncle, Randolph and Bertha Burdon, are attached to each other, a "suitable match that her parents had encouraged" but that precluded any experience of "what love was and what it could drive people to" (UA 223). Perhaps the most suitable attachment in the novel is that of Sophia's aunt in Ravello who has maintained for many years an illicit love affair with the Signor Dottore.

When she completed *An Unsuitable Attachment* in 1963, Pym sent it to Cape, who had published all six of the earlier novels. Cape rejected the novel, giving as their excuse that "they feared that with the increased cost of book production . . . they would not sell enough copies to make a profit."[17] After numerous attempts with other publishers, she put the novel aside. It was published finally in 1982, revised then by Hazel Holt, her literary executor, who indicates that cuts were made "along the lines" Pym herself "had been considering" and that short passages were deleted that had "dated" in a way that Pym "would have found unacceptable" (UA 9).

The writing of *An Unsuitable Attachment* and Pym's unsuccessful attempts to find a publisher for it mark the beginning of a sixteen-year eclipse in the publication of her novels. Although the comments in her journals and letters indicate that one reason the novel was not accepted for publication had to do with the reading public of the 1960s and publishers' awareness that it might not be commercially successful, critical response to the book indicates that it is probably inferior to the earlier novels. Jane Nardin, whose *Barbara Pym* (1985) was one of the first book-length critical studies of Pym's novels, writes in her preface that both *No Fond Return of Love* and *An Unsuitable Attachment* seem weaker than the first five novels published by Cape. Nardin writes that *No Fond Return of Love* "has a cumbersome and artificial plot" and that *An Unsuitable Attachment* "clearly lacks both conflict and direction." Both novels she sees as "products of a tired imagination." Robert Liddell, Pym's lifelong friend, writes that there is a "fatal flaw" in the structure of *An Unsuitable Attachment,* that several of its characters are "asking for development and needing a story of their own in which to show their paces" (*Mind at Ease* 90). Philip Larkin, who wrote the foreword for the 1982 Macmillan publication of *An Unsuitable Attachment,* finds that its "chief failing is that the 'unsuitable attachment' between Ianthe Broome . . . and . . . John Challow . . . is not sufficiently central to the story and not fully 'done' " (173).[18] Larkin also reports that his correspondence with Cape reflects that Cape reviewers had submitted negative responses on the novel. Nevertheless, Larkin praises *An Unsuitable Attachment,* writing that it is "richly redolent of her unique talent" as it was before her confidence was shaken by Cape's refusal to publish it (175). Pym fans who read the novel in context will for the most part agree. Rupert Stonebird is Pym's archetypal anthropologist and observer. Yet in developing his character, Pym extends her sympathy to males in ways not seen in the earlier novels. And her muted focus that avoids concentrating on a central protagonist reflects a mature interest in experimenting with the form of her novels.

During the years she was writing *An Unsuitable Attachment,* Pym developed a close friendship with Richard Roberts, a Bahamian antique dealer six years her junior. Roberts owned an antique shop in London and was interested in opera. Pym visited Keats's house in Hampstead with Roberts, had intimate dinners and exchanged gifts with him, and in one instance attended an auction at Sotheby's to bid on a pair of china birds for Roberts's mother.[19] Pym's diaries and letters reflect her fondness for Roberts, whom she called Skipper, and her disappointment as the relationship with him waned by the mid-1960s. The relationship with Roberts may have been reflected in the "unsuitable attachment" of Ianthe Broome and John Challow. Certainly it influenced the writing of her next novel, *The Sweet Dove Died* (VPE 213), written during the years 1963 to 1969 but not published until 1978.

In spite of her disappointment about the failure to publish *An Unsuitable Attachment,* Pym continued to write. Yet, the writing of *The Sweet Dove Died* marks the beginning of what critics have called her darker phase. Pym never loses her sense of irony, but noticeably missing from *The Sweet Dove Died* is the wit and humor that sparkle through line after line of the earlier novels. This novel offers an overt look at male homosexuality that intersects with an examination of the lives of older unmarried women. Although critics have suggested that Pym's treatment of homosexuality in this novel reflects her desire to write a novel that her publishers could market in the 1960s,[20] it is just as likely that she wrote about male homosexuality and the plight of the fiftyish unmarried woman because these were issues she was dealing with in her own life at the time.

The novel's protagonist is Leonora Eyre, whose name alludes to Beethoven's Leonora overtures and Jane Eyre—as one character in the novel points out, a somewhat disquieting mixture (SDD 85). A paragon of repression, Leonora's almost inhuman elegance evokes the adjectives ''cold and fossilized'' from her friend Meg, who as Leonora's foil suffers intensely from her passionate attachment to a young male homosexual. Leonora's search for perfection prevents her from accepting the reality of her own attachment to the much younger, sexually ambiguous James. Ironically, a large part of James's attraction to her, the fact that he feels comfortable in the company of older women, is the very aspect of her own existence—aging—that she is least able to accept. Having been left enough money to live on by her parents, she is not constrained by the alarm clock. Neither does she suffer the restraints of religion. Leonora is free, free of all but her own self-interest, the prison of her self.

James, likewise, is a prisoner. Young and unsure of his sexuality, he waivers from one potential partner to another. His vulnerability lands him in a series of prisons. He is attracted to Leonora in part because she reminds him of his mother, in part because he sees her as sexually safe. His excursions from the safety of her mothering include an overt sexual encounter with Phoebe Sharpe from which he withdraws because he fears entanglement. Freed momentarily from both Leonora and Phoebe when he goes abroad to Spain and Portugal, James experiences a ''sensation of freedom, almost of escape'' (SDD 83). Yet he becomes almost immediately involved in a liaison with Ned, the American assistant professor on sabbatical whose ''thin, gnat-like voice'' teases and probes and imprisons him in a sybaritic ''pad'' lined with synthetic fur, in colors of olive, red, and black (SDD 105). The jungle images of Ned's pad recall James's own comparison of himself with the young, neutered cats he sees at a cat show he attends with Leonora. Other images of his imprisonment include the hotel room in Lisbon that he shares with Ned, "covered in a kind of striped paper," that James compares with the inside of an old-fashioned suitcase both because of the stripes and because of "the heat and the general feeling of constriction which Ned's presence and his whining American voice gave" (SDD 106), and the barred window in the flat Leonora prepares for him on his return from abroad.

The prison motif is an important element of the novel, but the prisons are not so much prisons imposed by others, but prisons of the self, often assumed because of the characters' sense of vulnerability, their seeming inability to extend themselves imaginatively in the interest of others and to accept, as Meg points out in trying to console Leonora, that things, and human relationships, are never perfect. Pym took her title for this book from a poem by Keats:

> I had a dove, and the sweet dove died;
>   And I have thought it died of grieving;
> O, what could it grieve for? its feet were tied
>   With a single thread of my own hand's weaving . . .

The dove symbolizes both self-imprisonment and the relationship that cannot thrive because of that imprisonment.

After numerous publishers had rejected the book between 1968 and 1977, it became apparent that Pym would be unable to find a publisher for yet another of her novels. By July of 1970, her despair is evident when she writes in a letter to Larkin, "It is a wonder to me now that I ever published anything . . ." (VPE 257). Pym was aware that her novels were not trendy. And although there are indications that she tried to make some amends along these lines, she remained true to her own voice.

In spite of Pym's failure to publish during these years, there were some bright spots. In 1965, the BBC serialized *No Fond Return of Love* for its *Woman's Hour.* In addition, her novels remained available in public libraries in the Portway Reprint Series (VPE 213). In 1971, Robert Smith published the first critical appreciation of her novels, an article in the October 1971 issue of *Ariel* titled "How Pleasant to Know Miss Pym."[21] Smith praised Pym's "acute observation of a limited social scene." Her novels, he wrote, provide a "valuable record of their time, perhaps more valuable than anything an anthropological research team set to work in Surbiton could produce" (62).

Pym still did not stop writing. During the years from 1970 to 1972, she wrote *An Academic Question*, revised by Hazel Holt and published posthumously in 1986. Pym wrote the first draft of *An Academic Question* in first person and later went back and rewrote it in third person. Holt, in revising the novel, "amalgamated" the two drafts and made use of Pym's notes in an attempt to " 'smooth' " the drafts "into a coherent whole" (AQ vi).

An Academic Question sparkles with the wit and humor of Pym's earlier work, and the voice of its first-person protagonist recalls Mildred Lathbury of *Excellent Women*. This novel is significant in that it contains Pym's most extended treatment of young children. We see briefly Kate Grimstone, daughter of Caroline and Alan Grimstone, and her fleeting relationship with Luke and Alice Horniblow, the somewhat unruly children of Iris Horniblow, single mother and faculty colleague of Alan Grimstone. The novel, however, fails to develop the child characters. Other more fully developed themes include the passing of time and issues associated with aging and the plight of the academic wife, involved, but only peripherally, in the academic jungle of professional rivalry and publishing ritual.

The theme of time passing is evident in Pym's presentation of the three generations of women in Caroline (nicknamed Caro) Grimstone's family and in the characters of Dolly Arborfield and Daisy and Coco Jeffreys, Dolly's sister and nephew. It is also apparent in the treatment of Normanhurst, the old people's home, and in the retirement of Alan's department head, Crispin Maynard. The concept of family succession, though not fully developed, is useful in contrasting the social scene of Caroline's mother's generation, a world centered in the parish, with that of her daughters, Caro and Susan. At church with her mother, Caro reflects on generational change and the "liberal-minded people" of her generation, in particular her "own university with its undenominational meeting-house, the dead pigeon lying in the water and the obscenity scrawled on the piece of modern sculpture'' (AQ 121). Susan, who casually tells Caro of having an abortion but keeps the information from her mother, is a sociologist in the welfare state. She and her television-designer lover, Gary Carter, live in a squalid neighborhood conducive to her ''objective'' study of its social problems. Her expertise at ''interviewing problem families'' makes the discussion of abortion, contraceptives, and ''other intimate feminine matters'' seem almost inconsequential (AQ 69). The emphasis on the changing social scene is especially apparent in a scene where Caro and Susan are walking in the woods. Caro's interest is in the things of nature; Susan's is in ''some of the more dire aspects of her work from which she was obviously not to be distracted by any false nostalgia for the past.'' In this setting, and juxtaposed to Susan's announcement of her abortion, Caro notices that what she had thought to ''be a violet turned out to be a scrap of purple chocolate wrapper, while an unidentified flower was just a screwed-up pink paper tissue'' (AQ 70). Pym uses similar images of the litter of civilization mistaken for natural beauty again in her final novel to emphasize social deterioration with the passing of time.

Dolly Arborfield and the Jeffreys provide another contrast that points to Pym's concern with time passing. Both the fortyish Coco, whose sexuality is ambiguous, and his mother, Daisy, are fastidiously preoccupied with matters of dress and appearance, shying away from anything suggesting aging or death. Dolly, on the other hand, is an antique dealer who loves animals and is genuinely concerned about the care of the elderly. Under Dolly's influence, Caro finds herself involved in reading to the aging Dr. Stillingfleet. When Stillingfleet dies, Caro represents Alan at his cremation ceremony, where she reflects on the ''general sadness of life,'' the journey that the inhabitants of Normanhurst were all soon to make to the crematorium, and to the inappropriateness of modern television films to the interests of the elderly for whom television ''was their one pleasure'' (AQ 53). In addition to attending the Stillingfleet ceremony, Caro also represents Alan at Esther Clovis's memorial ceremony, a ceremony that Pym uses again in *A Few Green Leaves.*

Dr. Stillingfleet's death and his bequeathal of his papers to other scholars links the themes of time passing and academic rivalry. Academic rivalry motivates Alan to use Caro to retrieve the Stillingfleet manuscript from Stillingfleet's box of secret papers so that Alan can prevail in his scholarship over Crispin Maynard. The two men vie over their publications; nevertheless, when Maynard retires he does so with a "gesture of reconciliation" that seems to "open the way for Alan's advancement" (AQ 178), a sort of ironic shifting of the mantle from the shoulders of the older man to the younger.

Pym's irony in this novel is at its best in her treatment of academic competition and narrowness. Caro's response to Iris Horniblow's presentation at the Dabb's Memorial Lecture echoes the irony Pym expresses over Susan's social benevolence and Sister Dew's concern with keeping her old people clean—the potato crisps Dr. Stillingfleet craves are forbidden him because they dirty up his beard. Iris's subject is " 'patterns of neighbourhood behavior' in various suburban communities where Iris had done her fieldwork," a subject Caro thinks promises "to be interesting—for what could be more fascinating than the study of a community one actually knew?" "But," Caro narrates, "after a very few minutes it became apparent that the dead hand of the sociologist had been at work and as soon as I heard the words 'interaction,' 'in-depth' and 'grass-roots,' I knew that this lecture wasn't going to be any more compelling than the other two had been" (AQ 77).

Pym's ironic treatment of academic life takes into account the plight of the academic wife who exists on the fringes of the academic world, typing manuscripts, proofreading, filing note-cards, pasting stickers on books, entertaining guests, always striving to find some way to participate in her husband's work and ever on the alert for infidelities that might erupt between the husband and his female colleagues. Caro's desire to participate plunges her into the action of the novel, the central line of which is the filching of the Stillingfleet manuscript so that Alan can prevail over Crispin Maynard. When Alan makes her responsible for returning the manuscript to its place among the Stillingfleet papers, she takes a menial job at the library to have access to the papers, which have been moved to librarian Evan Cranton's office after Stillingfleet's death. In the end, her efforts prove irrelevant since the Stillingfleet papers are destroyed in a library fire set by young Guy Fawkes Day revelers. But it is that mission that brings her back to Alan after she discovers his infidelity with his editor's young assistant. In the end, Caro prevails. Crispin Maynard senses

her part in securing the manuscript and tells Alan how lucky he is
" 'to have a wife who would do that' " for him (AQ 177). And
Alan "graciously" acknowledges, when Caro considers remaining with her library job, that he " 'might occasionally have some
typing' " for her (AQ 178).

This novel, thinly developed though it is, conveys Pym's voice,
her wit and irony. Her experience with academics in the International African Institute clearly provides some of her source
material. Her focus on an academic wife in the character of Caro
Grimstone may reflect Pym's intention to explore what her own
life might have been had she married Henry Harvey. But Pym set
the novel aside to begin one of her finest—perhaps her best—
novels, *Quartet in Autumn.*

Not only was Pym down on her luck when it came to finding a
publisher in the early Seventies, but health problems were also
beginning to plague her. In 1971, she discovered a lump in her left
breast and underwent a mastectomy. In 1974, she suffered a mild
stroke that left her with dyslexia. Although she recovered quickly
from the stroke, she retired from her work at the International
African Institute and moved from her bed-sitting-room in London,
where she had been spending the week while she worked, to Barn
Cottage to live with Hilary, who had retired from the BBC in 1971
and moved to Finstock (VPE 214). There, she universalized her
experiences with illness and her concern with aging and the
inevitable approach of death in *Quartet in Autumn,*[22] a novel that
continues in the darker mode of *The Sweet Dove Died.* In its
treatment of social change and the plight of the aged, it exudes a
tragic irony that has been compared to Northrop Frye's sixth
phase of satire that "presents human life in terms of largely
unrelieved bondage" in which "suffering has an end in death."[23]

In *Quartet in Autumn,* Pym traces a little more than a year in the
lives of four aging office workers—two men and two women—
isolated in individual prisons, yet ironically brought together with
the death of one. In this novel, Pym presents her bleakest vision of
human life, as her characters pass like mummies through a world
filled with images of death.

The most communicative members of the quartet are Letty
Crowe and Edwin Braithwaite. Letty's existence is marked by
her homelessness. Displaced from her bed-sitter when her landlady sells out to the African Mr. Olatunde, whose rowdy religious

services she finds disturbing, Letty moves into a room with Mrs. Pope and tries to find a place for herself in the local parish life. Her plans to live out her retirement in the country with her friend Marjorie are upset when Marjorie decides to marry her vicar, David Lydell. Marjorie's solution for Letty is Holmhurst, the old folks' home. But Letty prefers, after visiting with Beth Doughty, Holmhurst's "resident warden," to "lie down in the wood under the beech leaves and bracken and wait quietly for death" (QA 150–51). Such images, reminders of her mortality, frequent Letty's life. She sees "a woman slumped on a seat on the Underground platform" during the rush hour and looks back to make sure it isn't her "school contemporary" Janet Belling (QA 17). Nevertheless, Letty sees the flowering laburnum and appreciates the wild garlic when she walks in the wood. She is concerned about the welfare of others and is aware of her failure "to make contact" (QA 4). Watching pigeons "picking at each other, presumably removing insects," she reflects that "[p]erhaps this is all that we as human beings can do for each other" (QA 9). Edwin, a widower, shares his jellybeans in the office and is the envy of the other three because of his church affiliation—"he was Master of Ceremonies (whatever that might be) and on the parochial church council (the PCC)" (QA 8). His concern for others brings him to arrange for Letty's room at Mrs. Pope's house when Letty is displaced by Mr. Olatunde's vigorous religion. It is Edwin who arrives with Father Gellibrand to find the collapsed and dying Marcia; and Edwin submits to being " 'her next of kin' " (QA 177), entailing the responsibility of arranging for her funeral.

Less outgoing are Norman and Marcia. Norman, small, wiry, and angry, cautions the others about the dangers of hypothermia to the elderly. He dislikes automobiles and gets his greatest thrill from seeing a wrecked automobile being towed away. Norman and Marcia share a large tin of Nescafe, but they convince themselves that they share only because it's cheaper to buy the larger-sized tin. Marcia, who has recently had a mastectomy, is obsessed with her hospital experience and her physician, Dr. Strong. Her other preoccupations include a dresser drawer full of neatly arranged plastic bags, classified by size, shelves of neatly arranged tins of food, and a shed full of sparkling clean milk bottles that she saves for emergencies. In her lunch hour excursions to the library, she collects pamphlets informing the elderly of available social services, yet fails to communicate what she learns from the pamphlets to her elderly colleagues and refuses to avail herself of the services.

The precipitating event in the novel is the retirement of Marcia and Letty, a ritual that involves a "lunchtime gathering" because as "ageing unskilled women" they were not entitled to an evening party (QA 100). The party is presided over by "the (acting) deputy assistant director" who "wasn't quite sure what it was that Miss Crowe and Miss Ivory did or had done during their working life" (QA 101). He notes in his presentation speech that they will be missed so much that "nobody has been found to replace them" and then quickly slips away to a luncheon engagement (QA 102). Pym details the events of the first days of their retirement. Marcia's is spent arranging her plastic bags and empty milk bottles. Letty's includes a trip to the library during which she passes the office building where they had worked and reflects that "it gave her the feeling that she and Marcia had been swept away as if they had never been" (QA 114).

Pym's irony is at its most tragic in this novel, developing in part out of her sense of aging, her illness and surgery, and her knowledge of the working world. In the end, Marcia dies of malnutrition. Janice Brabner, the social worker whom Marcia sees as an intruder, Edwin, and Father Gellibrand find her slumped over a partly opened tin of luncheon meat. Presumably, she was too weak to get to the nutrition she held in her hands and that was so plentifully and neatly stacked on her cupboard shelves. Marcia's death brings the others together, and their communion grows closer over a cup of coffee at Edwin's house before the funeral. An even deeper communion is shared when the three come together in Marcia's house to dispose of her belongings, deeply concerned that that disposition should be "what Marcia would have wished" (QA 216). As the novel ends, both Norman and Letty feel a sense of power in that others are to be affected by the choices they make. Norman, to whom Marcia leaves her house, can choose between his bed-sitter and living in the house, the latter to the distress of Priscilla and Nigel, Marcia's neighbors, who had hoped for a young family next door. Letty's choice is between Mrs. Pope's bed-sitter in London and a house in the country with Marjorie. As the novel ends, Marjorie, whose engagement to David Lydell has been broken, invites the three for lunch in the country, evoking from Letty a reflection that distills the tragic irony of the novel: "it made one realise that life still held infinite possibilities for change" (QA 218).

During the 1970s, Pym's intellectual interests were reflected in her reading and social life. Her diaries and letters indicate that her reading included James Baldwin's *Another Country,* Elizabeth Taylor's *The Soul of Kindness,* Charlotte M. Yonge's *The Daisy Chain, The Pillars of the House,* and *The Clever Women of the Family,* James's *The Golden Bowl,* novels by Anthony Powell, the letters of Sylvia Plath, and the poems and novels of Philip Larkin. Her friendship with Larkin grew largely through their correspondence. After years of writing to one another, they met for lunch at the Randolph Hotel in Oxford in April 1975. She also maintained her friendship and correspondence with Robert Smith. Her literary/social life included parties and other social functions that involved Elizabeth Taylor, Margaret Drabble, Elizabeth Bowen, and her old friends Jock Liddell and Henry Harvey. After her retirement she joined the Finstock Local History society and served as a preliminary judge for the Romantic Novelists Association (VPE 280).

Throughout these wilderness years, Pym never stopped writing and thinking about writing. In June 1964, she commented in a letter to Richard Roberts on how "full of fictional situations life is" (VPE 228). Later that year, she again wrote to him: "With a little polishing life could become literature, or at least fiction!" (VPE 231). In September 1965, writing to Larkin about the BBC decision to serialize *No Fond Return of Love* for its *Woman's Hour,* she writes, "Perhaps I can't stop writing after all. Even if no one will publish me" (VPE 238). In December 1967, she writes almost prophetically to Larkin: "In about ten years' time, perhaps somebody will be kind enough to discover *me*" (VPE 244). To Henry Harvey, in April 1976, she writes, "Novel writing is a kind of personal pleasure and satisfaction, even if nothing comes of it in worldly terms" (VPE 287).

REDISCOVERY: THE FINAL YEARS

Then on January 21, 1977, the *Times Literary Supplement* published a list of names solicited from prominent literary people of the most underrated and overrated writers of the twentieth century. Pym, designated underrated by both Philip Larkin and Lord David Cecil, was the only living writer to be named by two people (VPE 291). This incident marked an important turn in her literary career.

Pym became a celebrity. Macmillan called her on February 14, 1977, with an offer to publish *Quartet in Autumn,* and it was shortlisted for the Booker Prize for 1977. Macmillan also began making plans for the 1978 publication of the previously rejected *The Sweet Dove Died.* In May 1977, Pym had tea with Lord David Cecil, and in September of that year the BBC aired *Tea with Miss Pym,* a program about her life and literary career, filmed with Cecil in her garden at Finstock (Malloy, "Quest for a Career" 15–18). The *New Yorker* commissioned her to write a short story, published as "Across a Crowded Room" in their July 16, 1979, issue. In addition, at the request of the *Church Times* she wrote a short story, "The Christmas Visit," which appeared in their December 1978 issue. She broadcast a radio talk for the series *Finding a Voice,* and she appeared as a "guest on the BBC's *Desert Island Discs*" (VPE 291). Tullia Blundo, a doctoral candidate at the University of Pisa, wrote the first doctoral thesis, "La Narrativa di Barbara Pym," on Pym's novels (Heberlein, *Communities of Imaginative Participation* 88). Cape reissued her early novels, and in America, Dutton began publishing her work. In October 1978, she was made a Fellow of the Royal Society of Literature (VPE 321). A letter arrived "from the USA" asking her to " 'lecture' " (VPE 330), and Rota, an "antiquarian bookseller, acting on behalf of an American university" inquired about the disposition of her literary remains (VPE 314).

Although she appreciated the attention, Pym remained modest, almost self-deprecating. In a letter to Larkin, shortly after her recognition in the *Times Literary Supplement* article, she wrote, "I am really better at making marmalade (very successful this week!) and doing patchwork" (VPE 293). She continued her work with the Romantic Novelists Association and the Finstock History Society and served as a judge for the Southern Arts Association Prize, awarding the prize to Penelope Lively for *Nothing Missing but the Samovar* (VPE 325).

In January 1979, Pym discovered she had ovarian cancer. Her final year was spent racing with death to finish yet another novel,

A Few Green Leaves. Symbolically wrapping up the themes that governed her life and work, it reflects the final years of her life in Finstock and her awareness of "the mystery of life and death and the way we all pass through this world in a kind of procession" (VPE 331).

Pym's primary images in *A Few Green Leaves* reflect death and time passing, yet in writing this final novel she summons up images and themes from virtually all of her previous novels. Set in a small village based on Finstock where she was living with Hilary, *A Few Green Leaves* recalls the village setting of *Some Tame Gazelle.* In the earlier novel, life is centered around the parish, but in this final novel the doctor's surgery competes with the rector's study as the most important place in the village. Pym's excellent women, recalling the Bede sisters of *Some Tame Gazelle* and Mildred Lathbury of *Excellent Women,* exist in *A Few Green Leaves* in the ladies of Tom Dagnall's history society, who assist him in recording information from tombstones and searching public records. Although Tom, as rector, is one of Pym's more appealing male characters, he shares some of the same faults as the clergy of earlier novels, recalling the helplessness and ineffectuality of Archdeacon Hoccleve of *Some Tame Gazelle* and Mark Ainger of *An Unsuitable Attachment.* Adam Prince, good food inspector of *A Few Green Leaves,* ex-Anglican clergyman converted to Roman Catholicism, embodies the fear of "going over to Rome" that plagues several of Pym's clergymen. Further, Prince's epicurean tastes recall Father Thames and Marius Ransome of *A Glass of Blessings;* one of Prince's memories is of the sole nantua he was served by Wilf Bason at Father Thames's table. Prince's implied homosexuality recalls the theme of male homosexuality expressed through Piers Longridge and Keith of *A Glass of Blessings* and James and Ned of *The Sweet Dove Died.* Ianthe Potts's unrequited love for a male homosexual echoes the relationship between Leonora Eyre and James of *The Sweet Dove Died.*

The anthropology motif that runs through most of Pym's novels is an important element in *A Few Green Leaves.* The protagonist of this final novel, Emma Howick, is an anthropologist ostensibly studying the small village in which the novel is set. Emma's decision at the end of *A Few Green Leaves* to write a novel echoes the words of Alaric Lydgate of *Less Than Angels* who turns his attention from anthropology to novel writing with prompting from Catherine Oliphant. The darker tone of *A Few Green Leaves,* its focus on death and time passing, continues to some extent the dark tone of *Quartet in Autumn.* At the same time, Pym takes care to inject more wit in *A Few Green Leaves* than she did in *Quartet in Autumn,* thus linking this novel in its lighter tone to her earlier novels. Although Emma Howick is named after Jane Austen's character, it is her mother, Beatrix Howick, who is the Emma character in the Austen sense. Beatrix's attempts to bring Emma and Tom together recall Emma characters of earlier novels, including Jane of *Jane and Prudence* and Sophia Ainger of *An Unsuitable Attachment.* The death of Esther Clovis links this novel with several of the earlier novels, especially *An Unsuitable Attachment* and *Less Than Angels,* and recalls, too, the peripheral role of women in academe, including Dulcie and Viola of *No Fond Return of Love.* Even Fabian Driver's death announcement conjures up images of the past, adding significance to the dalliance of Graham Pettifer, whose estrangement from Claudia recalls Rockingham and Helena Napier of *Excellent Women.*

These links with the earlier novels are no accident. Rather they seem a deliberate attempt by Pym to unify her oeuvre and to clarify her role as a novelist as she carefully, deliberately prepared for death. Rossen has noted that the "intensely personal" quality of *A Few Green Leaves* "suggests—at least in part—an *apologia pro vita sua,* offering a summary of all her essential novelistic themes and a comment—however indirect—on her personal life" (*World of Barbara Pym* 156).

Although Pym finished the final draft of *A Few Green Leaves,* she did not live to see it in print. Knowing death was imminent and not wishing to be a burden to Hilary, she "arranged to go into Michael Sobell House, a hospice attached to the Churchill Hospital in Oxford" in January 1980. She died on January 11. Fittingly, her last visitor was Henry Harvey (VPE 291- 92), who by then was living nearby in the village of Willersey (Malloy, "Quest for a Career" 6).

POSTHUMOUSLY

In her lifetime Pym had written and prepared for publication ten novels. In addition, she had written a number of novels that would later see publication through the auspices of her literary executor, several radio plays, and some thirty short stories.

After her death, Pym's private papers were lodged at Oxford's Bodleian Library.[24] The collection includes drafts of both the unpublished and published novels, with the exception of the draft of *Jane and Prudence,* which has been lost; drafts of twenty-seven short stories, most submitted for publication and rejected; a notebook containing stories written while Pym was in her teens; her private diaries and notebooks; correspondence with friends and publishers, including letters from Robert Gleadow, novelist Elizabeth Taylor, Richard Roberts, Robert Smith, and Philip Larkin; and miscellaneous pieces including "The Magic Diamond" and photographs of the actors, a typescript of the Blundo doctoral thesis in Italian, typescripts of talks Pym gave to various groups, typescripts of several radio plays, and an index of her library made by Hilary in 1980. Of particular interest to scholars are Pym's literary notebooks, small spiral books in which she kept notes and observations that later went into the novels, as well as grocery lists, lists of books read, of clothes bought and made, of Christmas cards and gifts given and received, and of personal and household expenses, thus providing an intimate look at her composing process and the evolution of her books as well as a look at her everyday life (Heberlein, *Communities of Imaginative Participation* 26–27).

From the time of Pym's rediscovery in 1977, publishers have been eager to reissue and to publish her work. In 1977, Cape reissued *A Glass of Blessings,* and Macmillan (Great Britain) published *Quartet in Autumn.* In 1978, Cape reissued *Some Tame Gazelle, Excellent Women, Jane and Prudence,* and *Less Than Angels;* Macmillan published *The Sweet Dove Died;* and Dutton published *Quartet in Autumn* and offered the first United States publication of *Excellent Women.* In 1979, Dutton published *The Sweet Dove Died,* and Cape reissued *No Fond Return of Love.* Both Macmillan and Dutton published *A Few Green Leaves* in 1980; that same year, Dutton published *A Glass of Blessings* and *Less Than Angels,* and in 1981 Dutton published *Jane and Prudence.* In 1982, Hazel Holt prepared *An Unsuitable Attachment,* the novel that marked the beginning of Pym's publishing eclipse, for publication, and it was published in Great Britain by Macmillan. Dutton published *An Unsuitable Attachment* and

No Fond Return of Love that same year in the United States, following in 1983 with the publication of *Some Tame Gazelle.* During the years from 1977 to 1983, all ten of the novels that Pym herself had intended for publication were either reissued or published for the first time in Great Britain and the United States.

The following year, 1984, both Macmillan (Great Britain) and Dutton published *A Very Private Eye: An Autobiography in Diaries and Letters.* The editors, Hazel Holt and Hilary Pym, excerpted parts of Pym's diaries and letters, lacing them together with brief introductory and explanatory passages based on their close acquaintance with Pym to provide a chronicle of her life. This book, which the editors indicate contains a little more than half of the material lodged in the Bodleian, covers the years from 1932 through Pym's death in 1980, and is divided into three parts: Oxford, 1932–1939; The War, 1940–1945; and The Novelist.

The next three years saw the publication by Macmillan (Great Britain) and Dutton of three more volumes of Pym's work— *Crampton Hodnet* (1985), *An Academic Question* (1986), and *Civil to Strangers and Other Writings* (1987). These books were derived from manuscripts lodged in the Bodleian and revised for publication by Hazel Holt. Holt writes that in preparing *Crampton Hodnet* she attempted to eliminate some of the "over-writing and over-emphasis" that "led to repetition," and to revise the novel based on Pym's "own emendations (made in the 1950s)" and notes in her diary for 1939 (CH vi). Using Pym's notes and an original handwritten version, Holt "amalgamated" two drafts of *An Academic Question. Civil to Strangers and Other Writings* is in two parts. Part One contains the title novel; Part Two contains three additional novels—*Gervase and Flora,* the "Home Front" novel, and *So Very Secret;* four short stories—"So, Some Tempestuous Morn," "Goodbye Balkan Capital," "The Christmas Visit," and "Across a Crowded Room"); and the radio talk "Finding a Voice." Holt notes that the "Home Front" novel was incomplete and that all three of the novels in Part Two were "in a fairly 'raw' state and it was obviously impossible to include them in their entirety" (CS 3).

In 1988, Dutton published *The Barbara Pym Cookbook,* compiled by Hilary Pym and Honor Wyatt. The *Cookbook,* which has drawn favorable reviews in the *New York Times Book Review* (4

Dec. 1988: 86), *Publishers Weekly* (16 Sept. 1988: 81), and *Ms.*
(Dec. 1988: 41–42), is a compilation of recipes for dishes
mentioned in the novels interspersed with commentary by Hilary
and Honor Wyatt and excerpts from Pym's novels. Doreen
Alvarez Saar describes it as "subtle and tantalizing," a "mixture
of the unlikely ingredients of biography, literature, and cookery"
(*Barbara Pym Newsletter* 4.1 [1989]: 10).

REDISCOVERY AND RECEPTION

The response of Pym's reviewers since her rediscovery has
been enthusiastic, particularly with regard to the ten novels that
Pym herself prepared for publication—the seven "early" novels
written before her eclipse (*Some Tame Gazelle, Excellent Women,
Jane and Prudence, Less Than Angels, A Glass of Blessings, No
Fond Return of Love,* and *An Unsuitable Attachment*) and the
three later novels (*The Sweet Dove Died, Quartet in Autumn,* and
A Few Green Leaves). Of the early novels, *Excellent Women* and
Less Than Angels are generally acknowledged as the best, fol-
lowed by *Some Tame Gazelle* and *A Glass of Blessings. No Fond
Return of Love* and *An Unsuitable Attachment* seem to fall out as
the weakest of the ten novels Pym prepared for publication.
The early novels are praised highly for their comedy, and
reviews frequently compare Pym with other novelists, particularly
Jane Austen. Lord David Cecil, in "Reputations Revisited," the
21 January 1977 *Times Literary Supplement* piece that marked the
beginning of Pym's revival, called *Excellent Women* and *A Glass
of Blessings* "the finest examples of high comedy to have
appeared in England during the past seventy-five years." Rosalind Wade, in the January 1978 issue of *Contemporary Review,*
writes that *Excellent Women* "emerges as one of the most brilliant
comedy novels of the century" (46). A. L. Rowse, reviewing
Excellent Women and *A Glass of Blessings* for *Punch,* compares
Pym's "social realism" and understanding of society with the
work of Jane Austen and cites Pym's novels for their authentic
depiction of a society in transition (732–34). W. B. Hooper calls *A
Glass of Blessings* a "wonderful novel, reminiscent of Iris
Murdoch and Margaret Drabble" (*Booklist* 1 Apr. 1980: 1109),
and Ellen Fairbanks, noting Pym's "precise ear for the witty

exchanges and the small details that make up the fabric of
everyday English life,'' credits the novel with recalling ''the
works of Jane Austen and Margaret Drabble'' (*Ms.* July 1980: 30).
David Kubal, reviewing *A Glass of Blessings* in *The Hudson
Review,* finds Pym's view of society ''outdated'' but writes that
her ''complex and limited vision of human possibility, embodied
in a subtle comic art . . . will delight and console those who live in
parishes of one sort or another, as, if one thinks of it, nearly
everyone does'' (1980: 438–39).

Less Than Angels has been cited as ''perhaps Pym's subtlest
and strongest achievement'' (Binding 606). Edmund Fuller
greeted the Dutton publication of *Less Than Angels* with the
comment that Pym's ''growing audience'' would ''rejoice,'' and
praised her close observation ''of the comic both in the private
and professional behavior of her people'' (*Wall Street Journal* 2
Mar. 1981: 16). Jean Strouse, writing in *Newsweek,* hears in *Less
Than Angels* ''echoes of Jane Austen and Charlotte Brontë.''
Pym, Strouse writes, lays bare the structure of society ''with
surgical precision, and, like writers of the best romantic fiction,
makes it human and funny and sad'' (19 Jan. 1981: 84). Discussing Pym's treatment of male-female relationships in *The Hudson
Review,* Kubal suggests that this novel ''may be her best'' and
writes that Pym's ability to imagine a ''balance between the needs
of pleasure and of autonomy'' is ''a rare accomplishment in
contemporary literature'' (1981: 462–63).

Reviews of the 1983 Dutton publication of *Some Tame Gazelle*
are largely positive. Christine Vogel, comparing Pym with Austen,
writes that the ''circumscribed existence of Pym's characters serves
as a perfect backdrop for her finely targeted psychological portraits'' (*Washington Post Book World* 21 Aug. 1983: 14). Frances
Taliaferro compares Pym with Austen in the characterization of
Belinda and Harriet Bede and in the ''ironic symmetries'' of the
''gentle plot'' of *Some Tame Gazelle,* with Trollope in her ''gift for
distinguishing and choreographing a large cast of characters,'' and
with Angela Thirkell in her ''sense of humor that alternates between
donnish wordplay and a giddy appreciation of the ridiculous.'' The
novel, Taliaferro says, is ''a literary miracle, an entertaining novel
whose two central characters are intelligent, contented, and good''
(*Harpers* Aug. 1983: 75).

The reviews of *Jane and Prudence* are mixed. Anatole Broyard, writing for the *New York Times Book Review,* calls the novel Pym's "most brilliant achievement" (15 Aug. 1982: 27), and Stephen Harvey, in the *Village Voice,* writes that it is a "nearly perfect specimen of the lapidary fiction which can reveal more about the essence of things than can books with big, thumping ambition" (2 Dec. 1981: 56). On the other hand, Richard Dyer, in the *Boston Globe,* writes that in *Jane and Prudence* Pym "repeats some of her best effects, with diminishment, and there are signs of carelessness. . . . But the book will make you laugh aloud with delight, repeatedly, before boomeranging everything on you in the ending" (27 Oct. 1981: 16).

No Fond Return of Love seems a less satisfactory novel than the first five novels of Pym's early period, yet it has been generally well received. In addition to eliciting a significant number of positive reviews, it has helped to further the discussion of the Pym–Austen comparison. Among the more negative responses to this novel is that of Jay Halio, who finds Dulcie Mainwaring's life and loves "pleasantly amusing, nothing more." Halio writes that "the heavy helpings of poetic justice dished out to her and the other characters at the end of the novel strain credulity." As for the comparison to Jane Austen, Pym's writing might be "Jane Austenish in some respects, e.g., its representations of English middle-class society," but it "has none of Austen's depth and fine wit" (*Southern Review* Winter 1985: 210). Anatole Broyard, writing in the *New York Times,* finds Pym "funnier" than Jane Austen and notes that Pym "works more on the fringes of society. Her heroines are characterized by an irrepressible honesty—not the aggressive, hurtful kind, but the sort that involuntarily corrects a mistake simply because the truth is so much more interesting" (1 Jan. 83: 10). Anne Tyler, who praises the "unselfconscious-ness" of the humor and the "brilliantly defined" characters in the novel, also distinguishes between Pym and Austen: "With Jane Austen the man was well worth the trouble. With Barbara Pym half the point is the absurdity of any woman's making so much fuss over someone as vain and pretentious as, say, Aylwin Forbes, the so-called hero of *No Fond Return of Love*" (*New York Times Book Review* 13 Feb. 1983: 1, 22). And Pico Iyer finds the novel "solid, old-fashioned entertainment." Pym, he writes, "organizes her fiction with brisk aplomb and drives her story forward at a smart, spritely pace" (*Partisan Review* 1985: 289, 291).

In view of Pym's difficulty publishing *An Unsuitable Attach-ment*—the novel that marked the beginning of her publish-ing eclipse—one might expect a measure of negative comment from reviewers. Larkin's foreword to the Macmillan edition cites the novel's lack of a central coherence, noting that Pym failed to include enough about Ianthe's falling in love. Anne Duchêne concurs, pointing out that "[a]ll the book's energy lies in its peripheral characters" (*Times Literary Supplement* 26 Feb. 1982: 214). James Campbell seems in agreement with Larkin and Duchêne. Although Campbell sees much that is good in the novel, he finds "too many characters of approximately equal 'weight' . . . and the particular 'attachment' of the title . . . not developed sufficiently beyond the others," as well as "too many scenes which appear to have no justification other than adding length" (*New Statesman* 19 Feb. 1982: 25).

Other reviewers are more positive, taking care to discuss parallels between Pym and Austen and to note feminist themes and Pym's functionalist approach to the novel. Marilyn Butler, in the *London Review of Books,* notes parallels between Austen and Pym themes and characters. Both novelists are social anthropolo-gists in that they study "pre-marital relations" in their tribes, but Pym's knowledge of social anthropology differs significantly from Austen's and is reflected in the ideas of functionalism—social life as an "interaction of individuals and of the organized groups to which they belonged"—that she brings to the novel. *An Unsuitable Attachment,* Butler writes, "looks like a deliberate attempt at a functionalist novel, even if the experiment is leavened with irony" (6–19 May 1982: 16). Deirdre Donahue compares the novel with Austen's *Emma,* charting "the growth of a single woman from ignorance to self-knowledge," and allows that the "publisher must have been mad to reject the jewel" (*Washington Post Book World* 20 June 1982: 6). Penelope Lively finds it "a wonderful book: hilarious, unexpected, touching and occasionally faintly disturbing" and wonders "that the feminists have never claimed Barbara Pym" (*Encounter* Apr. 1982: 76). Mary Cantwell finds Pym a "descendant of Jane Austen" and writes that the novel is "vivid, sly and hard to net, and why her publishers turned it down can be clear only to them and God" (*New York Times* 10 May 82: C15).

Reviews of the three later novels that Pym prepared for

publication have been mixed but largely positive, with *The Sweet Dove Died* and *Quartet in Autumn* generally viewed more favorably than *A Few Green Leaves. The Sweet Dove Died,* however, has its detractors. Paul Ableman finds it a "slight romance, written in a virtually unbroken sequence of genteel clichés," with "hardly enough substance . . . to fill a medium-length short story in a woman's magazine" (*Spectator* 8 July 1978: 26). Peter Ackroyd criticizes Pym's treatment of homosexuality, which, he says, "in this novel is like a peculiarly fruity after-shave: sensed but never discussed," and concludes that Pym is "too close to her material to be a convincingly comic or perceptive novelist" (*Sunday Times* [London] 16 July 1978: 41).

Other reviewers are more positive. Shirley Toulson writes that *The Sweet Dove Died* can only enhance Pym's "reputation as a writer of stylized dark comedies whose ruthless compassion enables her to pierce the pretentious follies of the social scene and to entertain her readers with her penetrating observations of the ways and manners of the English middle classes" (*British Book News* Oct. 1978: 843). Walter Clemons finds the novel "lethally funny and subtly, very pronouncedly sensual to a degree new in Pym's work" (*Newsweek* 16 Apr. 1979: 92). Susannah Clapp, writing in the *Times Literary Supplement,* calls it a "graceful novel" (7 July 1978: 757), and Harriet Rosenstein writes that the novel is "virtually flawless: witty, perfectly constructed, without an extra ounce of verbiage" (*Ms.* May 1979: 35).

Quartet in Autumn, shortlisted for the Booker Prize in 1977, may take first place among Pym's later novels. Liddell calls it "her strongest, finest work" (*Mind at Ease* 122); Long calls it "one of Pym's finest achievements" and "the great triumph of her late period" (*Barbara Pym* 174, 188). Because Dutton's publication of *Excellent Women* coincided with their 1978 publication of *Quartet in Autumn,* reviewers tend to compare the two novels. Updike finds the earlier novel "very fine, and the newer even finer—stronger, sadder, funnier, bolder." He compares Mildred Lathbury with both Letty and Marcia of *Quartet in Autumn* and notes the likenesses between the two novels, "even to striking, on the last page, the identical muted chord" (*New Yorker* 26 Feb. 1979: 117). Duchêne also sees connections between the characters and tone of the two novels, writing that in the later novel "[t]he warm current of sympathy, and Mildred's amused appraisal of singleness, has chilled into angry, appalled contemplation of loneliness" (*Times Literary Supplement* 30 Sept. 1977: 1096).

Quartet in Autumn has elicited an occasional negative review. Wade finds it "uneven and fragmented," the quartet sometimes resembling "puppets rather than real people" ("Quarterly Fiction Review" 46). But most reviewers are enthusiastic about its merits. Duchêne praises Pym's "marvelously acute ear for the periphrases" with which her characters "fend off desolation" (*Times Literary Supplement* 30 Sept. 1977: 1096). Updike finds the novel "a marvel of fictional harmonics, a beautifully calm and rounded passage in and out of four isolated individuals as they feebly, fitfully grope toward an ideal solidarity" (*New Yorker* 26 Feb. 1979: 120). Paul Bailey calls it "an exquisite, even magnificent, work of art" (*Observer Review* 25 Sept. 1977: 25). Richard Boeth praises Pym's perceptiveness, citing her as "more knowing and more illuminating than any psychiatrist . . . on the numberless ways in which we allow ourselves to be defined, limited and victimized" by our imagination about what others imagine (*Newsweek* 23 Oct. 1978: 125). And Victoria Glendinning writes that "Marcia's craziness is what all solitary people fear, and it is tackled wittily but head-on" (*New York Times Book Review* 24 Dec. 1978: 8).

A Few Green Leaves, written and revised during the last months of Pym's life, elicited mixed reviews, and reviewers who compare it with the other novels sometimes note that it is not the best novel with which to make one's acquaintance with Pym. Elaine Feinstein is highly critical of this novel (*Times* [London] 17 July 1980: D11), as is Bernard Levin. Acknowledging that it is the first of Pym's novels he has read, Levin writes, "I cannot for the life of me understand what all the fuss was about; *A Few Green Leaves* seems to me thin, dull and very nearly pointless" (*Times* [London] 27 July 1980: 40). On the other hand, Penelope Fitzgerald remarks on its "delightful set pieces—a Hunger Lunch, a Flower Festival, blackberry picking" (*London Review of Books* 20 Nov.–4 Dec. 1980: 19). Paul Bailey finds the novel "notable . . . for the quiet confidence of its unhurried narrative, which accommodates a dozen or so sharply differentiated characters in a beguilingly comic manner" (*Observer* 27 July 1980: 29). Nicholas Shrimpton praises the minimalist nature of Pym's writing, noting that her irony "consists less of saying one thing and meaning another than of saying nothing and meaning a lot." "The consequence," he writes, "is a vivid sense of how we live now. If anything is picking up the neglected fragments which future social historians will seek, it is probably novels like this" (*New Statesman* 15 Aug. 1980: 17). And John Braine calls Pym's final novel a book of "epiphanies" and "showings-forth of joy" (*Sunday Telegraph* [London] 3 Aug. 1980: 10).

Reviewers of *A Few Green Leaves* repeatedly comment on the connections between Pym's work and that of other writers. In addition to the usual comparisons with Austen, reviewers point to her affinity with Virginia Woolf, Philip Larkin, and John Betjeman. Robert Phillips finds this novel "a book to be welcomed and savored, but perhaps not without" first coming to appreciate "her other, more major, novels." Nevertheless, he compares Pym's achievement in this final work with Virginia Woolf's *Between the Acts* in its pitting of "time present against time past" and its "parading history before us in the living flesh" (*Commonweal* 8 May 1981: 284–85). A. N. Wilson compares Pym's work with that of Larkin and Betjeman in her exploration of "the oddness and bleakness of solitary lives." Her characters, he adds, are "as real and as rounded as some of the best characters in nineteenth-century fiction" (*Times Literary Supplement* 18 July 1980: 799).

Reviews of the three books gleaned from the Pym archives—*Crampton Hodnet, An Academic Question,* and *Civil to Strangers and Other Writings*—understandably have lacked some of the enthusiasm exhibited in the reviews of the novels Pym prepared for publication. Of the three books, *Crampton Hodnet* has had the most positive reception. Among its detractors, however, is James Fenton, who finds it "unsatisfactory." Pym, he writes, is "obsessed with surfaces, with fabrics and foibles" (*Times* [London] 20 June 1985: 11). Michael Dorris, who finds in it a "freshness that is irresistible," writes that its "disparate parts . . . do not quite mesh into the seamless wonder of [Pym's] later works" (*New York Times Book Review* 1 Sept. 1985: 14). And Miranda Seymour wishes the editors had changed the title, notes that "[t]he plot is thin," and objects to Pym's "excessive eagerness to establish the looks, habits and clothes of each character as soon as his or her name is introduced" and to the too-frequent repetition of jokes and "tea-and-scandal sessions." At the same time, Seymour writes that "high spirits, a satirical eye and a sharply funny handling of dialogue carry the day" (*Times Literary Supplement* 28 June 1985: 720).

For the most part, *Crampton Hodnet* received high praise. Martha Duffy cites its "rare charm" in "the glimpse it offers of Pym's imagination as it pauses for a moment in perfect understanding of a character" (*Time* 24 June 1985: 81). Heather Henderson calls Pym "a quiet subversive, deliberately confining her art to a small canvas," with a "rare gift for observing small details that speak volumes" (*Macleans* 24 June 1985: 62). And Peter Kemp writes that *Crampton Hodnet* contains "all those enduring features that give Barbara Pym's fiction its characteristic appeal: a connoisseur's eye for the absurd, almost disconcerting candour, the ability to note shortcomings with amused equanimity, placidly sombre insights into life's graver aspects" (*Listener* 27 June 1985: 31).

An Academic Question has not fared so well. Reviewers repeatedly praise the quality of Holt's "amalgamation" of the two drafts; they also suggest that the novel should not have been published. A *New Yorker* reviewer calls the reconciled drafts a "wonderful result" (3 Nov. 1986: 165). Tim Satchell praises "Mrs. Holt's skilful amalgam of both drafts" (*Books and Bookmen* Aug. 1986: 4). And Genevieve Stuttaford affirms Holt's opting for the "first-person narrative, which forms a natural bridge between the early works and the more powerfully resonant novels of Pym's late career" (*Publishers Weekly* 11 July 1986: 54). On the other hand, Harriet Waugh calls the novel "a product" of "a literary industry," and its publication "morally reprehensible on the part of her executor, agent if she has one, and publisher" (*Illustrated London News* Oct. 1986: 80). Charles Barr finds the novel "fascinating . . . for its sourcebook quality," but allows that its publication is "in a way . . . a disservice" (*Listener* 31 July 1986: 24). On a more positive note, Merle Rubin supports publication of the book, writing that "[a]lthough the book, never fully revised, is one of Pym's paler efforts . . . , it would be foolish to complain that its publication does the author a disservice. The novel is interesting in its own right" and provides insight "about what can happen when a writer tries to work against her grain" (*New York Times Book Review* 7 Sept. 1986: 25).

Others, too, write positively about *An Academic Question.* Laura Shapiro finds *An Academic Question* "slightly more acid than Pym's usual work," but bearing "her characteristic wit" (*Newsweek* 10 Nov. 1986: 84). Dorris finds the flow of the novel "occasionally choppy," but he writes that the "effortless grace of Pym's language" and "the deadpan gaze with which she approaches her subject" involve the reader "almost as a participant in the milieu of the author's invention" (*Los Angeles Times Book Review* 14 Sept. 1986: 6). And Isabel Raphael cites Pym's "gentle cattiness . . . which beautifully deflates academic pretension and puts social trendiness in its place" (*Times* [London] 31 July 1986: 11).

Reviews of *Civil to Strangers and Other Writings* are mixed. Although there is some implied criticism of the procedure used in preparing the manuscripts, several of which were reduced from the "raw" state—a *Kirkus* reviewer calls the collection "a hodgepodge" (1 Nov. 1987: 1537), and Stephen Wall writes that the "other fragments accompanying *Civil to Strangers* look fumbling and will be of interest to enthusiasts only" (*London Review of Books* 3 Mar. 1988: 10). A *New Yorker* reviewer cites Holt's "impeccable" introductory comments and notes that "her editing seems judicious and discreet" (22 Feb. 1988: 117). Among the negative reviewers is Penelope Lively, who finds the title novel "a piece of quite attractive juvenilia." The "ensuing 'reductions' " she finds "more dubious." In concluding, Lively notes that "[f]ew writers would wish for such a remorseless exposure of early and inferior work. . . . Devotees will find occasional satisfaction; those who have not yet tried Pym should leave well alone [sic] and buy a copy of *Quartet in Autumn;* the scholars will no doubt snarl" (*Books* Nov. 1987: 21–22). Michele Slung also expresses negative sentiments, writing that only the most "diehard Pym pals" can appreciate *Civil to Strangers* and noting the sadness of having this volume of "unsatisfying prose" conclude with Pym's "assessment of her literary life" (*Washington Post Book World* 17 Jan. 1988: 3, 13).

Other reviewers are more positive. Claire Tomalin writes that "[n]ot quite everything in this collection . . . is vintage Pym, but most of it is too good to miss" (*Observer* 15 Nov. 1987: 26). Patricia O'Conner writes that although *Civil to Strangers* is "not among the strongest of Pym's novels," it "can take its place alongside her others with no apology'' (*New York Times Book Review* 17 Jan. 1988: 29). Dorris calls the title novel ''pure delight,'' though he admits that parts of it ''are almost certainly still in the draft stage,'' that ''[c]oincidence too often takes the place of plotting, and every loose end is tied up too neatly.'' The other pieces in the collection, he writes, ''are of interest primarily as supplements to more significant efforts'' (*Chicago Tribune* 3 Jan. 1988: Sect. 14, 4).

Of all of Pym's books, *A Very Private Eye* has been the most frequently reviewed. Negative reviews range in substance from James Fenton's somewhat flippant disparagement (*Times* [London] 19 July 1984: 10) to the scholarly assessment of Kate Browder Heberlein whose work among the Pym papers at the Bodleian adds credibility to her criticism. Heberlein estimates that *A Very Private Eye* contains no more than 15 percent of the material in the Bodleian, as opposed to the near 50 percent that the editors claim in the preface. Heberlein criticizes the ''disproportionate amount of space . . . given to [Pym's] early life and loves'' and the ''preponderance of letters to Harvey,'' which may result not so much from ''his importance in her life'' but from ''his making them available.'' Heberlein calls for more material from the literary notebooks to make the volume more useful to scholars, further coverage of the relationship of the details of Pym's life to the novels, more about the relationship with Jay and the connections between Richard Roberts and James and Ned of *The Sweet Dove Died* and Gordon Glover and Fabian Driver of *Jane and Prudence.* The friendships, she writes, need more explanation, particularly Pym's relationships with Honor Wyatt, Jock Liddell, and Bob Smith. Readers of *A Very Private Eye,* Heberlein says, will come away ''with a vague and misleading impression of [Pym's] personal life and little understanding of how she transmuted her odd, quiet, rather sad life into her odd, quietly comic fiction'' (*Contemporary Literature* 1985: 369–71).

Other reviewers are also critical of the editors' achievement. Barbara Everett points out that the reader is not told whether '' 'just over half of the material' '' from the Bodleian that the editors say they have used ''applies both to correspondence and to journal entries,'' making it difficult to ''judge the reticently intense relationships developing through some of the letters.'' Further, she writes, there is ''nothing like an appropriate shaping in the materials, which merely follow a loose chronological sequence'' (*London Review of Books* 6–19 Sept. 1984: 5). Peter Ackroyd calls the book an ''unwieldy mass of letters and documents'' (*Times Literary Supplement* 3 Aug. 1984: 861). Richard Widmayer writes that ''the work is often a delight'' but indicates that the substance ''proves a bit of a disappointment,'' perhaps because of its autobiographical concept. He adds that ''[t]he ironic judgment is what we want explored, not the color of her undergraduate underwear,'' and he calls for less material prior to 1948 and more on the later years (*Rocky Mountain Review of Language and Literature* 1985: 77–78).

At the same time, reviewers have praised the quality and substance of Pym's writing throughout the diary and letters. A *New Yorker* reviewer finds the first part of the book ''especially rich in comic characters'' and writes that ''in her diaries . . . one finds the essential Barbara Pym: curious and wry, and always gathering, sometimes grimly, grist for her mill'' (16 July 1984: 92). Richard Dyer writes that ''for all its artlessness, this is one of the best of the books by Barbara Pym.'' It ''brings us the personality of the 'real' Barbara Pym, but it also brings us something better, her character'' (*Boston Globe* 3 July 1984: 11). Victoria Glendinning appreciates the historical value of the book, writing that Pym's ''semicomic mania for detail, and her astonishing inventories of clothes, decor, food, hairstyles and cosmetics, give this marvelous compilation a secondary value as social history'' (*New York Times Book Review* 8 July 1984: 3).

Reviewers frequently point to the parallels between the life revealed in the ''autobiography'' and Pym's novels, noting at times that these parallels provide insight into Pym's writing process and the ways her writing influenced her life. Rosemary Dinnage, for example, remarks that the writings reveal that Pym ''seemed to foresee the shape of her life'' (*New York Review of Books* 16 Aug. 1984: 15). Especially insightful is Susan Mernit who writes that the early diaries not only depict Pym's social life but they ''also sketch out the genesis of another, more shadowy self, an alternative *persona* that she was creating.'' The shift in focus in the diaries from the personal to the literary after World War II suggests that ''Pym literally invented her mature self.'' Ambivalent about her ''singleness,'' she chose ''finally, work over love,'' but she wished ''continually for what she did not have." *A Very Private Eye,* Mernit concludes, provides "an opportunity to see the novelist invent herself" (*Women's Review of Books* Jan. 1985: 5–6).

The reviews of Pym's books number in the hundreds. Her novels are available in paperback, and they have been translated into French, Italian, German, Dutch, Portuguese, Hungarian, and Russian (Holt, *A Lot to Ask* 279). Yet her success as a novelist extends beyond the scope of the popular press. Her reception within the academic community suggests that the life she wrote in her books may indeed find its rightful place in the English literary canon. John Halperin, reviewing *A Very Private Eye* in *Modern Fiction Studies,* expresses the view that "Barbara Pym is one of the greatest modern British novelists." Her novels provide "unrivaled pictures of the middle classes of postwar England." "One could argue," he writes, that the ten novels Pym prepared for publication, "taken together, are the most striking examples of comic fiction to have appeared anywhere in the world in this century" (1984: 780).

Pym's novels are required reading in a number of undergraduate and graduate-level literature courses in the United States and Canada. Deborah J. Knuth of Colgate University, Eleanor Beiswenger of Austin Peay State University, and Anne C. Pilgrim of York University (Toronto) report in the June and December 1989 issues of the *Barbara Pym Newsletter* on courses in which they teach Pym's novels. The *Newsletter* itself, edited from 1986 to 1992 by Mary Anne Schofield and Doreen Alvarez Saar, attests to Pym's acceptance within the academic community. Since Pym's death in 1980, more than a dozen Ph.D. dissertations and sixteen books about her life and work have been published. In addition, more than seventy articles have appeared in scholarly journals and collections.

Pym's work merits study both in terms of its place in the English literary canon and because Pym's techniques as a writer writing her life are instructive to students of writing. Toward this end, Part II of this book explores some of the fictional techniques Pym employs in transmuting the raw materials of her life into her novels. Part III summarizes the scholarly treatment of her work. Part IV lists Pym's work as well as the secondary literature, including most of the substantive reviews of the novels, that her fiction has elicited.

Notes

[1]Anne M. Wyatt-Brown, "Ellipsis, Eccentricity and Evasion in the Diaries of Barbara Pym," writes that Frederick's apparent illegitimacy may have contributed to Irena's taking a leading position in the family's life. Drawing on Karen Horney's *Feminine Psychology* (1967; rpt. New York: Norton, 1973), Wyatt-Brown hypothesizes that Pym's family environment contributed to her developing "a sense of her own unworthiness" and to her overvaluing of love (29), an attitude that is manifest in the conversion of her negative experiences into "a comic literary receptacle" (30).

[2]Julian Amery, son of Leopold Amery, a member of Parliament for more than thirty years, was elected to Parliament in 1950. For a discussion of Pym's attachment to him and its effect on her writing, see Robert Emmet Long, *Barbara Pym,* 9–11; Hazel Holt, *A Lot to Ask,* 73–80; and Wyatt-Brown, *Barbara Pym: A Critical Biography,* 48–52.

[3]Long notes Simon Beddoes's "exact likeness to Julian Amery" (*Barbara Pym* 66).

[4]Wyatt-Brown suggests that Pym's Oxford relationship with Rupert Gleadow and her lack of sexual interest in him is reflected in Barbara Bird's reluctance to engage in a sexual relationship with Francis Cleveland ("Ellipsis, Eccentricity and Evasion in the Diaries of Barbara Pym" 44).

[5]Diana Benet, in *Something to Love: Barbara Pym's Novels,* discusses some of the flaws in *Crampton Hodnet.* Among them she cites "overplotting" as well as "too many characters, too many—and some too ominous—episodes" (29).

[6]Long indicates that "Beatrice Wyatt" reflects Pym's "unrequited attachment" to Amery (*Barbara Pym* 11).

[7]See Michael Cotsell, *Barbara Pym,* 30–31.

[8]Wyatt-Brown uses the lumber room metaphor to explain Pym's treatment of Barbara Bird's frigidity. This metaphor, Wyatt-Brown suggests, helps us to "better understand the forces that made her a writer" ("Ellipsis, Eccentricity and Evasion in the Diaries of Barbara Pym" 45).

[9]See Holt's "The Novelist in the Field" for an account of the years at the International African Institute and a discussion of the influence of Pym's experience with the anthropologists on her career as a novelist.

[10]For a discussion of some of the significant changes in *Some Tame Gazelle* from its early draft stage in 1934 to the final publication in 1950, see Cotsell, 19–22.

[11]See Glynn-Ellen Maria Fisichelli, *"The Trivial Round, the Common Task": Barbara Pym: The Development of a Writer,* 97–107, for a discussion and plot summaries of several of the short stories. Wyatt-Brown also discusses several of the short stories in *Barbara Pym: A Critical Biography.* See especially chapters 1, 2, 3, and 7.

[12]Robert Liddell, who discusses Pym's reuse of elements from *Crampton Hodnet* in *Jane and Prudence* in *A Mind at Ease: Barbara Pym and Her Novels,* writes that "[a]fter *Jane and Prudence* Barbara could not have intended that *Crampton Hodnet* should ever be published, but no doubt still kept it as a possibly useful quarry" (24).

[13]Denton Welch died in 1948 at the age of thirty-three. *The Last Sheaf,* a collection of his unpublished writings, was published by John Lehmann in 1951. Robert Phillips, in *Denton Welch* (New York: Twayne, 1974), describes Welch's "refusal to compromise facts and to fictionalize life," noting that "no one was certain whether [his writings] were fiction or autobiography" (158). Other qualities of Welch's writing noted by Phillips include his "deliberate juxtaposition of the important and the trivial," the "narrowness of his range," and his "personal, anecdotal narrative line" (159). His writing may be "repetitive and restrictive," but "so are the masters," and Phillips goes on to quote Proust, who wrote that the " 'great men of letters have never created more than a single work, or rather have never done more than refract through various mediums an identical beauty which they bring into the world' " (167).

[14]Holt writes that Pym "always had a passion for 'finding out' about people who interested or attracted her." Her " 'research into the lives of ordinary people' " ranged from looking them up "in *Who's Who, Crockford* or street directories to the actual 'tailing' of the object of her investigation" (VPE 10).

[15]Constance Malloy, "The Quest for a Career," 196n19, cites manuscripts in the Pym papers at the Bodleian.

[16]Benet, *Something to Love: Barbara Pym's Novels,* writes: "If Barbara Pym wrote about 'excellent men,' Rupert might be one of them . . ." (105).

[17]From a letter to Robert Smith, 19 March 1963, cited by Malloy, "The Quest for a Career," 9.

[18]Reprinted as "The Rejection of Barbara Pym" in Salwak, *The Life and Work of Barbara Pym*, 171–175. Page numbers in parentheses are from the reprint.

[19]See Janice Rossen, *The World of Barbara Pym*, 67–68; Long *Barbara Pym*, 159–63; and Wyatt-Brown, *Barbara Pym: A Critical Biography*, 115–17, for discussions of the relationship with Roberts and Pym's use of it in *The Sweet Dove Died*. Pym herself wrote that the novel "is a chunk of my life, in a sense!" (VPE 307).

[20]See, for example, Merritt Moseley, "Barbara Pym's Dark Novels," 3–4, and Jane Nardin, *Barbara Pym*, 5–6.

[21]Reprinted in Salwak, *The Life and Work of Barbara Pym*, 58–63. Citation is from the reprint.

[22]Snow, *One Little Room an Everywhere*, quotes Pym as saying, in response to a questionnaire sent by her publishers, that she had written *Quartet in Autumn* because she was "tired of the heavy-handed, humourless way" the subject of retirement and old age was treated, "especially by the media." Snow also notes Pym's identification with the "consciousness of mortality that she attributes to Letty" (84).

[23]*Anatomy of Criticism: Four Essays* (Princeton, N.J.: Princeton University Press, 1957), 238. See Bruce Richard Jacobs, *Elements of Satire in the Novels of Barbara Pym*.

[24]See Rossen, "The Pym Papers," for an overview and discussion of the papers and their relative usefulness to scholars. In addition, Wyatt-Brown includes a useful bibliography of the unpublished materials in *Barbara Pym: A Critical Biography*, pp. 187–90.

PART TWO—WRITING A LIFE: BARBARA PYM AND HER NOVELS

The publication of *A Very Private Eye: An Autobiography in Diaries and Letters* (1984) called attention to the close ties between Barbara Pym's fiction and the people and events in her life. In addition, a number of her critics have pointed to the close parallels between her life and her novels.[1] Yet the connections between Pym's life and her novels go beyond the rendering of people, events, and feelings into fiction. The repetition and evolution of the themes of her novels register an artist's struggle to come to terms with some of the underlying issues of her life. The iteration and evolution of theme throughout the Pym canon suggests that Pym used the novels, at least on an unconscious level and perhaps even consciously, to explore and shape the fundamental issues that governed her life.

In short, Pym wrote her life. At the same time, the autobiographical nature of her work in no way diminishes her art. Pym's novels reflect her awareness that the self is in many ways a fiction, and the autobiographical nature of her novels may have required "more, rather than less, artifice than the writing of other kinds of fiction" (Hite xv).

In writing her life in her novels, Pym avoided the problem of memoirs lamented by Virginia Woolf in "A Sketch of the Past," that they "leave out the person to whom things happened" (65). Through her novels Pym's readers come to know her, sometimes as narrator, sometimes as character, but more often in the tension that issues from her subtle irony. Pym's novels are a valuable testimony to the interplay between the artist and her art, the artist shaping her art and that in turn shaping the life that gives form to the art. This study traces the iteration and evolution of three major themes that dominated Pym's life and her novels, focusing on the ten novels that Pym herself prepared for publication, in an attempt to better understand some of the ways she used her fictional technique to interpret and articulate her experience.[2]

The themes of Pym's novels fall into three somewhat overlapping clusters related to romance, religion, and literature. Each cluster involves a complex interrelationship of subject matter and ideas that evolves throughout the novels, from *Some Tame Gazelle* to *A Few Green Leaves,* until in her final novel Pym achieves a resolution that suggests a similar working out in her life.

The first, romance, deals to a large extent with women's relationships with men, including the illusions of romantic love, the frustrations of unrequited love, and the associated need of an object on which to dote. Sometimes counterpointed to romantic love relationships are women's relationships with one another. Closely related to the theme of romantic love is Pym's treatment of the trivia of domestic life—the clothes, the food, the details of the commonplace that have come to mark her writing. In short, the romance theme includes Pym's realm of personal life and relationships.

The world of personal relationships overlaps with Pym's treatment of religion, which focuses primarily on the Church of England, the social unit that represents community life. Here Pym expresses the contradictions she perceives between the idealized role of the church and the actuality of a petty, ineffectual clergy—the frequent objects of women's doting—and a church regimen that often fails to meet the needs of its congregation.

Integrating both romance and religion is literature, which Pym uses in frequent quotations and allusions throughout the novels. Pym's Oxford degree in English literature was, no doubt, an important influence in the development of this focus for her work. But her concern with literature throughout the novels may reflect her search for meaning in her own life, a search that involves the function of literature itself and the need to discover her own niche in English literary history. This search is evident as Pym contrasts the work of the greater English poets and novelists with the work of the social scientist, particularly the anthropologist, and with the more superficial work of the romantic novelist.

SOME TAME GAZELLE

Pym's first published novel, *Some Tame Gazelle,* written in 1934–1935 shortly after she had come down from St. Hilda's College, Oxford, with a second in English literature, is, as Pym tells us, largely autobiographical, based on her unrequited love for Henry Harvey, with whom she had been close during her Oxford days. Pym describes the project as a "story about Hilary [her sister, three years younger] and me as spinsters of fiftyish" (VPE 44). The novel is about Belinda and Harriet Bede, spinster sisters, and their relationships, friendly and romantic, in a parish-centered village. The sisters are preoccupied with their attachments with the clergy, Belinda with the Archdeacon Henry Hoccleve, for whom she has for thirty years sustained an unrequited love, and Harriet with young curates. In the course of the novel a series of intruders with offers of marriage threaten these happily unmarried ladies. In the end, Belinda and Harriet (Barbara and Hilary) discover they prefer living together in spinsterhood to the unknown trials of matrimony. Ironically, the novel seems to anticipate the lives of Barbara and Hilary in that they lived together much of their lives and retired together in a cottage in the village of Finstock. Barbara remained a spinster and friends with Henry Harvey until her death. Hilary, married for a short time, separated from her husband in 1946 (VPE 184).

The theme of the questionable nature of matrimony pervades *Some Tame Gazelle.* The two marriages in the novel, the disquieting relationship of Archdeacon Henry Hoccleve and Agatha and the marriage of the Reverend Edgar Donne and Olivia Berridge that occurs in the final chapter, appear to have been arranged by the wives. Pym carefully ties the imagery of death to marriage in the gift presentation ceremony for Edgar and Olivia in the penultimate chapter of the novel. As they discuss Connie Aspinall's arrival for the ceremony, Edith Liversidge tells Harriet that Connie's train is " 'due in at a quarter to three, so I suppose she should be here for most of it—in at the death, you know.' " And Harriet sighs, " 'Poor Mr. Donne . . . one almost feels that it *is* a death' " (STG 231). At the ceremony, the Archdeacon brings in the gift, a "large square object [a clock] shrouded in a cloth" (STG 232). Later he flings aside the shroud after quoting from

Edward Young: " '*We take no note of time but from its loss . . .*' "
(STG 234).

Although the wedding chapter that follows opens on a brighter
note, Pym is careful to plant the seeds of ambivalence, to question
the myth of romantic love. The day of the wedding is "fine, one of
those unexpected spring days that come too soon and deceive one
into thinking that the winter is over" (STG 242). The music
selection includes *The voice that breathed o'er Eden* "sung to the
tune of *Brief life is here our portion,*" and during the ceremony
Belinda's attention strays to the "rows of memorial tablets to past
vicars" (STG 245). Pym ends the novel with a wedding, following
pastoral tradition, but the subversive allusions to death introduce an
ambiguity implying that with the passing of time the marriage of
Olivia Mary Berridge and Edgar Donne is likely to repeat the
undesirable pattern of the marriage of Agatha and Henry Hoccleve.
This marriage ceremony reverses the traditional celebratory marriage, celebrating "not marriage, but singleness" (Nardin 71).

Matrimony is the greatest threat to the comfortable lives of
Belinda and Harriet Bede. Proposals from suitors interrupt their
lives. Most frequent, but least threatening, are Ricardo Bianco's
courtly proposals to Harriet. Met with Harriet's perfunctory
rejection, they serve as a touchstone against which she can
compare the intruding Mr. Mold's "prosaic and casual" attitude
(STG 137). Similarly intrusive is Theodore Grote's proposal to
Belinda, tendered because " 'a man does need a helpmeet' "
(STG 224). Refused by Belinda, the undaunted Grote straight-
away proposes and is accepted by poor, elegiac Connie Aspinall
whose living arrangement with her relative Edith Liversidge is
less than satisfactory. The proposals of both Mold and Grote
reflect the cynicism of Dr. Nicholas Parnell, librarian and intruder
along with Mold and Grote, that sixty is a " 'good age for a man to
marry. He needs a woman to help him into his grave' " (STG
148). In summary, the love relationships in *Some Tame Gazelle*
indicate that Pym's sentiment about romantic love by the time she
published this novel may have been reflected in Parnell's quotation of Samuel Johnson—that it is "*only one of many passions
and it has no great influence on the sum of life*" (STG 144).

In *Some Tame Gazelle,* Pym's treatment of romantic love
overlaps her satiric comment on the Church of England, the latter

consisting largely of a humorous look at an inept, insensitive clergy. The novel's most prominent clergyman is the Archdeacon Henry Hoccleve whose insensitivity extends beyond his reproach of his wife Agatha for not keeping the moth out of his suit to a self-centered inability to anticipate the needs of his congregation. Afraid of being overworked, Henry seeks sympathy from Belinda, turns early morning services over to his curate so he can sleep late, and forces the cat from a chair so he can claim the warmest spot in the room. He looks to Bishop Grote's visit with "a kind of grim relish" (STG 161), reveling in the gloomy discomforts of the guest room with its sides-to-middle sheets, lumpy mattress, and carefully selected dull books on the bedside table. Seldom able to find the appropriate prayer for any occasion, his greatest act of insensitivity is his Judgment Day sermon, a litany of quotations from the English poets beginning in the seventeenth century and continuing through T. S. Eliot.

The other clergy in the novel are similarly insensitive. The Reverend Plowman, the Archdeacon's foil and rival, preaches homely sermons that his parishioners can understand. Plowman's "elaborate ritual" is "ample compensation for the intellectual poverty of his sermons" (STG 42). Nevertheless, he is excessively interested in refreshments, and he steals Henry's thunder by getting in the appropriate prayer and generally overstepping his authority at the presentation ceremony that precedes the wedding of Father Donne and Olivia Berridge. Bishop Grote with his bleating voice and sheeplike caricature is a foil to both Donne and Hoccleve. Grote decides at age sixty to marry for convenience. Donne, a young Henry Hoccleve, is caught up in marriage by Olivia almost unawares. Although Donne's reading preference is for detective novels and the questionable poems of the Earl of Rochester, Olivia has plans to encourage literary sermons.

Pym's use of literature is more pervasive in *Some Tame Gazelle* than in any of her subsequent novels. She uses numerous quotations from the English poets, beginning with the Thomas Haynes Bailey lines from which the novel derives its name to Keble's "the trivial round, the common task" that anticipates the subject matter of her *oeuvre* (STG 227). Hardly a page passes without some use of literature. Literature fosters a bond between characters in the novel as Henry reads Wordsworth's *Prelude* to Belinda and they reminisce about their college years. Literature provides a standard against which characters can weigh their own lives as well as counterpointing to provide ironic comment on the characters and action in the novel. Father Donne's name resonates with irony. The Archdeacon would pronounce it "Dunne," after the seventeenth-century poet; but Donne himself rejects that pronunciation, perhaps a reflection of his literary naïveté. Other literary allusions can be found in the names in the novel, including of course Father Plowman's name and the name Bede. Literature functions symbolically, and ironically, throughout *Some Tame Gazelle.* Quotations from and allusions to Milton and the Garden of Eden as well as the pastoral mode of the novel itself—the bucolic setting, a village "sealed off hermetically from the outside world," the quality of innocence that pervades the novel, its courtship theme, and the fact that it ends with a marriage celebration (Long, *Barbara Pym* 25)—all reflect Pym's skill at using symbols to convey her message that marriage is not the preferred state.

The most obvious explanation for the frequency of literary allusion in this first novel has to do with the fact that it was written when Pym was fresh from the study of English literature at Oxford. But more importantly, this must have been a time when Pym was struggling with the meaning of literature, meaning in the sense of how literature was to function for her personally and of its more general cultural functions. She may not have reached any long-lasting conclusions in writing *Some Tame Gazelle,* but the function of literature is an important concern as she explores the use of quotation and allusion within the novel itself.

Pym's first novel is her most overtly autobiographical piece in its characterization of the people in her life and in its treatment of unrequited love. The resolution of the novel reflects her awareness of the illusory nature of romantic love, perhaps even an acceptance of the blessings of spinsterhood. Pym struggles intensely with the conflicts facing her, with society's assumptions that young women must marry, and with her own need to become a writer. It would seem that she was dealing unconsciously, if not consciously, with her calling as a novelist and the conflict between a writing career and fulfilling the conventional role promised by the myth of romantic love.

EXCELLENT WOMEN

Excellent Women (1952), the second novel Pym published
during her lifetime, is less overtly autobiographical than *Some
Tame Gazelle*. Nevertheless, Pym continues to draw heavily on
her own experience, setting the novel in a London suburb, on the
"wrong" side of Victoria Station, a neighborhood much like that
in which she and Hilary lived—a flat in Pimlico—at the time she
was writing it. In *Excellent Women,* Pym undermines the value of
marriage throughout the novel so that the heroine's seeming
anticipation of marriage as the novel ends becomes an ironic
statement about conventional marriage (Nardin 82).

Romance becomes the dominant theme as Pym focuses her
attention on the negative aspects of spinsterism while comparing
it favorably with marriage and widowhood. The first-person
protagonist, Mildred Lathbury, daughter of a clergyman, is a
spinster in her mid-thirties, preoccupied with the lives of others,
prone to feelings of guilt and self-abnegation. Hers is the plight,
Pym seems to be telling us, of women who have not been chosen
or who have not snared a husband to validate their lives. Mildred's
foils are the married and unfaithful Helena Napier, the clergyman's widow Allegra Gray, who has had practice catching a
husband and who is bound to snare a new one, and Winifred
Malory, spinster sister of and housekeeper to the vicar Julian
Malory. Allegra's matrimonial plans for Julian render Winifred
superfluous and threaten her security in the vicarage. Allegra's
question, " 'What do women *do* if they don't marry' " (EW 129),
poses the problem that runs throughout the novel. The question is
pondered by Mildred, who has come to realize "that practically
anything may be the business of an unattached woman with no
troubles of her own, who takes a kindly interest in those of her
friends" (EW 47).

Mildred's kindly interest involves her as mediator in a series of
romance-related problems that bring her to the conclusion that
perhaps she "really enjoyed other people's lives more" than her
own (EW 222). Her service to others, set against the background
of her naïve yet at times cynical self-observation, provides much
of the humor of the novel as Pym studies, in more detail than she
did in *Some Tame Gazelle*, the foibles of married people. Here she
reuses the theme of marital infidelity that she practiced in

Crampton Hodnet. Rocky Napier's exploits with Wren officers, his Italian girlfriend, and Helena's affinity for her anthropological soulmate, Everard Bone, point to a major difficulty associated with married life. And although Rocky and Helena are reunited in the end, the reader holds little hope for an idyllic marriage in spite of their move to a country cottage. The Napiers, in short, awaken Mildred to the naïveté of her romantic ideas about marriage.

A large part of Mildred's diffidence derives from her sense of guilt about her spinster state. Self-conscious of her voyeuristic tendencies, reflected in her previous job with the Censorship where she had read about "the silly romantic way" (EW 25) people carried on and the "weaknesses of human nature" (EW 46), she takes care to tidy Rocky's desk, conscious that she might "come across something" that was none of her business (EW 172). She wonders why the information she finds in her bedtime reading of a book of household hints—that "a package or envelope sealed with white of egg cannot be steamed open"— would ever be of use to her (EW 171). As a spinster, Mildred appreciates her independence, coveting her solitary life. Yet her sense of inadequacy as an "unmarried and inexperienced woman" (EW 25) motivates her interest in three potential suitors: the dashing Rockingham Napier, associated with images of a goat, moths, and woodworm and who moves her emotions; Julian Malory, who "might need to be protected from the women who were going to live in his house" (EW 256); and Everard Bone, whose anthropological manuscripts, which she seems doomed to proofread and index, evoke despair. The ending of the novel leaves the reader fearful that she may indeed absolve her guilt and validate her existence by marrying Everard and, like the wife of the president of the Learned Society, spend her days proofreading, indexing, and knitting and nodding at meetings of the Learned Society.

The religion motif that originates in *Some Tame Gazelle* assumes greater consequence in *Excellent Women*. Although Pym makes no explicit statements about the Church of England in this novel, implied comparisons with the Learned Society and with Roman Catholicism cannot be overlooked. Helena Napier, anthropologist, expresses antipathy toward the vicarage and pits anthropology against religion with comments about Mildred's " 'churchgoing and good works' " (EW 177). Mildred points out to Helena that St. Ermin's, where Archdeacon Hoccleve delivers his Judgment Day Sermon, carried over from *Some Tame Gazelle,* is not far from "the premises of the Learned Society" (EW 87). Hoccleve's obscure service, which evokes the disgust of Mrs. Bonner and the mirth of Everard Bone, is juxtaposed with Helena and Everard's reading of their obscure paper to the Learned Society. At dinner afterward, Helena contrasts anthropologists with " 'so-called good people who go to church' " (EW 97). Although Everard Bone is a churchgoer—his mother, who is not a Christian, despairs that the " 'Jesuits got at my son' " (EW 150)—anthropologists as a group are associated with atheism, and their president, who looks "mild and benevolent," is a " 'militant atheist' " who in Mildred's imagination made his wife an unbeliever (EW 89).

In addition to implying that members of the Learned Society are to be compared with followers of the Church of England, Pym devotes considerable space to setting the Church of England off against Roman Catholicism, enough to suggest that her own religious affiliation may have been an important personal issue at the time she was writing *Excellent Women.* One implied criticism has to do with the failure of Church of England ritual to evoke an appropriate emotional response in its participants. Archdeacon Hoccleve's Judgment Day Sermon is not the only religious observance to disappoint Mildred. As she and Dora attend the window dedication ceremony for Miss Ridout, Mildred reflects on her confirmation service at age fifteen when she had "knelt, uncomfortably, expecting something that never quite came" (EW 111). Later, in a moment of emotional distress after saying good-bye to Rocky, Mildred seeks solace at St. Mary's. But her attempt to meditate is interrupted by Miss Statham, "polishing-cloth and a tin of Brasso in her hand," who stifles a giggle and remarks that " 'it seemed a bit funny to be sitting here on a nice afternoon thinking things over' " (EW 168).

The subject of Roman Catholicism, frequently accompanied by a comment on the emotional response it evokes in its followers, surfaces several times. Typically, Roman Catholicism is opposed to the Church of England with an implication that its followers might be lured into going over to Rome. The biography of Cardinal Newman that Mildred carries in her string bag on her dinner visit with Mrs. Bone is symbolic of the lure of Roman

Catholicism and of Mildred's (and possibly Pym's) temptation. When Mildred leaves for home she stuffs "some pamphlets about woodworms and Jesuits" into her "string bag with Cardinal Newman and the loaf" (EW 150). Later, meeting Everard at lunchtime, she reflects on the last time they had met and "Cardinal Newman and a loaf in my string bag" (EW 186). On holiday with Dora the two visit an Abbey with a group of priests from a Roman Catholic seminary. Inside the Abbey, Mildred is

> almost overwhelmed by the sudden impression of light and brilliance. The walls looked bright and clean, there was a glittering of much gold and the lingering smell of incense was almost hygienic. Not here, I thought, would one be sentimentally converted to Rome, for there was no warm rosy darkness to hide in, no comfortable confusion of doctrines and dogmas; all would be reasoned out and clearly explained, as indeed it should be. (EW 196)

Later, as they leave the Abbey, Mildred watches from the bus stop "a group of priests looking down on us from the upper deck" and feels that "somehow the Pope and his Dogmas had triumphed after all" (EW 202). Back at home, preparing to write to Rocky in the interest of reuniting him with Helena, Mildred goes over her notebooks, "turning the pages of a notebook" in which she "kept accounts and made shopping lists" and wondering if "perhaps there was matter for poetry in them." Here she runs across "the name of a well-known Roman Catholic bookshop" and recalls going into it at Christmas and finding it "a peaceful refuge from the shopping crowds" (EW 183). Finally, it must be significant that the new tenants who replace the Napiers and with whom Mildred feels pleased because she can anticipate a clean bathroom are Roman Catholics.

The bathroom imagery is, in fact, an important motif throughout *Excellent Women*. Bathrooms are associated with Mildred's self-image. Pym introduces the bathroom motif on the second page of the novel when Mildred describes her flat and the association of the need to share a bathroom with her sense of self-esteem: " 'I have to share a bathroom,' I had so often murmured, almost with shame, as if I personally had been found unworthy of a bathroom of my own" (EW 6). Mildred finds the "burden of keeping three people in toilet paper . . . rather a heavy one" (EW 10); Helena Napier's toilet paper contribution is "of a rather inferior brand"; and Helena's cleaning of the bath "was not as well done" as Mildred would "have liked to see it" (EW 21). The vicarage boasts "a large cold bathroom" (EW 16–17), perhaps in keeping with its inhabitants; and the bathroom of the Learned Society is a " 'repository for any junk that can't go anywhere else,' " a place where, as Helena explains, the users are at their " 'most primitive.' " Here, in the bathroom of the Learned Society, Helena and Mildred engage in girl talk about Rocky and Everard, and Mildred reflects on her own girlhood experience with bathrooms "where one has stayed there too long, though never long enough to last out the dance for which one hadn't a partner" (EW 95). At the train station, returning with Dora Caldicote from the window dedication ceremony for Miss Ridout, and having been enlightened by a Wren officer on the train about Rocky's exploits with women, Dora has to "go into the Ladies." Not wanting to go herself, perhaps not wanting to face her own affinity with Rocky's other women, Mildred follows meekly, noting that it "was a sobering kind of place to be in and a glance at my face in the dusty ill-lit mirror was enough to discourage anybody's romantic thoughts" (EW 115). The Ladies Room of the department store Mildred visits after the disconcerting news that Allegra Gray is engaged to Julian Malory provides another "sobering sight indeed":

> one to put us all in mind of the futility of material things and of our own mortality. *All flesh is but grass* . . . I thought, watching the women working at their faces with savage concentration, opening their mouths wide, biting and licking their lips, stabbing at their noses and chins with powder-puffs. Some, who had abandoned the struggle to keep up, sat in chairs, their bodies slumped down, their hands resting on their parcels. . . . (EW 131)

At the home of Everard Bone's mother, Mildred finds "a bathroom with much marble and mahogany and a stained-glass window," a place that evokes thought about the Oxford Movement and its architecture and seems "suitable" to the biography of Cardinal Newman she is carrying in her string bag (EW 146).

Even the Abbey Mildred visits on holiday with Dora is not without a notice that says "Ladies."

In more than one instance Pym connects bathrooms, in which one comes closest to one's true self, with Roman Catholicism. Thus it seems likely that the willingness of two Roman Catholic spinsters whose "rota for cleaning the bath" Mildred finds pleasant and cooperative is of significance in the novel (EW 243). Is Pym using a subversive text to suggest that the Roman Catholic Church spoke to her more primitive needs and that she found it inviting at this time in her life? At the very least, the bathroom imagery links two major themes in *Excellent Women*—romantic love and religion.

Pym uses literary quotation and allusion freely in *Excellent Women,* though not as pervasively as in *Some Tame Gazelle,* and it is still difficult to settle on any clear pattern for its use. Sometimes she uses it humorously as when Mildred, who keeps cookery and devotional books on the bookshelf for "comforting bedside reading," is glad to find she has selected *Chinese Cookery* instead of *Religio Medici* (EW 20), and Miss Clovis quotes from Anthony à Wood to describe the sudden death of the president of the Learned Society: " 'suddenly with meat in his mouth' " (EW 176). Christina Rossetti's *"Better by far you should forget and smile,/Than that you should remember and be sad. . . ."* is quoted twice. First Mildred uses it in reference to Winifred's spinsterish role as Julian's housekeeper. Later she thinks of the lines as she ponders Rocky's treatment of the Wren officers. In the latter instance, Mildred's familiarity with these lines from "a limp suede-bound volume" among her "bedside books" is a commentary on her own character that has permitted her to set aside memories of her youthful unrequited love for Bernard Hatherley (EW 171).

Milton, Shakespeare, Donne, Matthew Arnold, Pope, Trollope, Keats, and others make their way into this novel. But perhaps most telling with regard to Pym herself are the literary allusions that Mildred, who in some repects at least is Pym, makes with reference to herself. Already mentioned is Mildred's reference to her own notebooks as a source of poetry, notebooks that call to mind Pym's own journals that juxtaposed shopping lists with ideas for her novels.[3] At least one part of Mildred sees herself as observer and writer. As she stands over the kitchen sink resenting the presumption of Rocky and Julian, she muses on how she might write a stream-of-consciousness novel dealing with ''an hour in the life of a woman at the sink'' (EW 161). Talking with Everard about the conversation she had had with his mother, Mildred muses to herself, ''Birds, worms and Jesuits . . . it might almost have been a poem'' (EW 151). And consoling Julian Malory after Allegra Gray's departure she seizes on a line from Keats, remarking, '' 'I always think *Nor What Soft Incense* would be a splendid title for a novel. Perhaps about a village where there were two rival churches, one High and one Low' '' (EW 212). It is perhaps this sense of herself as author that explains Mildred's comment at the very beginning of the novel that ''I am not at all like Jane Eyre, who must have given hope to so many plain women who tell their stories in the first person'' (EW 7). Mildred's denial ironically betrays her naïveté, her frequent inability to see herself clearly. This passage so early in the novel also calls attention to its first-person narrator and to the autobiographical implications of the novel.

JANE AND PRUDENCE

Pym's next novel, *Jane and Prudence,* was published in 1953, just one year after *Excellent Women.* The close ties between the themes of romance, religion, and literature in the two novels suggest that Pym may have seen them as companion novels. In some respects the later novel comments on and augments the ideas presented in the earlier one. There seems little doubt that both novels reflect Pym's concern about issues of romance, religion, and literature in her own life.

The romance theme again focuses on the plight of the spinster, with women's options, and probably aspects of Pym's own personality depicted in the range of women who inhabit the novel. Each of these women, Jane Cleveland, Constance Driver, introduced posthumously, Prudence Bates, Jesse Morrow, Miss Doggett, Flora Cleveland, Eleanor Hitchens, and Mildred Lathbury Bone—carried over from *Excellent Women* and whose fate is revealed by Miss Doggett—illustrates an option. The title character Prudence Bates is seemingly doomed to a lifetime of unsatisfactory love affairs. Prudence's unrequited passion for her employer, Dr. Grampian, lasts until she becomes interested in the rakish Fabian Driver. Driver is the quintessential unfaithful husband to his wife Constance whose death came as a shock to him because he had almost forgotten her existence. In his egotism, he places his own photo over her grave. But when Driver succumbs to Jesse Morrow, who surreptitiously captures him so that she can avoid being a distressed gentlewoman in her old age, he takes his place in "the shrine" of Prudence's past loves, and Prudence moves on to Geoffrey Manifold and possibly an interlude with Grampian and an affair with Edward Lyall. The other unmarried women in the group are Miss Doggett, domineering and manipulative; Eleanor Hitchens, who has adjusted well to spinsterism, living a comfortable life and enjoying the company of her women friends; and nineteen-year-old Flora Cleveland, whose insatiable interest in young men suggests a future that parallels Prudence's life.

The married women seem to fare less well than the spinsters. Constance had had to endure Fabian's infidelity, even entertaining his paramours on needlework afternoons under the walnut tree. Jane Cleveland has given up her literary interests to minister awkwardly to a complacent vicar husband. Inept as a cook and homemaker, she dresses shabbily and offends family and guests with her misspoken attempts at conversation. Mildred Lathbury Bone has become the most useful wife of all, having learned to type so she can type Everard's manuscripts. This sort of devotion, Miss Morrow allows, " 'is worse than blackmail—a man has no escape from that' " (JP 126). And it is difficult to be optimistic about the marriage of Jesse Morrow and Fabian Driver as he is " 'led away captive by the women [Jesse and Miss Doggett]' " (JP 215). Of all the women in the novel, the one who seems to have fared best is the well-adjusted spinster Eleanor Hitchens.

Some of Pym's most effective humor is found in her use of the refrain "What do men need? What do men want?" that runs like a Greek chorus throughout *Jane and Prudence*. Pym introduces it in chapter 3 as the women gather in what Jane feels is "some primitive kind of ritual" to decorate the church for the Harvest Thanksgiving (JP 31). The subject of preparing meals is discussed, and Miss Mayhew, one of the church ladies and proprietor of a restaurant, pronounces, " 'Of course, a man must have meat' " (JP 30). In this same chapter, Mrs. Glaze, the Cleveland's

cook, reveals that Fabian Driver, who would have Jane believe he
cooked his own meals, has a housekeeper who is cooking him a
"casserole of hearts" (JP 33). When Jane and Nicholas must eat
lunch at the Mayhew/Crampton restaurant because of Jane's
ineptitude in the kitchen, Mrs. Crampton serves Nicholas a double
portion, telling them, " 'Oh, a man needs eggs!' " and Jane muses
that "[m]en needed meat and eggs—well, yes, that might be
allowed; but surely not more than women did?" (JP 51). In
chapter 7, Miss Doggett fills Jane in on Fabian's infidelity to
Constance, remarking that "men only want *one thing*—that's the
truth of the matter" and then looking puzzled as if she had
forgotten what that one thing might be (JP 70). A few pages later,
Jane responds to Nicholas's compliment on Flora's " 'shaping
very well as a cook' " with " '[b]ut men don't want only that.' "
Then remembering Miss Doggett's comment she leaves her
sentence incomplete as if she, too, had "difficulty in remembering
what it was that men wanted" (JP 82). Not without significance is
Jesse Morrow's smirking refrain in the next chapter as Mrs. Lyall,
Miss Doggett, and Jane discuss men's need for a good breakfast:
" 'Men seem to need a lot of food at all times' " (JP 90). In
chapter 13, as Miss Doggett, Miss Morrow, and Jane prepare the
dead Constance Driver's things to be given to the Society for the
Care of Aged Gentlewomen, they discuss Mildred Lathbury's fate
and the subject of what men want. This time, what men want is
expanded to "[t]yping a man's thesis, correcting proofs, putting
sheets sides-to-middle, bringing up children, balancing the housekeeping budget" (JP 127–28). A few pages later, on finding
Nicholas at home playing with animal-shaped "kiddisoaps," Jane
thinks, "If it is true that men only want one thing, . . . is it perhaps
just to be left to themselves with their soap animals or some other
harmless little trifle?" (JP 129). The subject of what men want
seems resolved to Jane's satisfaction as she reflects on Jesse
Morrow's shrewdness and how Jesse had managed to prevail over
Prudence in capturing Fabian Driver. But Jane's optimism is cast
against Fabian's recognition, as he reaches out and unseeingly
places his hand on the headless body of a dwarf in the vicarage
garden, that though Jesse may be what he needs, she is no longer
what he wants.

   Pym's treatment of religion in *Jane and Prudence* might seem
almost inconsequential if it were not for her somewhat subversive

treatment of it in *Excellent Women*. Even though Jane is a vicar's wife, and the church is central to her life, there are few direct references to religion. We are aware of Nicholas's relatively complacent attitude toward his position; his concerns with animal-shaped kiddisoaps, with playing golf, and with his tobacco culture seem more important than his church responsibilities. And even his church responsibility seems to be largely related to keeping peace among the members of the Parochial Church Council whose main interests are with trivia such as the illustration for the cover of the church magazine. The men on the council largely ignore the women, who are preoccupied with assessing one another's hats; until the women arrive the men gossip about inconsequential matters including a critical assessment of the Clevelands' eating habits and Jane's inability to cook. A major concern of church members is competition with Father Lomax's church, which is Higher than Nicholas's parish, and any sign that might imply sympathy with Roman Catholicism. When Mr. Oliver joins Father Lomax's congregation to fill the post of thurifer left vacant by a gentleman who has "embraced the Roman Faith" (JP 211), Nicholas is disconsolate.

Several characters comment or reflect on religious matters. Mrs. Glaze comments on the Romish inclinations of Father Lomax's church. Fabian compares the simplicity of Father Kinsella's Roman Catholic service, which lacked "the glamour of Rome," with the Church of England; he chooses the Parish Church over Father Lomax's church, even though the High Church service of the latter is more natural to his temperament, because "even if the service was less exotic, the yoke was easier" (JP 55).

Prudence's attitude toward religion reflects that of Mildred in *Excellent Women*. At one point Prudence proclaims the "whole business of religion" meaningless (JP 13). As the novel ends, she finds the glamour of Roman Catholicism enticing. She imagines herself "on holiday in Spain, a black lace mantilla draped over her hair, hurrying into some dark Cathedral" or "instructed by a calm pale Jesuit who would know the answers to all one's doubts" (JP 201). Yet, after pondering George Herbert's "Hope" and being reminded of "Jane and Nicholas, Morning Prayer and Matins and Evensong in a damp country church with pews, and dusty red hassocks," she concludes that "[p]erhaps the Anglican way was the best after all" (JP 202).

Jane expresses a similar ambivalence toward religion. As she browses in a bookstore in London near the close of the novel, an assistant offers help. Jane's unspoken response is

> 'No; thank you. I was just looking round,' was what one usually said. Just looking round the Anglican Church, from one extreme to the other, perhaps climbing higher and higher, peeping over the top to have a look at Rome on the other side, and then quickly drawing back. (JP 218)

One senses that both Prudence and Jane reflect Pym's resolution of the ambivalence she may have felt toward the Roman religion as she was writing *Excellent Women* and *Jane and Prudence*.

Pym's treatment of literature in *Jane and Prudence* is also closely tied to her treatment of it in *Excellent Women*. In *Excellent Women*, Pym hints briefly at the autobiographical nature of her novel with the reference to Jane Eyre. The implications of Mildred's denying that she is like Jane Eyre possibly allude to Pym's concerns regarding the nature of her writing. This seems even more likely if we recall that the original title of the Brontë novel was *Jane Eyre: An Autobiography* and that the Brontë novel reflects to some extent events from Charlotte's own life.

Jane and Prudence provides an even stronger statement about Pym's concern with the form of the novel and its relation to life. Pym begins and ends this novel with Jane comparing her clergyman's-wife role with what she had imagined it might be from reading the novels of Trollope and Yonge. Jane compares herself to Pandarus and Emma Woodhouse in her preoccupation with arranging Prudence's life. Prudence Bates is most likely named after Austen's Miss Bates in *Emma*. An inveterate novel reader, she forgets her longing for Dr. Grampian over a novel with an "inevitable but satisfying unhappy ending" (JP 47). Her reading preference is for novels that are "well written and tortuous, with a good dash of culture and the inevitable unhappy or indefinite ending, which was so like life" (JP 156). Novels are not all that Prudence reads. She reads Coventry Patmore, and Marvell, and Herbert. In fact, Pym laces *Jane and Prudence* with literature from allusions to Milton's *Comus* to references to Matthew Arnold and quotations from Patmore, Marvell, Herbert, and Keats. The allusions and quotations enhance and counterpoint the text in various ways. But what stands out in this novel is the frequency of Pym's references and allusions to novels, perhaps because she was moving toward a greater sense of her own niche in the history of English literature.

When read alongside *Excellent Women, Jane and Prudence* is remarkable for the way it plays upon, sometimes revising, sometimes developing in greater depth, the themes and motifs of the earlier novel. Pym's conclusions are not yet firm. Yet, she is clearly exploring the issues with which she was concerned in her daily life. These included woman's lot—What did a woman do if she didn't marry? What could she expect if she did?—the efficacy of the Anglican Church, and the function of literature and Pym's own role in its creation. Jane, Prudence, and Jesse Morrow all represent paths that Pym herself might have taken. Not without significance is Jane's statement as she reflects over the work she had put aside when she married: "Creative work, that was the thing, if you could do that nothing else mattered" (JP 131).

LESS THAN ANGELS

Pym's next novel, *Less Than Angels,* first published in 1955, contains one of her clearest statements about her role as a novelist. In a journal entry in March of 1940, Pym indicates she has been struggling with questions about her future as a writer, noting, "I seem to have decided already the sort of novels I want to write" (VPE 103), and expressing happiness in dealing with the trivialities associated with a woman's life. By the 1950s, as she comes to write *Less Than Angels,* Pym's concept of herself as a novelist evolves into a metaphoric statement about the purpose of her creative work.

In *Less Than Angels,* Pym focuses her treatment of romance, religion, and literature into a quasi-anthropological treatment of English society, including its anthropologists, in an attempt to define a means of providing people's needs for "a guide to the deeper or higher things of life" (LTA 194). Pym continues her characteristic comic treatment of the clergy and of men and women in a variety of roles. She also seasons her text with quotations, allusions, and references to literature. But this novel exhibits a more complex symbolism as Pym explores the function of the novel and her role as novelist.

Pym's protagonist in *Less Than Angels* is Catherine Oliphant, her name possibly an allusion to Margaret Oliphant, the nineteenth-century journalist/novelist of English provincial society. Catherine Oliphant, who thought of herself as "looking like Jane Eyre or a Victorian child whose head has been cropped because of scarlet fever," earns her living "writing stories and articles for women's magazines," drawing "her inspiration from everyday life, though life itself was sometimes too strong and raw and must be made palatable by fancy" (LTA 7). Catherine's use of fancy to make life palatable in her fictions is set against anthropologists' detached attempts at describing civilization. Representative of the anthropologists is Catherine's lover Tom Mallow. Tom, who might have "entered the Colonial Service" and married his well-to-do childhood sweetheart, Elaine, is a great disappointment to his family because he takes up anthropology to study the role of the mother's brother in an African tribe (LTA 30). Tom, however, is ineffectual as an anthropologist. Having lost his faith in anthropology, he wonders about " 'the use of it all' " (LTA 105). Tom's thesis, when he finishes it after much struggle, is poorly written and boring. In the end he dies in Africa, "accidentally shot in a political riot, in which he had become involved more out of curiosity than passionate conviction" (LTA 231).

Tom comes to realize before his death, as Catherine has known all along, that English provincial life has its ritual and ceremony every bit as deserving of study, and every bit as primitive, as the Africa upon which the anthropologists have seized. In addition to the anthropologists who have their own rituals of paper reading and giving of offprints, Pym shows us the ritual aspects of Tom's home village, a Shropshire market town, and of a London suburb. Once the burden of his thesis is behind him, Tom is able to look with detachment at the life he has turned from and to see the irony in a debutante dance his aunt, Mrs. Beddoes, gives for her daughter. Searching for the right men, who are right because they are taller than her daughter, Mrs. Beddoes invites the young anthropologist Mark Penfield, who attends in his hired clothes, "like a kind of male Cinderella" (LTA 164). And Tom comes to question "what could be more primitive than the rigid ceremonial of launching a debutante on the marriage market?" (LTA 165).

When he visits his home village on the afternoon of a carnival and flower show, he is reminded "of the African festivals he used to attend" (LTA 177). Looking around the effects of his childhood home he feels "as if he were observing some aspect of a culture as alien to him as any he had seen in Africa." The television set he sees in a "central position in the room like a kind of altar" (LTA 180), and his uncle (ironically, his mother's brother), who preferred the television to the afternoon carnival and flower show, Tom sees as "a kind of prisoner, or a sacrifice laid before the altar of the television set which demanded a constant tribute of victims" (LTA 181). Yet, as Catherine points out, Tom leaves the complexity of personal relationships entailed in involvement in Shropshire, or with Catherine, or with his new love Deirdre Swan, for the " 'simplicity of a primitive tribe, whose only complications' " were " 'in their kinship structure and rules of land tenure,' " which he could " 'observe with the anthropologist's calm detachment' " (LTA 186).

Pym's study also includes the London suburb that is the home of Deirdre Swan. To emphasize the ritual aspect of life in the suburbs, Pym employs the comic character of a French anthropologist, Jean-Pierre le Rossignol, whose anthropological studies are not of Africans but of the English. Jean-Pierre, whose studies include a trip to Bournemouth to study the English on holiday, attends Whitsunday services in the suburbs, and in an attempt to "command a good view of the proceedings" unwittingly occupies the Dulkes' pew. Deirdre and her brother Malcolm, not to speak of the Dulkes, are somewhat disconcerted, thinking he should be asked to move (LTA 81). After the service, Jean-Pierre has Sunday lunch with Deirdre and her family, where he plies them with "questions about English suburban life" (LTA 84), including sleeping habits on Sunday afternoon and the practice of the older female relatives doing the kitchen work in households where there are no servants. Pym's attention to suburban practice includes teatime rituals, the proper time of day to beat rugs, proper table setting, and ritual associated with courtship and marriage in the suburbs. Presented in a quasi-anthropological light, her description of commonplace activities in *Less Than Angels* infuses her treatment of the commonplace throughout the corpus of her work with archetypal significance.

Pym's juxtaposition of religious themes with anthropology in

Less Than Angels suggests that the two are dialectically opposed to the romance novel as means toward understanding life. Father Gemini, a Roman Catholic priest, is both missionary and linguistic expert. Gertrude Lydgate is a missionary turned linguist and anthropologist. And Father Tulliver, clergyman in the suburbs, lets it be known that he is at some risk of being called into the Mission Field in darkest Africa. Priests and anthropologists are compared as Professor Mainwaring interviews the research grant applicants, and Miss Clovis asks the applicants if they "don't regard the anthropologist as a dedicated being very much like a priest" (LTA 205). In this same chapter, Professor Mainwaring tells the applicants that he has given all his anthropological books to the Foresight Research Centre, that he can "do very well without them" as "[t]hey are not the kind of reading to see me into my grave" (LTA 209). The books he turns to are Shakespeare, the Bible, and Anthony à Wood's *Athenae Oxoniensis*. And in attempting to explain his predicament in no longer having the research grant to award, he uses as metaphor Shakespeare's *Timon of Athens*.

Through Catherine Oliphant, Pym arrives at a synthesis derived from religion/anthropology and romantic fiction. Catherine's development in the novel shows her moving in her own writing from romance to realism. Early in the novel, Digby voyeuristically reads a sheet in her typewriter that cloys with romance. Although Catherine is a strong character throughout the novel, at this early stage she envies Tom his large family, and her visit to the suburbs for tea with Mabel Swan and Rhoda Fleming involves a nostalgic curiosity for the suburban environment and concern with a seeming lacuna in her own life because she has no close family members. Discussing her role as a writer with Mabel Swan, she tells Mabel she writes " 'trite little stories for women, generally with happy endings' " and agrees with Mabel that life may not be " 'so unpleasant as some writers make out,' " that for most people, except for the very young, it is " 'comic and sad and indefinite—dull, sometimes, but seldom really tragic or deliriously happy' " (LTA 89). Aware of the discrepancy between her romantic fiction and the reality of life, she muses that "[t]he small things of life were often so much bigger than the great things . . ." (LTA 104). Like Tom who loses faith in his anthropological work, Catherine loses faith in her romantic fiction, aware that her "falsely happy" endings are "unbearably trite and removed from life" (LTA 27). Her desire for realism and her attraction to Alaric Lydgate lead her to ask him to verify the details of one of her stories. In the end, she convinces him to burn his field notes and relieve himself of the burden of his procrastinated anthropological writing. Satisfied by two weeks of mothering by Rhoda and Mabel after Tom's death, Catherine recognizes that she must have her own space, that she must maintain some distance as she resumes her writing. In the end Catherine returns to her flat and to a greater understanding of her role as a writer.

Both Tom Mallow and Alaric Lydgate serve as symbolic characters in marking Catherine's growth as a writer. Tom's loss of faith in anthropology and his death in Africa represent for Catherine, and for Pym, a denial of the usefulness of anthropological study with its objectivity and detachment. Alaric Lydgate's ritual burning of his field notes and his exclamation that he might write a novel signal Catherine's realization that neither the romantic novelist nor the anthropologist held the solution for providing a "guide to the deeper or higher things of life" (LTA 194) and that in her role as a novelist she had to seek a mean between romance writing and the detachment of the anthropologist.

Through Catherine, Pym expresses her theory about her own technique as a novelist. Catherine's reflection on the layering of her thought provides a metaphor for Pym's technique. Musing to herself as she rides the bus after Tom's departure for Africa, Catherine's

> thoughts seemed to be in three layers. On the top layer she was saying over to herself like a chant two lines of verse which often, though for no apparent reason, came into her mind at moments of stress or emotional upheaval
>
> > *What was he doing, the great god Pan,*
> > *Down in the reeds by the river . . .*
>
> It was a jingle, perhaps with some forgotten comic significance, but it persisted, over and over again like a blue-bottle buzzing in a closed room. The middle layer was a preoccupation with a series of beauty articles she was writing for one of her magazines. . . . Underneath all this, in the bottom layer of her thoughts, was a dark and confused sadness about Tom which she did not attempt to bring out and analyze. (LTA 194)

The top layer of Catherine's thoughts reflects the social background, the context and tradition within which life is lived,
including accepted notions about life that include religion and
literature. Pym's fictional technique sets off the trivia of daily
living and the realities of romantic love—the middle layer of
Catherine's thoughts—against context and tradition to illuminate
the comic ironies of life. The bottom layer of Catherine's thought
corresponds to the emotional tone, achieved through imagery and
metaphor, that reflects life's underlying tragedy. This explication
of her theories about her work as a novelist enriches Pym's
characteristic comic treatment of life's commonplaces in *Less
Than Angels,* making this novel one of her best.

It is apparent that by the mid-Fifties, when she was writing *Less
Than Angels* and *A Glass of Blessings,* Pym had come to see her
work within the tradition of the English novel of manners,
particularly as it was developed by Austen, Trollope, and Brontë.
Her frequent allusions to her predecessors in *Excellent Women,
Jane and Prudence,* and *Less Than Angels* and her focus on the
novelist's function in *Less Than Angels* indicate the direction she
saw her own work taking. As a novelist of manners, she knew that
if she were to gain the perspective she needed to study English
society, she had to find a position somewhere between the
distance achieved by the anthropologist and the emotional involvement of the romantic novelist.

A GLASS OF BLESSINGS

In *A Glass of Blessings,* Pym returns to Jane Austen to explore
her own technique as a novelist. Her first-person narrator and
protagonist, Wilmet Forsyth, an Emma character, blunders about
trying to be useful to others yet is handicapped by her limited
knowledge of herself and hence of others. Pym continues to study
contradictions between illusion and expectation and the actualities of life in male-female relationships and in the Church of
England. Literature as subject matter becomes less explicit as she
consciously employs more complex techniques and thereby subtly makes a statement about the nature of her fiction. Especially
effective throughout *A Glass of Blessings* is Pym's use of exterior

space to demonstrate the state of mind of her characters. In this novel the reader enters the rooms of most of the characters, all perceived through Wilmet's eyes, eyes that sometimes distort the significance of what they see. Because the reader is privy to details that Wilmet doesn't see, the reading is infused with humor and dramatic irony.

Pym's treatment of romance in this novel focuses less on the plight of the spinster and more on marital relationships. In addition, homosexuality becomes an important motif, one that enters into her commentary on romance—in this case marriage— and on religion.

The two married couples of the novel are Wilmet and her civil-servant husband, Rodney, and Wilmet's friend Rowena and husband, Henry. Significantly, we know nothing of their rooms, perhaps because in view of their marital status none has a room of her or his own. The two husbands are steady, reliable providers, preoccupied with the business world and occasional romantic fantasies. Wilmet believes them captive, roving "only within the limits of their chains" and compares them to "the dark blundering badgers" they had watched on a television show (GB 43), little discerning the extent of their romantic fantasies and the parallels between the blundering of the badgers and her own blundering about in the affairs of others. Wilmet appreciates the guest room provided for her when she visits Rowena and Harry, finding it "so very comfortable, somehow even more than my room at home— perhaps because I could be alone in it" (GB 34). Childless, Wilmet's main concern in the novel is her sense of guilt about her own uselessness. The need to be useful involves her in the affairs of the parish and in the lives of several of her friends, almost to the point of infidelity.

Wilmet's foil is Mary Beamish who for years has devoted her life to caring for her invalid mother. Wilmet visits Mary's room after Mrs. Beamish's death; contrasted with the "heavy formality of old Mrs. Beamish's drawing-room," Mary's room is still furnished with her girlhood furniture. The room is a mess, the bed "strewn with black clothing of various kinds" (GB 124). Wilmet in her interest with matters of dress seizes on the black clothing, noting only in passing the spire of St. Luke's that can be seen from the window, novels by women writers, and anthologies of poetry, details that reflect the conflicts facing Mary, who tries the life of the convent briefly before deciding to marry the curate Marius Ransome.

Wilmet's self-centeredness makes her insensitive to the reality of the relationship between Mary and Marius Ransome. In addition, she toys with the idea of an affair with Piers Longridge, oblivious, in spite of multiple signs, to the fact that he is homosexual. Curious to see Piers's room, she is shocked by the presence of his friend Keith and resents that Keith had helped to bring order both to Piers's life and to his room. Yet she sees only the tidiness in the rooms of Piers and Keith, glossing over the books and art that reveal their deeper sensibilities. Piers, from whom Wilmet takes Portuguese lessons, becomes her teacher in other ways as well. Aware of her self-centeredness, he provokes her to some insight by pointing out that there were " 'others in the world—in fact quite a few million people outside the narrow select little circle that makes up Wilmet's world' " (GB 199). When she implies that in letting her believe he lived with a colleague Piers has not been quite truthful to her, he asks if we are not " 'all colleagues, in a sense, in this grim business of getting through life as best we can' " (GB 198). It is these words that come to mind as Wilmet discusses with Mary the unexpected news that her mother-in-law, Sybil, is to marry Professor Root.

In short, the unions of Piers and Keith, Mary and Marius, and Sybil and Professor Root all come as a surprise to Wilmet, reflecting her insensitivity to the actuality of their needs. Marriage, though it entails much compromise, in this novel becomes a stabilizing force, a means of getting through life. Sybil and Professor Root, in Mary's words, will " 'be able to comfort each other in their old age' " (GB 227). And Wilmet and Rodney, forced out of the house by Sybil's marriage, must find their own rooms, and in the process find that they are closer than they have been in years.

Homosexuality, presented sympathetically in the relationship of Piers and Keith, takes on a less positive note when Pym connects it with the clergy. Sybil, agnostic and social worker, whose name and insights imply a sort of pagan knowing, alludes to priestly perversion in commenting on an advertisement in the *Church Times* offering "opportunities for youth work." Commenting that " 'we know the kind of thing that sometimes happens: the lurid headlines in the gutter press or the small sad paragraph in the better papers,' " she goes on to wonder " 'how these poor creatures fare afterwards. I suppose they would be unfrocked' " (GB 15). This comment juxtaposed with mention of Father Thames and Father Bode raises a question about Father Thames, whose study " 'has a very pagan look,' " including "a piece of statuary" brought from Italy of "a young boy, the features blunted with wear and age, but very pleasing none the less" (GB 109).

Thames's study reflects his love of beautiful things, including Dresden china and a Fabergé egg. In contrast, Father Bode, who, Mary relates, was " 'full of *practical* sympathy' " and a great comfort to her in her bereavement (GB 126), inhabits a study whose personal touches are "of the simplest and cheapest" (GB 110). Wilf Bason, who is a steady customer in the establishment where Keith works as waiter and for whom Wilmet in her usefulness to the parish arranges a position as cook for the clergyhouse, caters to the epicurean tastes of Father Thames, cooking shrimp scampi and other gourmet seafood treats during Lent. Bason points out the affinity between Father Thames and the curate Marius Ransome, noting that the austere guest room at the clergyhouse would not have suited Ransome, that " 'he and Father Thames are in some ways too much alike—they would have vied with each other' " (GB 111).

Marius Lovejoy Ransome, associated by Rodney with Pater's Marius the Epicurean, unites the romantic and religious themes in the novel. His marriage to Mary Beamish will stabilize his life and help him resist the temptation of going over to Rome that had overcome his friend Father Edwin Sainsbury. And Mary's money will provide additional comfort. Both marriage and the Church of England, Pym seems to say, are stabilizing forces. Like the first layer of Catherine Oliphant's thoughts in *Less Than Angels,* they provide a context against which the reality of everyday life must be lived. Marriage, like the game of Patience that Wilmet plays as Rodney gathers the courage to tell her about his dalliance with Prudence Bates (whose name Wilmet ironically remembers as Patience), involves intricate moves that are sometimes blocked by another card a player fails to notice. Significantly, the name of the game and the name that Wilmet wants to give Prudence Bates echo Wilmet's use of the word "patience" when "the elderly bent shabby priest," whom Wilmet compares to Father Bode, takes the swarm of bees in the " 'pagan part' " of the retreat garden: " 'Fancy his knowing about bees . . . . I can imagine it might be a test of saintliness—certainly of patience' " (GB 232–33). The pagan element of the retreat garden, its "compost heap under the apple tree and the drama of bees swarming at unexpected times" (GB 247), and the "fungus on the wall" in the choir vestry in Father Ransome's new church (GB 254), represent the realities of human life signified by the second level of Catherine's thoughts, realities that contradict and require compromise within the context of institutions.

Pym's most significant use of literature in *A Glass of Blessings* centers around her covert reference to Jane Austen's *Emma* in Wilmet's gradual coming to self-knowledge in the course of the novel.[4] The pagan garden scene at the retreat house with its compost heap and swarming bees serves as the confessional at which Wilmet leaves her guilt, marking the beginning of her regeneration (Long, *Barbara Pym* 124). The theme of regeneration is also reflected in the novel's Cinderella motif—Father Thames will retire to the Villa Cenerentola and Piers's friend Keith works in the Cenerentola coffee bar, a scene that reminds Wilmet of the garden and the compost heap—and in the egg imagery that unites Wilf Bason and Father Thames. The garden scene, juxtaposed with Mary's revelation of her engagement to Marius Ransome, brings together the motifs of romantic love and the Church. Afterward, Wilmet reflects that "[i]t seemed as if life had been going on around me without my knowing it" (GB 230). The following day, she expresses admiration for the "elderly bent shabby priest" who takes the swarm of bees and reminds her of Father Bode (GB 232), Pym's symbol of stability in the Church. In the end, Wilmet comes to recognize the needs of others and that her own life, as well as Mary's, may be a glass of blessings.[5]

NO FOND RETURN OF LOVE

Pym returns to the theme of unrequited love in her next novel, *No Fond Return of Love,* published in 1961; at the same time she weaves into the novel some wry commentary on the Anglican clergy and academic life along with observations about the novel and its relation to life. In this novel Pym uses people, animals, and objects to symbolize characters and their relationships and extends her exploration of character motivation.

In *No Fond Return of Love,* Dulcie Mainwaring and Viola Dace, two thirtyish spinsters suffering from unrequited love, pursue Aylwin Forbes, a fiftyish scholar of English literature. The egotistical Aylwin, like "many of his middle-aged colleagues in the academic world" (NFRL 118), prefers pretty young girls to women his own age, believes women's lives to be empty if they are unmarried, and expects to be waited on by women, from the serving of tea to the indexing and proofing of his books, the latter performed by women like Dulcie and Viola who work on the "dustier fringes of the academic world" (NFRL 13). In the course of the novel, Aylwin dissolves a marriage with his too-young wife, Marjorie, with whom he decides he has "[n]othing in common but a stone squirrel" (NFRL 211), a symbol of their brief romantic relationship; proposes to Laurel, Dulcie's nineteen-year-old niece; and resolves finally to propose to Dulcie, a more suitable mate because she "could help him with his work" (NFRL 253). Aylwin's egotism and lack of self-awareness leave him without a genuine sense of self so that he returns from a vacation in Tuscany and a rereading of James's *Portrait of a Lady* talking in an "odd pseudo-Henry-Jamesian way" (NFRL 218) and intent on proposing to Laurel. When she turns him down, he shifts his focus to Dulcie, justifiying the "curious change in his feelings" by comparing his situation with that of Edmund in *Mansfield Park,* who "fell out of love with Mary Crawford and came to care for Fanny" (NFRL 253).

Aylwin's handsome brother, Neville, is an Anglican clergyman who finds it necessary to leave his church and go home to mother in the West Country at Easter, the most critical time in the church year, to escape the attention of Miss Spicer, one of his parishioners. Both Aylwin and Neville have "trouble" with women— Aylwin's wife, Marjorie, has left him because she perceives his infidelity, and Viola suffers from her unrequited love for Aylwin. Pym's extended treatment of the two men's family background, in the characterization of their mother, Mrs. Horatia M. Forbes, helps to explain their motivation. Mrs. Forbes is a domineering woman whose character is reflected in the fierce-looking stuffed eagle for which her Eagle House Private Hotel is named, a bird that "attacks" the "woman wielding the Hoover attachment" (NFRL 157). Her husband, father of Aylwin and Neville, had married against his parents' will and died when the boys were children. Both sons continue to live in fear of her, Neville of her comments about his persistent trouble with women and Aylwin of what she will say about his whiskey. Pym reinforces the significance of this relationship between mother and sons in a scene in the dining room of The Anchorage, where Dulcie and Viola stay in Taviscombe before they move to the Eagle House. There a family party of mother, father, two daughters, and "a boy of about fifteen who glared resentfully round the room" (NFRL 174) is overheard by the other diners when the mother admonishes the boy. Also mirroring the character of Mrs. Forbes is Mrs. Williton, Marjorie's mother, who takes it upon herself to resolve Marjorie's marital problem with Aylwin. Little wonder, then, that both Neville and Aylwin feel that women should not allow "themselves to be much seen" (NFRL 213).

In the end, Dulcie can choose either of the brothers. Neville offers her the opportunity to move into the flat left vacant by Miss Spicer's move, where she can become more involved in the parish of St. Ivel's and perhaps repeat Miss Spicer's offense by falling in love with Neville. Or she can choose to be useful to Aylwin, who needs her to index and proofread his books.

Dulcie rejects Neville's offer, and it seems doubtful that she will fall for Aylwin's ploy in view of her experience with Maurice and some of her earlier reflections on marriage and on the advantages of living independently. In lucid moments she recognizes that Maurice, who preferred older women, was childlike. When after months of separation, imposed by Maurice's excuse that he was not good enough for her, he suggests they renew their relationship, she understands that it is because she is "older and duller and with the added interest of being somebody to be won back again" (NFRL 128). Dulcie sees in the bickering of her Aunt Hermione and Uncle Bertram "what growing old with somebody" can do to one (NFRL 100), and when Hermione is too eager to "find out if there is *anything*" she can do to help her Vicar whose sister has died, Dulcie finds it "sad . . . how women longed to be needed and useful and how seldom most of them really were" (NFRL 103). Aylwin and Neville, having experienced their mother's domination, avoid women like Viola and

Miss Spicer, and even Uncle Bertram looks forward to escaping from Hermione to live with a community of monks where he will find "good food, central heating, no women" (NFRL 98). Dulcie also muses over her sister Charlotte's acquiescence to Laurel's request to move into her own apartment, noting Charlotte's "long suppressed desire to live a 'bachelor girl's' life in London," explained by her husband's preoccupation with his hobby collecting "Masai warriors' spears and shields" (NFRL 115). The recovery of the crippled beggar, seen early in the novel "selling matches; both legs . . . in irons . . . sitting on a little stool, hugging himself as if in pain" (NFRL 39), and encountered again in the final chapter, walking "briskly in the evening sunshine, wearing a good suit and smoking a cigarette, not shaking at all" (NFRL 252), is symbolic of Dulcie's recovery from the need to ingratiate herself with others.

Pym's attitude toward marriage is less positive in *No Fond Return of Love* than in *A Glass of Blessings,* where marriage is seen as a stabilizing institution. Accordingly, the ending of *No Fond Return of Love* is somewhat ambiguous. Faced with the marriages of Viola and Bill Sedge and Aunt Hermione and her Vicar, both of which reflect Viola's observation that "[p]erhaps all love had something of the ridiculous in it," one tends to assume that for some people marriage is right. In spite of Bill Sedge's seeming unsuitability as her mate, he makes Viola "feel that she was a *woman*" (NFRL 169). And Hermione's relationship with her Vicar develops "in the way things do" (NFRL 239) after she intercedes to suggest he send his surplices to the cleaners to keep them white. But Dulcie's recovery emphasizes the positive aspects of spinsterhood, and the positive experiences of other singles in the novel iterate similar advantages to living independently. Senhor MacBride-Pereira knowingly sidesteps any temptation to marry Mrs. Beltane, even though it would mean living rent free. He knows marriage is not for him and is content to respond to her request for an increase in his rent, to live his own quiet life wearing his kilt in the evenings and munching mauve sugared almonds while he observes the romantic overtures of others from his upstairs window. Similarly independent is Miss Randall, whom Aylwin avoids on the train to Taviscombe. She prefers a book by her favorite author to chatting with Aylwin about editing problems, an indication that "there may be mutual avoidance between men and women, the men not always realizing that they are not the only ones to be practising the avoidance'' (NFRL 208).

Pym's treatment of the Anglican Church is slight in *No Fond Return of Love*. She iterates themes used in earlier novels of the seeming helplessness of the clergy and of their need for protection from women in the parish. In this novel, Neville Forbes is a splendid sight walking in his cassock among the tombstones at Taviscombe and conducting an evening service at St. Ivels, but he is not a "particularly good preacher" (NFRL 247). His concern with the church heating system brings him to post a note forbidding anyone to tamper with the electric heating apparatus. Similarly preoccupied with his church's heating apparatus is the clergyman Dulcie and Viola encounter at the West Country Cemetery who invites them to visit his church and to " 'look out for' " its " 'main feature, . . . the unique oil-fired system' " (NFRL 184). In another instance Dulcie and Viola overhear two clergymen cattily discussing the unsuitability of a candidate being inducted into their brotherhood. And Uncle Bertram, reflecting on his desire to be useful to the abbey, notes that "[w]eeds grow, even in a religous community" (NFRL 99).

No Fond Return of Love reflects Pym's genuine concern with literature, particularly her need to see her own work in the English literary tradition. This novel is seasoned with reference and allusion. Titles are read from Dulcie's bathroom shelves— including Pym's *Some Tame Gazelle,* Denton Welch's *A Voice Through a Cloud,* and Coventry Patmore's *The Angel in the House,* from the shelves in Aylwin's study, and from shelves in the lounge of the Eagle House Private Hotel. Aylwin is compared to Rupert Brooke and is named after the title character of a Theodore-Watts Dunton novel. Others are quoted, including Marlowe, Tennyson, and Matthew Arnold.

The most interesting use of literature in this novel, however, is in Pym's allusions to the merging of literature, particularly the novel, and life. Already noted is Aylwin's confusion of himself with characters in *Portrait of a Lady* and *Mansfield Park.* Pym includes allusions to herself or her novels at least three times—in listing *Some Tame Gazelle* as one of the books on Dulcie's bathroom shelves, in the encounter with Wilmet, Rodney, Piers, and Keith from *A Glass of Blessings* in the Forbes Castle at

Taviscombe, and in a character who enters the dining room of The Anchorage in Taviscombe. This character, a novelist and presumably Pym, is described as

> a woman of about forty, ordinary-looking and unaccompanied, nobody took much notice of her. As it happened, she was a novelist; indeed some of the occupants of the tables had read and enjoyed her books, but it would never have occurred to them to connect her name, even had they ascertained it from the hotel register, with that of the author they admired. They ate their stewed plums and custard and drank their thimble-sized cups of coffee, quite unconscious that they were being observed. (NFRL 176)

Pym's own concept of the novel and her role as a novelist may have coincided with some of Dulcie's comparisons between life and the novel. At the very least, these allusions reflect Pym's self-consciousness about her art. Upon receiving the invitation to the Private View in the gallery where Maurice worked, Dulcie reflects that "[p]erhaps there was some kind of pattern in life after all. It might be like a well-thought-out novel, where every incident had its own particular significance and was essential to the plot" (NFRL 89). Later, disappointed at Viola's failure to respond adequately to her interest in making marmalade or her commentary on the significance of the trivial, Dulcie concludes that

> Viola had turned out to be a disappointment. In a sense, Dulcie felt as if she had created her and that she had not come up to expectations, like a character in a book who had failed to come alive, and how many people in life, if one transferred them to fiction just as they were, would fail to do that! (NFRL 167–68)

After touring the Victorian Gothic environment of the Forbes castle in Taviscombe, Viola notes disbelievingly that the Forbes family history " 'all sounds like a Victorian novel' " and that the people they encountered there—Wilmet and Rodney, Piers and Keith from *A Glass of Blessings*—are odd, " '[l]ike characters in a novel.' " Dulcie responds: " 'This whole afternoon has been rather like a novel . . . I feel as if I'd been rushed through to the end without having read the middle properly' " (NFRL 193). Later, after telling Aylwin that Laurel was much too young for him, that he should find himself a more suitable wife, Dulcie compares her state of embarrassment and what Aylwin must think of her with the reaction that might have occurred had it all taken place in a romantic novel. And on arriving home, reproached by Miss Lord for not making more of herself so that men will notice her, Dulcie defends her reading, noting to herself that "the world of the book began to seem the real one" (NFRL 232). This sense of the overlapping between fiction and actuality, a blurring of the margins of reality and the written life, Pym expresses in one of her notebooks in October 1964 when she dramatizes a scene from her own life and sends it to Richard Roberts with the note: "So you see, my dear, how with a little polishing life could become literature, or at least fiction!" (VPE 231).

AN UNSUITABLE ATTACHMENT

In *An Unsuitable Attachment,* written in the early Sixties and published posthumously, Pym continues the exploration of male-female relationships that dominates *No Fond Return of Love,* returning particularly to the idea expressed by Viola that all love has something of the ridiculous in it. In the later novel, two primary images convey the predicament of its characters. One is the animal imagery that extends beyond the cat Faustina and the cats boarded at Daisy and Edwin Pettigrew's cattery to the descriptions of human characters in the book. The second image is Pym's symbol of the suitable attachment, the bundles of lemon leaves containing, wrapped within, "the deliciously flavoured raisins at the heart" (UA 196).

The animal imagery is most obvious in Faustina, whose haughty distance preoccupies Sophia throughout the novel, and the cats in the Pettigrew cattery. But Rupert Stonebird, anthropologist and observer of humans, whose name contains animal imagery, opens the novel by comparing humans with animals as he watches Sophia and Penelope walking down the road: "They are watching me . . . . But no doubt I am watching them too, he decided, for as an anthropologist he knew that men and women may observe each other as warily as wild animals hidden in long grass" (UA 13). Daisy Pettigrew, who jealously watches the vicarage garden convinced that a wooden stump over which Sophia had spread a blue cloth to dry is a statue of the Virgin Mary and an indication of some leaning toward Rome, is compared to "an animal . . . , moving sometimes like a slow marmalade cat, other times like a bustling sheep dog" (UA 23). Father Anstruther, the retired vicar who substitutes for Mark Ainger when Mark is on holiday to Rome, describes his visits to the parish as " 'the dog returning to his vomit' " (UA 65). Sophia on more than one occasion compares the distance in her relationship with her vicar-husband Mark to her inability to reach Faustina. When Ianthe visits John Challow during his illness, she and the clergyman who answers the door stand "for a moment in mutual silence and surprise . . . like two strange cats meeting each other for the first time" (UA 111). Mrs. Purry, Rupert's housekeeper and sometimes cook, looks "suitably like a black Persian cat" (UA 130). The wall of the room in the restaurant where the parish party dines in Rome is covered with signed photographs of celebrities that Sophia compares with the photos of " 'animal celebrities' " that decorate the wall of Edwin Pettigrew's waiting room (UA 177). Signor Dottore in Ravello wears a suit that looks "like the distinctively marked skin of some wild animal" (UA 189). Robina Fairfax sees the communicants at the Learned Society garden party as " '[w]ild animals in their natural setting.' " Even Esther Clovis who appears in character at the garden party, a "short, rough-haired woman" playing matchmaker for Rupert and Ianthe in the interests of anthropology, exclaims that she has been " 'barking up the wrong tree' " (UA 213–14). In the final chapter of the novel Rupert, still observing, takes refuge in a corner with Edwin and Daisy Pettigrew because being with them was restful, "for they were quiet like animals" (UA 252). And Daisy explains to Rupert that she had felt that he and Ianthe would marry but that "feelings aren't always right. Yet the instincts of *animals* are unfailing. . ." (UA 253).

What humans and animals seem to share most in this novel is a wariness of one another. Pym's characters need one another. They need attachments for various reasons, but their preoccupation with making what they perceive a suitable attachment often blinds them to types of attachments symbolized by the fragrant raisins embedded deep in lemon leaves. Like animals, Pym's characters observe and stalk one another, but unlike animals their instincts fail them as they attempt to manipulate others to suit their needs. Their wariness and desire to manipulate frequently prevents their unrolling the lemon leaves to get down to the fragrant raisin heart of the bundle.

The two characters who attract the most sympathy in this novel are Rupert Stonebird and Ianthe Broome. They contend as protagonists and would seem to be candidates for a suitable attachment. Yet, Rupert, ironically an anthropologist, an observer by profession, is observed and carefully stalked by Sophia Ainger, who assumes the responsibility of matchmaker for her sister Penelope Grandison. Sophia and Penelope both watch Rupert and Ianthe. They watch Rupert because they find him a suitable mate for Penelope; they watch Ianthe because they see her in competition with Penelope. Rupert is rather vaguely aware that he needs a suitable wife; hence he expresses a mild interest in eligible women. Yet shyness and indifference inhibit his relations with them. He finds it difficult to remember Penelope's name. He has occasional rushes of feeling for Penelope when, for example, he sees her dress is split or when she cries in frustration on the Spanish Steps in Rome. But fearing complications he retreats, in the latter instance to the Vatican Library, "convenient hiding place and haven of scholars" (UA 183). When he needs a companion for the anthropological garden party he invites Penelope. When Penelope can't attend, he perfunctorily turns to Ianthe, takes her to the garden party, and when she withdraws from his attempt to kiss her, explaining there is someone else, he finds it difficult to believe she could be in love with someone else. Seeing himself as the "meekest and kindest of men," he is insensitive to the effect of his linguistic blunders on both Penelope and Ianthe (UA 217).

Ianthe, like Rupert, sees herself as genteel, as "an Elizabeth Bowen heroine" (UA 26), expecting courtesy from men and often receiving it. She is observed as a possible mate not only by Rupert but by Mervyn Cantrell, her librarian colleague, who covets her Pembroke table and Hepplewhite chairs, and by John Challow, five years her junior, whose desire for attachment seems unsuitable in part because of his financial insecurity. Ianthe, less detached and observant than Rupert, falls in love with John Challow. It is the relationship of Ianthe and John that seems most likely associated with the central symbol of the raisins wrapped in lemon leaves. Nevertheless, their relationship, primarily because of their age difference and differing degrees of gentility, evokes a chorus of "unsuitable" from several characters, including Ianthe's aunt and uncle, Randolph and Bertha Burdon, who share a questionably suitable marriage, and Sophia, who suggests that Ianthe is not the sort to marry. The marriages of Mark and Sophia Ainger and of the Burdons contrast with the relationship of Ianthe and John. Mark, like Rupert, is detached, leaving Sophia to form an unsuitable attachment to her cat Faustina. The Burdons, assumed a "good and suitable match" by Bertha's parents, also share an arid, detached marriage, and in contemplating "Ianthe's foolishness," Bertha realizes "almost with regret that she herself had never loved" (UA 223). Thus Pym poses the question of what constitutes a "suitable attachment."

The nature of romantic love and its presence or absence in marriage was of intense interest to Pym, possibly because of her own romantic affinities, but most likely because of her concern with the plight of women betrayed by a culture that sees an unrealistic goal of love and marriage as the primary means of validating a woman's life. This same ethic persuades many women to be like Penelope, to look "for a husband . . . systematically" (UA 37–38), to dress like pre-Raphaelite beat-niks in a "kind of armour remembered from childhood play-acting" (UA 123), and to see all other women as competitors for men. The result is that women in their relationships with one another may never develop friendships that permit them to unroll the lemon leaves to find the delicately flavored raisins at the heart.[6]

Consequently, Sophia Ainger, who needs a friend—as Mark notes when he and Sophia pay their first parochial visit to Ianthe after she moves into her house, is unable to set aside her matchmaker's suspicion for friendly communion with Ianthe. In Ravello, Sophia is so set on making suitable matches—Ianthe with Basil Branche thus leaving Rupert for Penelope—that she fails to perceive the deeper significance of Ianthe's need to reveal that she is in love. When Sophia comes to understand that it is John Challow and not the more suitable Mervyn Cantrell to whom Ianthe is attracted, instead of trying to understand Ianthe's feelings, she blurts out that Challow " 'isn't the sort of person one would *marry*' " and seems unable to comprehend the "love"

Ianthe is attempting to convey. She tells Ianthe that she is " 'one of those women who shouldn't marry,' " seems to be " 'somehow *destined* not to marry' " (UA 194), will " 'grow into one of those splendid spinsters . . . who are pillars of the church' " (UA 195). Juxtaposed to this scene is one in which Sophia, her thoughts returning to Ianthe, unties a bundle of lemon leaves, removing "leaf after leaf until the fragrant raisins were revealed at the centre" (UA 196). By thus connecting Sophia, Ianthe, and John with this central symbol, Pym creates a triangle suggesting that the emotional attachment symbolized by the raisins wrapped in lemon leaves can occur between women friends as well as between heterosexual lovers.

As a character Sophia is a study in irony. Akin to Emma Woodhouse in her matchmaking manipulation, she is insensitive to others, yet she sees herself as a paragon of wisdom, a trait suggested by her name. She feels qualified to arrange the affairs of others and has a high estimation of herself and her influence on others. But Pym includes clues in her text that reveal that though this is Sophia's perception of herself, the narrator and reader may have different perceptions of what actually has taken place. Sophia's egotism is evident as she unwraps the lemon leaves, comparing the process to "uncovering the secrets of the heart, as Ianthe, aided by Sophia's probings, had uncovered hers." A few sentences later Pym's irony reinforces Sophia's egotism: "Having settled Ianthe, Sophia turned her thoughts to the others" (UA 196).

Penelope, like Sophia, tries to manipulate others to her own ends, thus cutting herself off from genuine communion. In Rome, Penelope contemplates arranging so that Basil Branche and Ianthe pair off, thus leaving herself free when Rupert joins them. Sharing a room with Ianthe, she quickly claims the best bed and lights up a cigarette, even though she thinks Ianthe probably would not approve of her smoking. Her jealousy of Ianthe and her competitive attitude prevent the development of friendship between the two women.

Although Pym's explicit commentary on religion seems slight in this book, she suggests through the parallels drawn between anthropology and the church a major problem related to the clergy and their inefficacy in ministering to their communicants.

Daisy Pettigrew echoes a familiar theme in the Pym canon, that of the threat Roman Catholicism poses to the Anglican Church. Daisy's myopic observation of the vicarage garden convinces her that a "tree stump with a blue cloth spread over it to dry" is a "statue of the Virgin Mary," a "popish image" (UA 22–23). Later in the novel, in a café, Daisy races with a clergyman to sit at a table with an African—so that the African might "not feel slighted in any way" (UA 235). Managing to get there first, she puts her bag on a chair to prevent the clergyman from sitting at the same table, telling herself, "One never knew—he might be a Roman Catholic or Oxford Group" (UA 236). Pym seems to be using this quirkish fear of Daisy's merely to add to the humor of her characterization; it seems little connected to any serious criticism of the Anglican Church.

Somewhat more serious is the issue of class as it pertains to the parish membership. Mark Ainger's parish, somewhat undesirable, "much too near the Harrow Road and *North* Kensington to be the kind of district one liked to think of one's daughter living in" (UA 19), is contrasted with the more affluent parish of Randolph Burdon where the " 'church wardens are titled men.' " Father Burdon bears the burden of having to minister to the rich—" 'My particular cross is to be a 'fashionable preacher,' " he tells Ianthe (UA 92)—and can't perform Ianthe's marriage ceremony because his " 'church is always closed in August' "—none of his " 'parishioners would *dream* of being in London in August,' " and he and Bertha " 'always go either to the Riviera or the Italian Lakes at that time' " (UA 224).

A similar remoteness from pastoral responsibilities is reflected in Mark Ainger's inability to suitably address his own parish. This inability to communicate with one's parishioners is a theme that runs throughout Pym's novels, beginning with Archdeacon Hoccleve's Judgment Day sermon in *Some Tame Gazelle*. Unsuited to his congregation because of his superior intelligence, Mark finds it necessary to dilute and sweeten his "rather dry instructive sermons." This he does with his famous openings—"an arresting beginning, nearly always of the same type, asking his congregation to imagine themselves standing gazing at the Pyramids or the Acropolis or even the New York skyline" (UA 53). Unfortunately, Mark needs Sophia to tell him that these attempts to dilute and sweeten his sermons have little effect since the majority of members of his congregation are unfamiliar with the sights to which he refers.

This inability to communicate, to anticipate one's audience, links the anthropological community with the clergy. Ianthe compares the anthropological garden party to parish functions, and Rupert and Sophia compare the lack of audience response received by the clergyman and by the anthropologist in the field. This comparison is reinforced by the detachment of both Mark and Rupert, who have difficulty communicating both profession-ally and personally. Like Mark, Rupert, in spite of his intelligence, commits linguistic blunders. He seldom remembers Penelope's name and offends her when he calls her " 'a jolly little thing' " on the Spanish Steps in Rome (UA 182). His blundering attempt at communication when he invites Penelope to the garden party over the phone results in her misapprehension of "talk" for "walk" and does little to narrow the gap between them. Both anthropolo-gist and clergyman fail linguistically, in part because they fail to participate imaginatively. In short, they fail to use the same imagination with their communicants that Mark expects his congregation to use in hearing his sermon openings.

Anthropology also provides the link by which Pym continues her commentary on the novel. Significantly, Rupert occasionally finds literature instrumental in understanding his own feelings. Ianthe brings to his mind lines from Landor, and as the novel closes he thinks that loving her might have resembled a "garland of red roses on the habit of a nun" (UA 254). In wondering if Ianthe had ever loved or been loved Rupert recalls lines from Wordsworth: "A maid whom there were none to praise/And very few to love . . ." (UA 89), lines recalled when he finds Ianthe reading Tennyson, whose lines she had heard John Challow citing in the early days of their acquaintance. In trying to express to Ianthe his opinions about Sophia, Rupert thinks of Matthew Arnold, using words from "Dover Beach" to express himself: " 'I think she sometimes feels that there really is neither joy nor love nor light . . .' " (UA 216). Ironically, Rupert's best efforts at communication derive not from the language of the anthropolo-gist but rather from the language of poetry.

Pym explicitly links literature and anthropology in the discus-sion of anthropology over dinner at Rupert's dinner party. Here at the heart of her novel, Pym has guests Everard Bone and Gervase and Robina Fairfax discuss with Ianthe, Penelope, and Rupert the problems of anthropologists who make " 'only one short field trip' " and yet go on using the material from that one trip " 'in articles and even books for the rest of their lives.' " It's like adding vegetables to yesterday's stew, Penelope asserts. And when Gervase protests that "novelists were just as bad, writing the same book over and over again," Ianthe points out that " 'life can be interpreted in so many different ways' " (UA 127). Everard concludes this segment of the conversation by pointing to the fact that the novelist and the anthropologist have " 'more in common than some people think,' " that " 'both study life in communities, though the novelist need not be so accurate or bother with statistics and kinship tables' " (UA 127–28). Here Pym seems to be commenting on her own work, establishing herself as one who studies life in communities, but who, because her work is not bound by the factuality that separates the anthropologist from his subject matter, can enter into her study imaginatively, interpreting it with the benefit of both reason and emotion, and thereby unrolling the lemon leaves to participate in the sweetness of the raisins at the heart. Pym may also have been answering any critics who might have wagged a finger at the consistency of setting and subject in her novels, calling attention to the opportunities her consistency offered for reinterpretation and for looking at multiple facets of life, always from a slightly shifting perspective.

For the reader who reads Pym's novels consecutively, the significance of her reuse of characters from earlier novels is by now apparent.[7] In *An Unsuitable Attachment,* the use of characters such as Everard Bone, the Fairfaxes, and Esther Clovis from *Excellent Women* and *Less Than Angels* helps to establish Rupert as a part of a larger community of anthropologists and adds depth to his character. Randolph Burdon mentions Ossie Thames, who offered lunchtime Lenten services at St. Luke's, thereby allying himself with the epicurean tastes and wiles not only of Oswald Thames but of Wilf Bason and Marius Ransome of *A Glass of Blessings.* Although Pym herself played down her use of carry-over characters as related to her laziness in developing charac-ters,[8] the reader is well aware by this time of the resonance these characters add to succeeding novels. In spite of her modesty, Pym's knowledge of English literary tradition and her frequent

mention of Trollope's novels, especially seen in *Jane and Prudence,* bespeak at least some perception of her work in the
tradition of Trollope's.

THE SWEET DOVE DIED

Pym's next novel, *The Sweet Dove Died,* written in the 1960s
but not published until 1978, offers yet another interpretation of a
facet of her own life. As Pym moves into what critics have
referred to as the darker phase of her writing career, she pulls out
the field notes of her own life to study and interpret relationships
that center around male homosexuals and the problems of women
in their fifties. These two motifs are linked in the novel through
the protagonist, fiftyish Leonora Eyre, whose self-repression and
search for perfection motivate her affinity for James, age twenty-
five, naive, and uncertain of his sexuality.

Most of the male characters in *The Sweet Dove Died* are either
homosexual or bisexual. They tend to have had close relationships
with their mothers and to be perfectionists, self-conscious, and of
somewhat elegant artistic taste. Their symbol is the cat, who
appears in various guises throughout the novel. James, who had
been close to his mother but whose parents are both dead, is more
comfortable talking to older women. His brief affair with Phoebe
Sharpe, a young English major who is editing the literary remains
of one Anthea Wedge, is in large part an act of rebellion resulting
from a need to assert his independence from his uncle, Humphrey
Boyce, and from Leonora. Secretly, he makes love to Phoebe in
Vine Cottage, yet he fears entanglement and loses interest in her
once he discovers their relationship is no longer a secret. James's
uncertainty about his sexuality leaves him vulnerable to both
women and men. He considers an assignation with a man who
comes into his uncle's antique shop to proposition him, and when
free from both Leonora and Phoebe on a trip to Spain and Portugal
falls into yet another trap in a relationship with Ned, a young
American, who manipulates him until he severs his relationship
with Leonora. Then Ned drops James and returns to America.
Ned, one of Pym's most despicable male characters, is an assistant
professor at a small New England college. He is on sabbatical at
Oxford completing a doctoral thesis on Keats's minor poems,

loves elegant English ladies, and writes to his mother twice a week. It is his mother's needs that he uses as an excuse in breaking off his relationship with James.

One of the most perceptive characters in the novel is Phoebe Sharpe. Although she naïvely fails to accept the threats to her relationship with James posed by Ned—he's safe since he's male—and by Leonora—she's only an older woman—Phoebe comes to see that part of James's attraction to Leonora has to do with Leonora's resemblance to his mother. And wondering if the two ever made love to each other, she finds the idea distasteful and perceives with some accuracy that "[n]o doubt the marble cheek would lean itself to be kissed, and perhaps that was enough for James" (SDD 126). Phoebe is significant in the novel as a foil to Leonora. James and Phoebe connect in a physical act of love; not so James and Leonora. Where a desire for perfection is the key to Leonora's personality—her dress, her demeanor, and the things she takes into keeping—Phoebe's existence is marked by imperfection. James finds the general untidiness of her cottage and her carelessness in handling food deplorable, more than once comparing Phoebe's untidiness with Leonora's elegance. After James and Phoebe first make love, he compares Phoebe to a cracked china castle he discovers at a jumble sale, as opposed to Leonora who was like a "piece of Meissen without flaw" (SDD 47). He notes that the "plastic tablecloths, artificial flowers and bottles of sauce" on the tables of the Leopard Dining Rooms where he and Phoebe have a strong cup of tea after an auction is "Phoebe's setting," but that "[c]ertainly it could never be Leonora's" (SDD 62).

Phoebe's insight into James's character is evident in the poem she writes him in which a cat's "spreading body was like a great empty wineskin or bladder being filled with Mendelssohn" (SDD 64). This association of James with a cat is juxtaposed to an episode in which Leonora takes James to a cat show specializing in "kittens and neuter cats" where James declines to buy a cat, "imagining the malevolent creature ruling his life that the kitten might become" and where he sees his own plight as like that of a caged cat (SDD 65–66). The preferred stance, he muses, is to "sit stolidly in one's earth tray, unmoved by the comments of passers-by. Yet too often, like some of the more exotic breeds, one prowled uneasily round one's cage uttering loud plaintive cries"

(SDD 68). Clearly, the cat metaphor applies to James, caught in the prison of his uncertain sexuality, wavering among Phoebe, Leonora, and Ned. It applies also to James's relationship with Ned, who quickly becomes a "malevolent creature ruling his life." And cats as kittens, immature and without gender, are associated with the relationship that exists between the older woman and the younger man. Both men and cats are pets, and younger men can be mothered and cared for without the threat of sexual relationship. Thus parallel relationships exist between Leonora and James, between Meg and the young homosexual Colin, and between Liz and her Siamese cats.

The predicament of the aging unmarried woman comes into focus in Pym's use of several older women who, in addition to Phoebe, serve as foils to Leonora. In chapter 12, Pym juxtaposes a mirror scene in which Leonora views herself realistically for the first time with Leonora's encounters with several women, all of whom reflect facets of her predicament. The fruitwood mirror is symbolic of Leonora's search for perfection. She acquires a fruitwood mirror from James's belongings when he goes abroad to Spain and Portugal. Its glass "had some slight flaw in it" so that "if she placed it in a certain light she saw looking back at her the face of a woman from another century, fascinating and ageless" (SDD 87). Leonora considers using it for putting on her makeup so she will be less able to see the flaws in her own reflection brought about by aging. She is shocked at finding that James has reclaimed the mirror when he moves out of her upstairs flat, and Humphrey finds another for her "tolerably like James's" but which gives back a different reflection, one that displeases her because her face seems "shrunken and almost old" (SDD 182). Significantly, it is the mirror furnished by the older man, Humphrey, as opposed to James's mirror, in which Leonora sees herself realistically. Juxtaposed to this recognition is Leonora's "full realisation of her unhappiness" that brings her to enter a self-service cafe. There, watching an elderly woman clearing a table, she becomes aware that "she herself belonged here too, with the sad jewellery and the old woman and the air of things that had seen better days" (SDD 183–84). Feeling "utterly alone," she encounters her cousin Daphne and accepts an invitation to Daphne's club for lunch, where she finds it "a little unnerving to see quite so many women gathered together in one place" (SDD 185). Recognizing her affinity with this group of women, Leonora, in spite of

Daphne's attempts to draw her out, refuses to admit to her loneliness. In the same chapter, Leonora has Christmas dinner with Liz, who has only her "cats and unhappy memories" of her "cad of a husband for company" (SDD 180). On Christmas evening she has supper with Meg, whose attachment to Colin parallels Leonora's relationship with James. Leonora recalls the "dreadful woman— 'Ba' " (SDD 181), whom she had met at the home of friends Richard and Joan Murray, where she had hidden while James moved out of her upstairs flat. Ba's suggestion to Leonora had been to involve herself in useful volunteer work.

By juxtaposing Leonora's encounters with this group of women and the mirror recognition scene, Pym emphasizes the loneliness they share and some of the options they face. They may "fill the emptiness of their lives with an animal" (SDD 188) or do volunteer work. Or like Meg and Leonora they may opt for a motherly attachment to a younger man. The latter has its hazards as Meg's and Leonora's experiences show. For women like Meg who are able to accept the imperfection of human relationships, it may be an acceptable option. Leonora, in her repressive search for perfection, suffers and yet fails to submit. As the novel ends, she remains aloof. Watching Humphrey arrive with a bouquet of peonies, she reflects that the Chelsea Flower Show he would be taking her to "was the kind of thing one liked to go to," that the perfection of the flowers

> was a comfort and satisfaction to one who loved perfection as she did. Yet, when one came to think of it, the only flowers that were really perfect were those, like the peonies that went so well with one's charming room, that possessed the added grace of having been presented to oneself. (SDD 208)

The Sweet Dove Died is, in short, about the human failure to connect, a failure brought about in part by preoccupation with things, with possessions, and by a search for perfection that fails to perceive that human relationships are largely imperfect.

Pym's treatment of religion is so slight in this novel as to seem almost nonexistent. It is seen peripherally through the character of Miss Caton, the typist at Humphrey's antique shop, and through Miss Foxe, when Leonora evicts her so as to have her flat for

James. Miss Caton has a friend who is "receiving instruction in the Roman Catholic faith" about whom James does not wish to hear her talk, reflecting that "[e]ven with the relaxation of the fasting rules Miss Caton would still have too much to say" (SDD 74). And when Miss Caton returns from her holiday, she annoys James once more with her account of her friend's dislike of Continental Catholicism and expresses relief at her own return to "good plain food and the Anglican Church" (SDD 132). Miss Foxe's association with the Anglican Church is also affirmative. Faced with eviction from her flat, she tells Leonora that, with Mrs. Ainger's help, she has been able to secure shelter with the nuns at St. Basil's Priory, " '[a] delightful country house for elderly people run by Anglican nuns' " (SDD 110). Pym doesn't omit the Anglican Church even from this novel that concentrates primarily on a group of men and women whose focus on elegance and possession renders the church irrelevant to their lives. But for Miss Foxe, less aware of the worth of her possessions, and for Miss Caton, who prefers to drink her tea from a white crockery cup, the Church of England is still important.

Pym's treatment of literature in *The Sweet Dove Died* seems slighter than in most of the other novels, yet she uses literary quotations and allusion at strategic points for enhancement, to inject irony, and to add depth to her characterization. Most obvious is her use of the Keats quotation

> I had a dove and the sweet dove died;
> And I have thought it died of grieving;
> O, what could it *grieve* for? its feet were *tied*
> With a single thread of my *own hand's* weaving. . .
> (SDD 146)
> [emphasis added]

from which the novel's title is taken. Pym emphasizes the dove image and gives the imagery an ironic twist by having Ned, an expert in love's cruelty, recite the poem to Leonora, bringing her to question her own relationship with James. The trio, Ned, James, and Leonora, visit Keats's house, where "simple bare rooms" are in stark contrast to the elegant things the three seek after (SDD 155). Leonora Eyre's name is sharply ironic both in its explicit connection with Jane Eyre, whose character contrasts with Leonora's, and in its connection with Beethoven's Leonora—from *Fidelio,* who is intent on freeing her husband from prison, whereas Pym's Leonora is imprisoned by her narcissism and intent on imprisoning James (Long, *Barbara Pym* 168). Leonora's attempt to read *In Memoriam* ironically enhances the idea of passing time, a concept Leonora tries not to dwell upon. Also telling is Ned's comparison of Leonora's implied refusal to forgive James to Henry James's *Washington Square,* reinforcing the narcissistic plight of Leonora, and of Humphrey, James, and Ned, all unable to connect with one another.

This novel, written during the years when Pym held little hope for getting it published, is almost certainly about her concern with options in her own life. The characters of James and Ned both allude to her experiences with Richard Roberts, some eighteen years her junior, who introduced her to the "world of antiques and the salesroom."[9] In March 1962, Pym wrote in her diary:

> In Gamage's basement I buy (for 1/-) a little Italian bowl with a lemon and leaves painted inside it. It really pleases me, although it is chipped and I begin to wonder if I am getting to the stage when objects could please more than people or (specifically) men. (VPE 206)

These lines indicate Pym's awareness of a part of herself that she objectifies in Leonora, thereby exploring the consequences for herself had she given herself over to a love of things. Thus this novel becomes to some extent a study not of the author but of what she might have become.

QUARTET IN AUTUMN

Self-imprisoned by their concern with possessions and the desire to manipulate others, Leonora, Ned, and James fail to connect. The failure to connect is also a major theme of *Quartet in Autumn,* written in the mid-Seventies and first published in 1977, the second of Pym's darker novels. This time the characters imprisoned by tragic isolation are a quartet of two men and two women on the verge of retirement. Romantic love seems nearly irrelevant, and the welfare state has usurped the responsibilities of the Anglican Church in this novel that exhibits Pym's most extensive innovation with the novel form.

Although the "phenomenon of 'romantic love' " (SDD 195) takes up little space in *Quartet in Autumn,* its effect can be seen on at least two of the characters, Letty Crowe, the most "normal" of the quartet, and her friend Marjorie. Marjorie, who is Letty's contemporary, is still engaged in the quest for romance, hopeful her provision of food and drink will prevail over that of Beth Doughty, resident warden of Holmhurst—an old people's home—and net her David Lydell, a vicar several years her junior. Letty is embarrassed by the lovemaking of the two and reflects that she herself had never married because she had thought that love, a "mystery she had never experienced" (QA 54), was a "necessary ingredient for marriage." "All those years wasted," she thinks, "looking for love" (QA 66). In one sense, the quest for romance can be seen as having inhibited Letty's engagement in meaningful relationships.[10] Marjorie's quest for love is so intense that when she seems to be succeeding with Lydell, she reneges on a long-held plan to live in retirement with Letty in a house in the country. Her insensitive solution for Letty is a room in Holmhurst. But Letty prefers to await death lying "in the wood under the beech leaves and bracken" (QA 151).

The theme of love in this novel is marked by love's absence, by the failure of the characters to emerge from isolating prisons of the self to communicate meaningfully with one another. Letty is the one member of the four aware of her failure to connect, an awareness reflected in her lunchtime encounter with hurried patrons in the ironically named Rendezvous restaurant. The failure to connect is symbolized in the mummy image that surfaces several times in the novel. For Norman, the "angry little man" of the quartet (QA 35), the British Museum is one of his "lunchtime stamping-grounds" (QA 2), where he contemplates mummified animals. Norman's vague interest in the neighborhood where Marcia lives turns to "stunned fascination, very much as he had gazed at the mummified animals in the British Museum" (QA 145). When he discovers Marcia emerging from her garden shed, the two stare at each other, again "like the British Museum encounter with the mummified animals—giving no sign of mutual recognition" (QA 146). And as Marcia lies in the hospital dying of malnutrition, she recalls having once followed him to the British Museum where she had watched him "sitting looking at the mummified animals with a crowd of school children" (QA 180). Four characters brought together by the accident of having to work together in an office communicate in the vaguest of ways, giving no sign of the "mutual recognition" of their inner selves. Although they meet briefly for lunch after Letty and Marcia retire, and Edwin, the more sociable of the two males, expresses concern for the others—for Letty by finding a room for her to move into when Mr. Olatunde's vigorous religion renders the house where she lives in a bed-sitter untenable and for Marcia by submitting to being Marcia's next-of-kin for practical reasons when she is hospitalized—the group manage to penetrate the isolating barriers that seem to have grown more staunch with age only with Marcia's death. Ironically, having to contemplate the reality of their own impending deaths they seem more able to extend genuine sympathy toward one another.

Images of death and aging dominate the novel, and the difficulties of all four characters in achieving communion and in participating in available social services are in many ways related to the walls that have grown up around them as a part of the aging process. Pym, who was likely struggling with her own questions about aging and her sense of time passing, leaves the reader with questions about the extent to which this isolation is itself a natural part of the aging process and whether it is indeed preventable. The isolation relates at least in part to the seeming inability of human beings to truly extend sympathy across the generation gap, a failure that Pym addresses in her treatment of a welfare state that has taken over many of the social responsibilities once assumed by the church.[11]

The Church of England plays a more prominent role in *Quartet in Autumn* than it did in *The Sweet Dove Died*. In the later novel, Pym uses the state of affairs within the church to reflect the deterioration of society with the passing of time. By the 1970s much of the social work that had once been seen to by the church has become the responsibility of the welfare state with its net of social services. The clergy of *Quartet in Autumn* are the Reverend David Lydell and Edwin's friend Father Gellibrand. Lydell is plagued with "diarrhaea," and preoccupied with his health, wine, and good food. His activities include eating at the tables of Marjorie and Beth Doughty, and one suspects his decision to

marry Beth instead of Marjorie is based on the quality of the tables
the two women set. Father Gellibrand is also concerned about
food, wondering when Marcia's funeral arrangements are made
how food might be served afterward and relieved the meal was
taken in a restaurant instead of a crowded "suburban sitting-room
or 'lounge,' invariably furnished in appalling taste," where he
would be "forced to drink sweet sherry or the inevitable cups of
tea" (QA 190). Father Gellibrand is well-meaning but ineffectual,
reflecting the Church's general lack of effectiveness in dealing
with contemporary social problems. Father Gellibrand also reflects the attitude of the younger generation, shying away from
Letty at dinner after the funeral so that she is aware that he does
"not much care for the aged, the elderly, or just 'old people,'
whatever you liked to call them" (QA 192–93).

But if the church is no longer responsible for old people, the
welfare state has its net organized and spread with well-meaning,
self-important workers like Janice Brabner, officiously striving to
meet the needs of the elderly. Unfortunately for Marcia the wall
she has built up around herself is impermeable, and the efforts of
social workers—even her neighbors Priscilla and Nigel—become
intrusions into her privacy. Pym is careful to emphasize through
Janice Brabner the social change that is taking place to shift the
samaritan efforts of the church to the state. We learn through
Father Gellibrand that the vicar who presides over Marcia's parish
is a trendy, long-haired young man who does not go in for
parochial visiting. Even Father Gellibrand prefers arriving at
people's houses when they are dead or "on the point of death" to
"normal parish visiting, with its awkward conversation and the
inevitable cups of tea and sweet biscuits" (QA 164). Janice
Brabner, Marcia's social worker, has been well trained, an older
colleague having impressed her with the need to "*make contact,*
by force, if necessary" (QA 32). But Janice's force is ineffectual,
and it is not until Marcia has succumbed to malnutrition that
Janice penetrates the barriers Marcia builds around herself. Janice,
who has "little use for the Church of England" (QA 163), finds
herself annoyed because one of her old people "had been taken
off for a drive by one of the enthusiastic amateur do-gooders from
the church" (QA 200). At Marcia's funeral, Janice, her thoughts
"clothed . . . in the language of a report," reviews Marcia's case,
reflecting that it "could be quoted in years to come as an example

of the kind of difficulties encountered by the voluntary social worker'' (QA 187).

Part of the message Pym seems to be conveying is that there are too few enthusiastic do-gooders; part of it has to do with the fact that both the church and the individual citizen seem to feel that with the welfare state in place the efforts of other organizations and of individual citizens are no longer required. Consequently, when Marcia and Letty retire, their employer and the people with whom they work assume that ''the State would provide for their basic needs which could not be all that great,'' that ''the social services were so much better now, there was no need for anyone to starve or freeze'' (QA 101). Even Norman and Edwin, whose conversations about Letty and Marcia are cloaked in self-conscious laughter, feel relieved of responsibility because they assume that Marcia has a social worker looking after her.

Yet in spite of the shortcomings of the church in looking after the needs of its parishioners, Pym is careful to defend it for the pattern it provides for life through ''the soothing rhythm of the church's year'' (QA 73). Edwin, as the one member of the quartet who enjoys ''the stable background of the church'' (QA 8), provides a link between the church and the social services through his church activities and his efforts to help others. Edwin brings Father Gellibrand and Janice Brabner together over the dying Marcia. And Edwin saves Letty from the vigorous religious practices of Mr. Olatunde and his followers, practices that Letty contrasts with ''her own blend of Christianity—a grey, formal, respectable thing of measured observances and mild general undemanding kindness to all'' (QA 66)—a concept of Christianity most likely in tune with Pym's own appreciation of the Anglican Church.

Pym's use of English literature in *Quartet in Autumn* is slight. Quotation and allusion play a minor role. Letty quotes to herself lines from Wordsworth, and Marcia, who keeps a book of poetry on her bedside table, no longer reads poetry but ''sometimes she remembered the odd tag'' (QA 20), including a line from Donne in her terminal ambulance ride. What is more significant is the role of literature in Letty's life. All four members of the quartet visit the library on their lunch hours, but Letty is the only one who goes there to read. Although she likes to read novels—but feels that she shouldn't read them before noon, even after her retirement—she fails to find what she needs in romantic novels and turns instead to biography, which she considers "true" and hence better than fiction. Pym tells us that if Letty hoped to find a novel "which reflected her own sort of life she had come to realise that the position of an unmarried, unattached, ageing woman is of no interest whatever to the writer of modern fiction" (QA 3). After Letty retires she sets out to do "some serious reading" (QA 112), but her attempts at reading sociology books leave her "frozen with boredom, baffled and bogged down by incomprehensible jargon" (QA 117).

Through Letty, Pym conveys some of her own attitudes toward the novel, attitudes accumulated through the years as a result of her association with social scientists in the International African Institute and as a result perhaps of her failure to publish—by the time she was writing *Quartet in Autumn* she had not published a novel in over a decade. Her own shifting interests associated with her illness and age were likely brought to bear. In essence, she sets aside the work of the social scientist, preferring her role as novelist. Her reference to the truth of biography is a somewhat ironic slap at those who fail to appreciate the truth of fiction and a reference to her own novelistic stance that abjures romantic fantasy in favor of realism, topics that were important themes some twenty years earlier when she was writing *Less Than Angels*. In *Quartet in Autumn,* Pym experiments self-consciously with the novel form to write a novel that objectified some of her own experiences with aging, a novel that was indeed relevant to the "unmarried, unattached, ageing woman."[12] In addition, her experimentation takes on the form of a musical piece, a fugue, in which the impressions of four aging characters form motifs that are interwoven in "one unified melody" (Fisichelli, *"The Trivial Round, The Common Task"* 156).

A FEW GREEN LEAVES

Between the writing of *Quartet in Autumn* and her final novel, *A Few Green Leaves,* two major changes occurred in Pym's life. An article in the January 21, 1977, *Times Literary Supplement* called attention to her novels—both Philip Larkin and Lord David Cecil named her the century's most underrated novelist—and publishers began reprinting her novels and soliciting work from her. On a less positive note, she discovered in 1979 that she had ovarian cancer. Pym had a strong sense of her achievement as a novelist and of her own mortality as she came to the writing of her final novel. Consequently, *A Few Green Leaves* constitutes a summary statement about her work, bringing into play once again, but with a sureness not seen before, the themes that dominated her life and work. As one might expect, the phenomenon of romantic love, although a part of *A Few Green Leaves,* is a minor theme. Pym's sense of time passing and social change are major topics in her treatment of the Anglican Church in this final novel. Most important in this novel is Pym's treatment of the role of the novelist, presumably a self-reference, iterating some of the issues she expressed in *Less Than Angels* and paying special tribute to the significance of history and autobiography as it relates to the form of the novel.[13]

The phenomenon of romantic love ostensibly dominates the relationships between Emma Howick, the novel's protagonist, and her two male suitors, Tom Dagnall, parish rector, and Graham Pettifer, anthropologist. As we shall see later, this relationship becomes a metaphor for Pym's statement about her work as a novelist; nevertheless, the interchange between Emma and Tom and Graham offers insight to Pym's ideas about relationships between men and women. Emma's ironic view of the relationship contrasts sharply with the naïve need to mother that marks Belinda and Harriet Bede in *Some Tame Gazelle.*[14] Although Emma carries food to both Graham and Tom and invites them both for meals, she does it aware of the injustice of their expectations. When Graham is critical of the groceries she sends to the ruined cottage where he writes his anthropological book, Emma feels nettled and chides him for his criticism. She decides "that she couldn't always be carrying food to Graham. Sometimes he would have to be content with her company only . . ." (FGL 146). In reviewing her parting with Graham she is aware of the superficiality of his display of warmth, affection, and gratitude, of the fact that, though he has not mentioned his wife, Claudia, "except by implication," he is returning to her. And seeing that he had picked all the tomatoes— even the green ones—that she had planted in pots in front of the cottage, she notes ironically that "[f]riendship between men and women was a fine thing" (FGL 191).

Pym uses other opportunities to comment on male-female relationships through the character of Beatrix Howick, Emma's mother, a manipulator reminiscent of Jane Austen's Emma. Beatrix, who is grateful to be a widow and hence free of the responsibility to marry, is happy pursuing her career in English literature. In spite of her recognition that relationships between men and women are ridiculous, she believes that "a woman should marry or at least have some kind of relationship with a man" and is disappointed in Emma's "high-minded dowdiness" that had produced "only a few unreadable anthropological papers" (FGL 98–100).

In addition to the phenomenon of romantic love, Pym takes a critical look at relationships between women who live together through the characters of Miss Lee and Miss Grundy and Daphne Dagnall and Heather Blenkinsop. The relationship between Miss Lee and Miss Grundy is marked by Miss Lee's bossiness over Miss Grundy. Miss Lee's remonstrance, " 'I *told* you not to wear those shoes,' " elicits from Emma the thought that "when two people lived together one must always dominate or boss . . ." (FGL 57). A similar relationship develops between Daphne and Heather once they move in together. Pym almost never broaches the subject of lesbianism, but in this novel she introduces the subject in the Daphne-Heather relationship through the speculation of the young physician Dr. Shrubsole about whether Daphne might be a lesbian. Daphne, who had moved into the rectory to care for Tom when his wife, Laura, died ten years earlier, feels the strain of her self-imposed sacrifice and, dreaming of a cottage in Greece, moves into a flat with her girlhood friend Heather Blenkinsop. Pym makes a point of Tom's indifference to Daphne as a person—like many of Pym's male characters, he tends to see women mainly in terms of their usefulness to him. Daphne's life with Heather is marked by conflicts and hurt feelings similar to those experienced by Miss Grundy, whose personality, like Daphne's, looks toward the romantic aspects of life. Daphne yearns for a dog—a desire she becomes aware of upon finding among jumble sale donations a picture of a Scottie "bearing the legend 'Thy Servant a Dog' " (FGL 45). Daphne's romantic aspirations are dashed by actualities. Instead of a cottage in Greece, she goes to live with Heather in a flat in Birmingham and suffers Heather's bossiness, including Heather's complaints that she is unable to sleep when Daphne attends Midnight Mass on Christmas Eve. Even her dog, Bruce, is a disappointment when she discovers in caring for him that she, not the dog, is truly the servant.

In her treatment of the Anglican Church in *A Few Green Leaves,* Pym integrates a conflict between the church and the pastor's study with the themes of death and time passing that unify the novel. The village boasts two physicians, the older Dr. Gellibrand, who prefers not to treat old people, and Dr. Shrubsole, the new, young doctor whose interest is geriatrics. Both compete with Tom Dagnall, the rector. Gellibrand has a brother who is vicar of a London parish, and "people often said that he [the physician] looked more like a clergyman than the rector did" (FGL 18). Both he and Tom have a special interest in the De Tankerville mausoleum, one of the symbols of death that dominate the novel. Tom's interest is related to his penchant for the seventeenth-century past; Gellibrand's interest concerns his acquaintance with members of the De Tankerville family interred in the recent past.

The two doctors, Gellibrand and Shrubsole, represent the old and new approaches to medicine. Gellibrand's older patients have gravitated toward the "new" doctor because Shrubsole takes their blood pressure and gives them a prescription as opposed to Gellibrand whose medical advice might be no more than a few sympathetic words, including the advice to " 'go and buy yourself a new hat, my dear' " (FGL 15). Martin Shrubsole takes blood pressure, appears sympathetic, and hands out prescriptions. Monday was "always a busy day at the surgery" because the patients who had not "been to church the previous day . . . atoned for this" by visiting the doctor's surgery, an act that afforded them advice and consolation and "the ritual scrap of paper" (FGL 13). In short, the doctor's surgery is replacing the rector's study and the confessional. Ironically, it is the young doctor whose interest is in geriatrics, yet his interest in the elderly is "detached and clinical." He likes taking blood pressure but is disinclined to involve himself in other aspects of people's lives, feeling "that the drugs prescribed to control high blood pressure should also damp down emotional excesses and those fires of youth that could still— regrettably—burn in the dried-up hearts of those approaching old age" (FGL 5). Shrubsole conscientiously attends to the nutrition and activities of his mother-in-law, Magdalen Raven, in spite of his awareness that his life would be less complicated and their house less crowded if "she were to drop down dead" (FGL 53). The crowded conditions at home place Shrubsole in materialistic competition with Tom since Shrubsole and his wife, Avice—with mother-in-law and three children—see themselves as in greater need of the living space in the rectory than the rector himself. The significance of this conflict between physicians and rector is reflected in a conversation between Emma and Daphne over who is the most important person in the village. Daphne suggests that it is the doctor; Emma supposes the rector is more important than the doctor. Then Daphne recalls a rhyme she used to say as a child containing the line " 'Out goes old Tom . . .' " (FGL 49).

Although the surgery seems to have usurped the confessional, Pym reflects the timelessness of the church in the funeral for Miss Lickerish, where Tom comes into his own. Miss Lickerish's death brings people to church who normally would not have been there, and Tom assures Emma that

> it was customary for the mourners to be present in church on the Sunday after the funeral. These particular people would not be seen at a service again until the next funeral, marriage or christening. When Emma expressed indignation, Tom, in his kinder and more tolerant way, pointed out that it gave a kind of continuity to village life, like the seasons—the cutting and harvesting of the crops, then the new sowing and the springing up again. (FGL 233)

Tom's steady assurance reflects Pym's own faith in the Anglican Church and in the continuity it provided in her life. Significantly, Martin Shrubsole and his family may covet the rectory, but they do not move into it.

In addition to the evolving dominance of the surgery over the rectory, themes of death and time passing are reflected in images and characters throughout the novel. The novel opens with the village parish group walking in the park and woods surrounding the De Tankerville manor house, a "right dating from the seventeenth century" (FGL 1). The De Tankerville manor house and mausoleum are central images in the novel, representing both the seventeenth-century past and the recent past. Tom's preoccupation is with the seventeenth-century past, but his history society ladies are nostalgically preoccupied with the recent past, the 1930s and 1940s. Although Miss Vereker, the legendary De Tankerville governess, does not appear until near the end of the novel, her exhaustion in the woods, where she is found by Emma and Avice Shrubsole, results in Tom's finding the deserted medieval village, thus symbolically uniting the recent past, represented by Miss Vereker and the nostalgia-ridden women of the history society, with the seventeenth-century past, the object of Tom's preoccupation (Rossen, *World of Barbara Pym* 171). Other reminders of death and time passing include the "dire" Mrs. Dyer, whose son Jason turns from chicken raising to a "second-hand junk trade" called "Deceased Effects Cleared" (FGL 173); the "derelict motor-cars" in the garden opposite the church that remind Emma of "old animals, or even old people, being sheltered in a kind of rest-home" (FGL 119); and the deaths of Miss Lickerish, of Esther Clovis, the formidable advocate of anthropology, and of Fabian Driver, husband of Constance and Jessie of *Jane and Prudence.*

Pym's mingling of past and present, her treatment of death and time passing, pay tribute to the passing of her own life and her recognition of mutability. There are numerous indications of the passing of the old and of the dubious character of the consumer society that replaces it. Village youths shatter the quiet of the park and woods with their transistor radio, and television complicates the rector's parochial visiting. Other images of the present include the concealed gender of the golden-haired Terry Skate; the intellectual, "rather hippy-looking" Barracloughs; and the lonely epicure Adam Prince, "good-food inspector and former C. of E. clergyman" (FGL 39). Change has brought with it a littered landscape: a "twist of purple on the ground" in the woods that Daphne optimistically takes to be a " 'patch of violets' " is only "the discarded wrapping of a chocolate bar" (FGL 4). The age of patronage represented by the De Tankerville manor house has given way to an age of welfare and social services.

The closing chapter of *A Few Green Leaves* brings together the members of the village to hear Dr. Gellibrand, invited by Tom to speak on "the history of medicine, starting in the seventeenth century and working up to date" (FGL 241). The seventeenth-century past and the recent past, the present, and the future are

united. Tom reflects on Anthony à Wood's death, and Dr.
Gellibrand forgets the seventeenth century to talk about "the
'good old days' of the nineteen thirties before the introduction of
the National Health Service" (FGL 243). Tom and Emma look
over the display of Gellibrand's antique surgical instruments, and
Tom suggests that Emma might address the society—" 'even
speculate on the future—what *might* happen in the years to
come' " (FGL 249).

In *A Few Green Leaves,* Pym iterates themes she explored in
her earlier novels to make a metaphorical statement about her own
choices as a novelist. In *Less Than Angels* Pym explores the role
of the novelist in the character of Catherine Oliphant, the romantic
novelist, contrasting the work of the anthropologist to that of the
romantic novelist to find a mean between the two. In *A Few Green
Leaves,* Pym brings a new dimension to the role of the novelist. In
a symbolic use of characters, through Emma's acceptance of Tom
Dagnall and her decision to write a novel, Pym pays tribute to her
own type of realistic fiction and to the autobiographical nature of
her work.

At the romantic-novel end of the spectrum is Miss Grundy, who
it is rumored "had once written a romantic historical novel."
Miss Grundy's romantic nature is reflected in implied comparisons between her and the romantically inclined Daphne Dagnall
and in Miss Grundy's High-Church preference, her "pining for
incense" (FGL 40). At the other end of the continuum are the
academics, Graham Pettifer and Tamsin and Robbie Barraclough.
Representing history and autobiographical writing is Tom Dagnall, whose interest in the seventeenth-century past dominates the
novel. But more significantly, Tom has "attempted to keep a
diary himself, the kind of record of his daily life that could rival
famous clerical diarists of the past" (FGL 137). On more than one
occasion we find him worrying over his responsibility to record
life for posterity, yet he is disappointed by the "uniform dullness" of life (FGL 110). Pym's frequent allusions to Anthony à
Wood through the character of Tom are particularly significant if
one considers her lifelong interest in à Wood. In a diary entry for
30 August 1936, she writes, "I wish my diary were as interesting
and instructive as Anthony à Wood's" (VPE 61). She remarks in
a letter to Henry and Elsie in July 1942 that she reads Jane Austen,
Byron, and Anthony à Wood at night in bed. And in a diary entry

for 19 July 1976, she writes: "Anthony à Wood died at 63, my
present age" (VPE 287). What Anthony à Wood, and hence Tom
in *A Few Green Leaves,* represents is Pym's own interest in
autobiography, and Tom's difficulty in writing his diary may
reflect a concern Pym experienced with the difficulty of expressing the essence of her life through her journals. She may have
found herself feeling, as Virginia Woolf expressed in *Moments of
Being,* that the real person was not there.

Moving among a cast of symbolic characters is Pym's protagonist, Emma, a somewhat ineffectual anthropologist who has come
to observe and write about the village. From the beginning of her
project Emma finds it difficult to remain uninvolved so that she
can maintain the distance she needs to study the village as an
anthropologist, and she reflects that it "might have been better" if
she had "been a novelist" (FGL 37). Even the jargon of
anthropology is troubling to her as she tries to select a title for her
paper, aware that anthropological tradition would require the
word "community" in lieu of the more cozy "village." Emma's
study takes her to a number of community activities, including a
sherry party given by Christabel Gellibrand, ostensibly to wel-
come newcomers to the community but in reality a means of
recruiting assistance for the flower festival, a Bring and Buy Sale,
and a hunger lunch. At the sherry party Emma rescues Miss
Grundy, who stumbles and nearly falls, and is aware of the irony
that it was she, an anthropologist and observer of human behavior,
not the son of the house or a romantic stranger, who had come to
the assistance of the author of the romantic novel. At the flower
festival, Emma finds herself considering the ritual significance of
the festival, yet she realizes her interest is less than scientific,
more appropriate to a romantic novel. Nevertheless, at this point
she rejects the idea of writing fiction, in part because she "tended
to despise her mother's studies of the Victorian novel" (FGL 86).

As she moves among the villagers, attending social functions,
participating in the life of the village, Emma's attitudes about her
work and her relationships with the primary characters move
along lines that reflect the symbolic nature of the characters
themselves. Emma is drawn to Graham Pettifer because of a
romantic attachment from the past. As her sympathy with Tom
grows, her resentment of Graham increases, a shift that Pym
emphasizes by juxtaposition and through the use of similar yet

contrasting settings. Chapter 21 ends with a walk around the manor, Miss Grundy and Miss Lee relating events of the recent past, Tom preoccupied with the seventeenth century. As the talk turns to trivialities, a growing sympathy develops between Emma and Tom. Chapter 22 begins with another walk, this time Graham and Emma walking in the woods—the Sangreal Copse. Graham's thoughts are of his disappointment with the Emma situation, which he blames on his wife, Claudia, and Emma. The imagery associated with this walk is one of squalor, stench, and death. They pass the cluster of bungalows that dispel Emma's " 'romantic ideas about Sangreal Copse' " and are appalled by the stench of a poultry house, deserted Emma recalls by Jason Dyer when he turned to his antique business, "Deceased Effects Cleared" (FGL 172–73). Returning to Graham's cottage, Emma thinks for a moment that Graham's invitation to come in for a drink may mean he has set aside his work with the idea of making love to her. Instead, he has invited the Barracloughs, whose academic shop-talk repulses Emma so that she wishes she might leave and "get on with her own work." When Robbie asks how her work is going, Emma replies, " 'It seems to be changing direction,' " and "unbearably irritated" departs (FGL 174–75). There ensues a third walk, this time with Tom, who walks her home through the woods and stops in for a drink and a comfortable chat.

Tom's historical quest in *A Few Green Leaves* is for the Deserted Medieval Village. Miss Vereker, symbol of the recent past, chooses the site of the Deserted Medieval Village for her resting place, thus uniting the recent past with the seventeenth-century past. Significantly, it is Emma, accompanied by Avice Shrubsole, who discovers Miss Vereker in the clearing that turns out to be the Deserted Medieval Village site. Tom finds the village; he also comes into his own, presiding over the death of Miss Lickerish. And as the novel closes, Emma decides to stay in the village—"*She* could write a novel and even, as she was beginning to realise, embark on a love affair which need not necessarily be an unhappy one" (FGL 249–50). Pym's ending, as usual, is ambiguous. Emma on one level accepts Tom, with whom she may embark on a love affair. But on a symbolic level, her acceptance of Tom signals the coming together of romance, realism, and autobiography. In determining to write a novel, Emma mitigates the techniques of the anthropologist with those of the romantic novelist. The synthesis represents the realistic novel of manners, replete with autobiographical influence and historical significance, a form that Pym herself had mastered.

CONCLUSION

As Pym's career as a novelist culminates in *A Few Green Leaves,* her thematic emphasis has evolved from the phenomenon of romantic love to literature. In *Some Tame Gazelle,* the emphasis turned toward the personal issue of unrequited love; literature in the form of allusion, quotation, even the form of the novel itself, was a vehicle, sometimes a metaphor, and certainly a significant element in a subversive subtext that Pym used to convey the ironies of romantic relationships. By the time she writes *A Few Green Leaves,* Pym's emphasis turns toward literature and its role in the human scheme and specifically toward her own role as a novelist; in the end romantic love becomes the vehicle for conveying her message about her own calling as a novelist. Literature subsumes both romantic and religious themes.

The theme of romantic love, and the absence of it, is an important element of Pym's irony that functions in large part through a dual-voiced narrative throughout the corpus of her work. Ostensibly, most of the novels are about conventional romantic love—from Belinda's unrequited love to Emma's realization that she could "embark on a love affair [with Tom Dagnall] which need not necessarily be an unhappy one" (FGL 250). Although Pym overtly points to problems associated with marriage, for example, the infidelities of Helena and Rocky Napier and Jane Cleveland's misapplication of her interests in her own marriage, on the surface she appears to celebrate the idea of conventional marriage. All in all, it is the happily married state toward which most of her heroines strive, and those like Letty Crowe who have no hope of achieving it at least review their lives in an attempt to understand why it never happened for them. But as several critics have pointed out, Pym uses a subversive subtext through which she conveys the fundamental conflicts of her life (Doan, "Text and the Single Man"; Bowman, "Barbara Pym's Subversive Subtext"). The most basic of these conflicts had to do with her choice, in the face of convention, to remain a spinster and

to write her novels. Consequently, a reading of the novels in terms
of the subtext, which appears in a number of techniques from the
counterpointing of her characters' internal monologue against
their dialogue with others to her parody of literary forms, reveals
a conflicting message that most likely conveys Pym's own beliefs.
It thus becomes apparent that Pym does not "fully countenance"
romantic attachment in her novels, perhaps because she believed
that "life can be lived without the fulfillment of romantic ideals"
(Rossen, "On Not Being Jane Eyre" 154).[15] In short, Pym's
lasting attitude toward romantic love may have been expressed in
her first published novel by having Parnell reflect on Samuel
Johnson's "*Love is only one of many passions and it has no great
influence on the sum of life*" (STG 144). As her fiction progresses,
Pym's serious treatment of romantic love shifts toward its failures, reaching a climax in the narcissistic failures of the characters
in *The Sweet Dove Died* to connect in meaningful relationships.
Perhaps even more extreme is the isolation experienced by Letty,
Marcia, Norman, and Edwin of *Quartet in Autumn*. Finally, in *A
Few Green Leaves,* romantic love becomes the metaphor or
vehicle Pym uses to convey Emma's coming to know herself as a
novelist, one whose powers offer possibilities for breaking down
the barriers that preclude communication or love.

  The Anglican Church is another major concern throughout
Pym's novels and her life. Thematically, it, too, is finally
subsumed by her focus on literature. Pym never stops poking fun
at the Anglican clergy. From *Some Tame Gazelle* to *A Few Green
Leaves* the clergy have their foibles. But they are only human and
in some ways victimized by the expectations of the church
hierarchy as well as by their parishioners who expect them to be
superhuman, hence making their shortcomings seem the more
despicable. As clergy they attract the attention of women who,
like Harriet and Belinda Bede, need someone to love, thus putting
them even more at risk. Pym's lifelong association with the
Anglican Church kept her aware of the special problems the
clergy faced. In a February 1968 letter to Robert Smith, who
seems to have been entertaining the idea of becoming a clergyman, she writes, "I am under no illusion about church people, on
the whole, and the dullness and pettiness and dreariness of all the
things a clergyman would have to do" (VPE 245). Pym's attitude
toward the clergy seems best expressed in Letty of *Quartet in*

Autumn, who "had an old-fashioned respect for the clergy which seemed outmoded in the seventies, when it was continually being brought home to her that in many ways they were just like other men, or even more so" (QA 205).

One facet of Pym's concern with the Anglican Church seems to have been with the threat posed to it by Roman Catholicism, and there is evidence in the novels, particularly in *Excellent Women* and in *Jane and Prudence,* that Pym may have felt lured by Roman Catholicism, whose ritual she may have suspected as more inspiring than that of the Church of England. She hints of her disappointment with the Church of England in a July 1944 diary account of "a Day of religions" that took her from "a service in the [WRNS] Mess" to "the Cathedral," where

> [w]e sang and prayed and there was a dry theological sermon about original sin from an old withered man. . . . What can one get from this but peace and the pleasure of music and the loftiness of the Cathedral? You couldn't expect anyone to come in and be inspired or even very much comforted—at the best soothed a little. (VPE 148)

One suspects that the inspiration Pym sought from the Church may sometimes have failed her as it did Mildred in *Excellent Women.* And Pym's implied comparison of the clergy and the anthropologists in *Less Than Angels* suggests that she may have found herself at times in Tom Mallow's predicament when he finds he has lost his faith in anthropology. Certainly her treatment of the Church in *Quartet in Autumn* and *A Few Green Leaves* leaves little doubt that Pym was concerned with the failure of the Church to meet the social and spiritual needs of its parishioners.

Nevertheless, Pym was keenly aware of the importance of ritual in people's lives, and her novels provide evidence of her sense that it was critical to human well-being even in the absence of meaningful words or content. The chronology of the novels, with few exceptions, emphasizes the passage of the church year. The ritual nature of flower arranging, a topic iterated throughout the canon, as well as other comparisons of the religious with the pagan, all point to a basic human need, whether religious or secular, for ritual.[16]

Pym's resolution of her concern about the Church of England

seems best expressed in her treatment of Letty and Edwin in *Quartet in Autumn* and in Tom Dagnall's position in *A Few Green Leaves*. Letty, who muses upon seeing pigeons picking insects from one another that "[p]erhaps this is all that we as human beings can do for each other" (QA 9), finds Mr. Olatunde's religion too noisy and in conflict with "her own blend of Christianity—a grey, formal, respectable thing of measured observances and mild general undemanding kindness to all" (QA 66). Edwin rescues her by finding her a room with Mrs. Pope, where her life can be "governed by the soothing rhythm of the church's year" (QA 73), from All Saints' Day to Christmas, and on through Lent, Palm Sunday and Holy Week to Ascension Day, Pentecost, Corpus Christi and Trinity Sunday—"That was how it had always been and how it would go on in spite of trendy clergy trying to introduce so-called up-to-date forms of worship . . ." (QA 74). Finally, in *A Few Green Leaves,* Tom Dagnall comes into his own when Miss Lickerish dies, resigned to the fact that many of her mourners would not be "seen at a service again until the next funeral, marriage, or christening" and assuring Emma that this practice "gave a kind of continuity to village life, like the seasons—the cutting and harvesting of the crops, then the new sowing and the springing up again" (FGL 233).

Because she believed that ritual was essential to human well-being, Pym must have considered literature an important means of complementing the work of the Church of England to provide the ritual that all humans need, perhaps even a means of infusing the ritual with some of the meaning that she felt might have been missing in Church ritual.[17] Consequently, in *A Few Green Leaves* Pym uses the metaphor of romantic love as well as the literary model of Jane Austen's *Emma* to convey her own sense of her role as a novelist and to make a statement about the significance of literature as a teacher, in that "it teaches us about individual people in a way that social science cannot rival" and "its material is forever new, no matter how many times it has been 'done' before" (Nardin, *Barbara Pym* 144).[18]

In *A Few Green Leaves,* Pym's idea of her role as a novelist is expressed in the convergence of romantic idealism, anthropological distance, and autobiographical (and historical) realism. Time is a significant element in the novel. Tom's preoccupation with the seventeenth century extends the perspective of time passing over several generations, thus providing a more expansive and a more complex sense of mutability. Change occurs in minute and particular ways when seen from the distance of one generation, but these particulars seem less significant within a scope of 300 years. Conversely, even over a length of 300 years, much remains constant. Church rituals, even when the participants fail to appreciate the immediate content, have archetypal significance that wields power over the participants. Even some of the clergy who confer the rituals share in common with their predecessors the desire to preserve an account of daily life to share in turn with those who come after—just as Tom wishes his diaries to be as meaningful as the diaries of Anthony à Wood.

Similarly, Pym's novels represent her lifelong need to write her life and in that writing communicate a ritual or structure infused with meaning that would help to give a sense of purpose to human existence. In the process she gained perspective on herself, indeed created herself—the novelist Barbara Pym—and left a legacy that in accepting the rituals of everyday life helps to validate the commonplaces of women's lives, hers and ours.

Notes

[1]See, for example, Charles Burkhart, *The Pleasure of Miss Pym,* Robert Emmet Long, *Barbara Pym,* Janice Rossen, *The World of Barbara Pym,* and Anne M. Wyatt-Brown, *Barbara Pym: A Critical Biography.*

[2]These ten novels, which I consider the Pym "canon," include *Some Tame Gazelle, Excellent Women, Jane and Prudence, Less Than Angels, A Glass of Blessings, No Fond Return of Love, An Unsuitable Attachment, The Sweet Dove Died, Quartet in Autumn,* and *A Few Green Leaves.* I have not included *Crampton Hodnet, An Academic Question,* and *Civil to Strangers* in this study because they are not of the same caliber as the novels Pym prepared for publication. To some extent Pym uses them as source material for characters and events that she develops more fully in subsequent novels in ways that suggest immature articulation in the earlier work. Consequently, including these three novels introduces contradictions into the canon. For example, Pym's inconsistent characterization of Miss Morrow in *Crampton Hodnet* and *Jane and Prudence* introduces an anomaly that does not exist if one considers only those novels that Pym clearly intended for publication.

[3]Rossen, "The Pym Papers," describes Pym's "small, spiral-bound 'little notebooks'. . . part diary and part working-notebooks for novel-writing," which she carried "in her handbag as a useful repository for thoughts, possible plot summaries, grocery lists, details of expenses, and humorous descriptions of people" (162).

[4]Jan Fergus, "*A Glass of Blessings,* Jane Austen's *Emma,* and Barbara Pym's Art of Allusion," writes that *A Glass of Blessings* "includes no overt allusions" to Austen's novels, but "its covert references to *Emma* partially control both form and content so extensively that Pym can almost be said to have rewritten that novel" (110). Fergus sees the retreat house episode as marking the symbolic regeneration of Wilmet and suggests that the queen bee may refer to the Church as the organizing center, combining "pagan, natural, sexual and Christian elements" (127).

[5]Fergus notes that this is "the happiest ending that Pym's novels afford" ("*A Glass of Blessings,* Jane Austen's *Emma,* and Barbara Pym's Art of Allusion" 131–32).

[6]Kathleen Browder Heberlein, *Communities of Imaginative Participation* (62), notes that Pym considered "A Friend for Sophia"

as a possible title for this novel. This indicates to me that friendship between women may have been uppermost in Pym's mind as she wrote the novel.

[7]See Lotus Snow, *One Little Room an Everywhere: Barbara Pym's Novels,* 67–76, for a catalogue of characters that Pym carries over from one novel to another. Snow writes, "Whatever her motive was in carrying over characters from one novel to another, she created of London and its environs her own Yoknaptawpha County." This "revivalist impulse" reinforces the individuality of characters and unifies her work, creating "a world distinctly recognizable as Barbara Pym's" (76).

[8]In a letter to Philip Larkin, Pym writes:

> I'm considering what you said about bringing characters from one's earlier books into later ones and I agree that one does have to be careful. It can be a tiresome affectation. With me it's sometimes laziness—if I need a casual clergyman or anthropologist I just take one from an earlier book. (VPE 203).

[9]Hazel Holt, *A Lot to Ask: A Life of Barbara Pym,* notes that James and Ned both exhibit elements of Richard Roberts and points to other parallels between the novel and Pym's life including the episode of borrowing furniture from storage only to find that " 'another lady' had also been enquiring about it" (215).

[10]Diana Benet, *Something to Love: Barbara Pym's Novels,* notes that in *The Sweet Dove Died* and *Quartet in Autumn* " 'romance' can inhibit the expression of unifying love" (159) and that in *Quartet in Autumn* "appearance of romantic interest impedes . . . ordinary human responsiveness" (161).

[11]Critics have responded in various ways to Pym's treatment of the predicament of the quartet in *Quartet in Autumn.* Benet, *Something to Love,* sees their "denial of need" as the "result of pride and ideas about self-sufficiency," noting that "values of independence and privacy are related to pride and mean being blind to the others' needs as well as being mute about their own" (160). Rossen, *The World of Barbara Pym,* discussing the problem of extending social services to the elderly, writes that Marcia's rejection of Janice Brabner suggests that Marcia is both insisting on "living life her own way" and asserting her "will to

die'' (172). Wyatt-Brown, *Barbara Pym: A Critical Biography,*
affirms that ''[r]ather than pitying Marcia, Pym accepted her
desire to die'' (132). Mason Cooley, *The Comic Art of Barbara
Pym,* supports the characters' isolation and their need to maintain
selfhood, noting that they make ''a successful stand against
obliteration'' (240). Pym's friend Robert Liddell, *A Mind at Ease,*
would seem to agree, writing that the four exhibit a ''sturdy
independence'' (132), that their ''stern obstinacy . . . secures for
them an idiosyncratic independence and gives hope to us all''
(135).

[12]See Margaret Diane Stetz, ''*Quartet in Autumn:* New Light on
Barbara Pym as a Modernist,'' for discussion of Pym's experimental treatment of time in this novel.

[13]Both Rossen and Jane Nardin find Emma representative of Pym
as novelist. Rossen writes that *A Few Green Leaves* ''serves as an
apologia, by reaffirming through its heroine's choice the author's
personal choice to devote her life to writing fiction'' (*World of
Barbara Pym* 5). Nardin writes that Emma's sensibility as a
novelist is like Pym's own and that ''she becomes increasingly a
spokeswoman for the author as the novel progresses'' (*Barbara
Pym* 141).

[14]One wonders if Pym is not intentionally reversing the technique
she used in *Some Tame Gazelle,* subtracting thirty years from her
life in characterizing Emma Howick to correspond with the thirty
years she added to her life in drawing the character of Belinda.

[15]Constance Malloy cites one of Pym's notebook entries written
when she was twenty-one in which Pym copied a passage from
Virginia Woolf's *To the Lighthouse:* '' 'It had flashed upon her
that she . . . need never marry anybody, and she had felt an
enormous exultation' '' (''Quest for a Career'' 195n5). Laura L.
Doan, ''Pym's Singular Interest: The Self as Spinster,'' sees this
quotation, among other diary entries and letters, as evidence to
confirm that Pym made a deliberate choice early in her life to
remain a spinster (140).

[16]Eleanor Wymard has noted that Pym's ''sense of ritual [is] the
most important organizing principle of her fiction,'' revealing
''the evolving complexity of her work'' and bringing ''us closer
to its significance'' (''Secular Faith in Barbara Pym'' 19). June
Singer, in *Androgyny: Toward a New Theory of Sexuality* (New
York: Anchor, 1976), writes that ''[a] ritual, even when its myth

has disappeared and its *raison d'etre* has been forgotten, still has its effect upon the human spirit, if only to remind us that we are connected to a sphere beyond the boundaries of consciousness, and even beyond the boundaries of sex and gender'' (161).

[17]Rossen, *The World of Barbara Pym,* writes that both English literature and the church ''provide a structure for living that can be imposed to give expression, coherence and stability to a sometimes desolate existence'' (92).

[18]See Nardin, *Barbara Pym* (143–46), for a discussion of parallels between *A Few Green Leaves* and *Emma.*

PART THREE—CRITICAL APPROACHES TO BARBARA PYM AND HER NOVELS: A BIBLIOGRAPHICAL ESSAY

In 1984, Lorna Peterson summarized the state of Pym criticism, noting that Barbara Pym had not "received the scholarly attention she deserves," that no "book-length work of criticism" had been published about her and that fewer than five articles about her novels had been "published in scholarly journals" (201). Eight years later, we can count at least sixteen books on Pym and her work, including two collections of critical articles, more than seventy articles in scholarly journals and collections, more than a dozen dissertations, and hundreds of reviews of her novels. Now, a little more than ten years after Pym's death, it seems appropriate to review the substance and extent of the criticism and scholarly work that exists on "one of the most original comic novelists to have written in England in the last thirty years" (Long, *Barbara Pym* 211–12).

BOOKS

Of the sixteen books devoted to Barbara Pym, two are collections of essays; one is an annotated bibliography; the others are book-length works by a single author. First to appear was Jane Nardin's *Barbara Pym*, published by G. K. Hall and Company (Twayne's English Author Series 406) in 1985. Nardin's 154-page book provides an overview of Pym's life and publication history and discusses her characteristic themes as they evolve in the novels. Nardin's purpose is to illuminate "fundamental issues of theme and technique" in Pym's novels. She includes brief readings of eight of the novels—*Some Tame Gazelle, Excellent Women, Jane and Prudence, Less Than Angels, A Glass of Blessings, The Sweet Dove*

Died, Quartet in Autumn, and *A Few Green Leaves*—limiting her discussion of *No Fond Return of Love* and *An Unsuitable Attachment* because she considers them "products of a tired imagination" (Preface).

Two book-length critical works were published in 1986: Diana Benet's *Something to Love: Barbara Pym's Novels* (Columbia: University of Missouri Press) and Robert Emmet Long's *Barbara Pym* (New York: Ungar—Literature and Life Series). Benet's *Something to Love* (164 pages) traces Pym's development "from the comic to the tragic, and from a feminine to a universal vision" (3). Pym's early novels, Benet says, reflect a concentration on the inner lives of women, but as Pym grows more confident in the "universality of her vision," her "men become more prominent citizens" (2). Long's *Barbara Pym* (256 pages) provides a chronology of Pym's life and publication history noting parallels between her experience and her fiction, followed by a reading of *Some Tame Gazelle, Excellent Women, Crampton Hodnet, Jane and Prudence, Less Than Angels, A Glass of Blessings, No Fond Return of Love, An Unsuitable Attachment, The Sweet Dove Died, Quartet in Autumn,* and *A Few Green Leaves.*

Charles Burkhart's *The Pleasure of Miss Pym* (Austin: University of Texas Press), Janice Rossen's *The World of Barbara Pym* (London: Macmillan; New York: St. Martin's), *The Life and Work of Barbara Pym* (London: Macmillan; Iowa City: University of Iowa Press), edited by Dale Salwak, and Lotus Snow's *One Little Room an Everywhere: Barbara Pym's Novels* (Orono, ME: Puckerbrush) were all published in 1987.

Burkhart's *The Pleasure of Miss Pym* (120 pages) purports to "show just where and in what her pleasure lies, and ours" (x). He divides his book into six chapters. "Miss Pym and the World" summarizes Pym's life and publishing history, discusses characteristics of her novels, and relates Pym's work to that of other novelists. "Miss Pym and the World of Her Novels" discusses the subject matter of Pym's novels and offers brief readings of *Some Tame Gazelle, Crampton Hodnet, Excellent Women, Jane and Prudence, Less Than Angels, A Glass of Blessings, No Fond Return of Love, An Unsuitable Attachment, The Sweet Dove Died, An Academic Question, Quartet in Autumn,* and *A Few Green Leaves.* "Miss Pym and the Africans," a reprint of a 1983 article in *Twentieth-Century Literature,* discusses Pym's treatment of

anthropology and Africa in the novels. "Miss Pym and the Comic
Muse" focuses on Pym's comic technique. "Miss Pym and Men
and Women" discusses various forms of male/female relationships in the novels. And "God and Miss Pym" focuses on Pym's
association with the Anglican Church.

Rossen's *The World of Barbara Pym* (193 pages) offers "an
extended analysis" of Pym's novels designed to lay a "ground-
work for more detailed studies of her work." Rossen discusses
Pym's "fundamental ideas and perspective" and shows the close
relationship between Pym's life and her novels (4). The book
contains an introduction and seven chapters, whose titles reflect
their concentration. The first, "A Style of One's Own," discusses
major influences on Pym's writing and narrative technique.
Chapter 2, "Love in the Great Libraries," reprinted from a 1985
article in the *Journal of Modern Literature,* discusses Pym's
experiences at Oxford and their reflection in themes of romance
and scholarship in *Some Tame Gazelle, Crampton Hodnet, Jane
and Prudence,* and *No Fond Return of Love.* Subsequent chapters
deal with topics of spinsterhood, the Anglican Church, and
anthropology as factors in Pym's life and her treatment of them in
the novels. Chapter 6, "The Artist as Observer," "examines
Pym's conception of the artist" and its reflection in her narrative
technique in *Some Tame Gazelle, Excellent Women, Less Than
Angels,* and *A Glass of Blessings.* The final chapter, "*A Few
Green Leaves* as Apologia," explores the "themes of loneliness,
mortality, ageing, and rejection" in *The Sweet Dove Died, A
Quartet in Autumn,* and *A Few Green Leaves* (5).

Salwak's *The Life and Work of Barbara Pym* (210 pages) is a
collection of nineteen essays aimed at a "comprehensive, up-to-
date survey of her life and work" (ix). The collection is in three
parts: "The Life," "The Work," and "In Retrospect." "The
Life" comprises four pieces: four brief laudatory paragraphs by
Shirley Hazzard—originally presented at "A Celebration of
Barbara Pym," Gramercy Park Hotel, October 1984; a scholarly
essay by Constance Malloy that traces Pym's writing career from
1934 to her death in 1980; an account by Hazel Holt of working
alongside Pym at the International African Institute, with discussion of how Pym's experience at the Institute is reflected in the
novels; and an account by Gilbert Phelps of his acquaintance with
Pym, whom he met in Finstock during the last years of her life.

Part Two, "The Work," contains eleven pieces, including a short piece by Joyce Carol Oates (from "A Celebration of Barbara Pym") and one by Penelope Lively. This section reprints the first critical article on Pym's novels, Robert Smith's "How Pleasant to Know Miss Pym," from *Ariel*, 1971. Several essays discuss the subject matter of Pym's novels: John Bayley discusses "the Pym world"; Mary Strauss-Noll discusses "love and marriage"; John Halperin, "the war of the sexes"; and Muriel Schulz, anthropology. Essays by Lotus Snow and Robert Graham discuss Pym's narrative technique—her use of literary allusion and her "narrative manner," respectively. An essay by Rossen provides a useful overview of the Pym collection at the Bodleian Library. The final section of Salwak's book contains four short pieces, two by Pym's close friends Philip Larkin and Robert Liddell. Larkin gives an account of Pym's rejection by her publishers, and Liddell discusses Pym's career as a novelist, noting some of the relationships between her life and her novels. An essay by Frances Bachelder notes connections among the novels themselves, and Gail Godwin closes the collection with two paragraphs of praise, originally presented at "A Celebration of Barbara Pym."

Lotus Snow's *One Little Room an Everywhere: Barbara Pym's Novels* (101 pages) consists of seven essays on a variety of subjects related to Pym's novels. The first, " 'The Trivial Round, the Common Task': The Subject of the Novels," reprinted from a 1980 article in *Research Studies,* discusses Pym's treatment of the ordinary in her novels. "Some Namesakes in the Novels" notes sources and significance of names in the novels. " 'Some Small Smattering of Culture': Literary Allusions in the Novels," reprinted from Salwak's collection, catalogs Pym's allusions to English poets and novelists in the novels. "More Than Angels: Men" discusses Pym's treatment of gender relationships. "The Revivalist Impulse" discusses the motives for and the unifying effect of Pym's "habit of carrying over" characters from one novel to another (67). " 'Colleagues in a Grim Business': the Tragicomic Vision" offers comparisons between the novelistic visions of Austen and Pym. And "Toward Ranking the Novels" summarizes Pym's publishing career and offers assessments of individual novels.

Rossen's second book on Pym, *Independent Women: The Function of Gender in the Novels of Barbara Pym* (Brighton:

Harvester; New York: St. Martin's), was published in 1988. This
collection of ten essays (172 pages) uses "biographical, historical, and feminist approaches" to analyze "Pym's literary achievement" (ix). Rossen also seeks to "re-examine the nature of Pym's
accomplishments and the usefulness of further comment on her
work," for which, she writes, the essays in her book "make an
excellent case for continuing the discussion" (2). Rossen divides
the essays into four groups. The first section, titled "The Creative
Process" and containing pieces by Barbara Everett, Anne M.
Wyatt-Brown, and Hazel Holt, considers Pym's novels in a
biographical context, suggesting "various perspectives on Pym's
creative process and the shaping of her novelistic imagination"
(7). The second group, "New Approaches," comprising essays by
Laura L. Doan, Barbara Bowman, and Charles Burkhart, focuses
on Pym's attitude toward men, sometimes from a feminist
perspective, revealing a "narrative strategy which marginalizes
the bachelor" (61). Part Three, "Literary Heritage," contains
essays by Jan Fergus and Rossen that discuss, respectively, Pym's
allusions to and reworking of *Emma* in *A Glass of Blessings* and of
Jane Eyre in several of the novels. The final section, "Reminis-
cences," contains short pieces by Robert Smith and Roger Till
recollecting their acquaintance with Pym.

Three Pym books were published in 1989: Katherine Anne
Ackley's *The Novels of Barbara Pym* (New York: Garland),
Michael Cotsell's *Barbara Pym* (London: Macmillan; New York:
St. Martin's), and Robert Liddell's *A Mind at Ease: Barbara Pym
and Her Novels* (London: Peter Owen).

Ackley's *The Novels of Barbara Pym* (209 pages) contains
seven chapters, the first of which includes "a general introduction" to the novels. Although Ackley considers all of the published novels, she focuses on nine that Pym herself prepared for
publication—*Some Tame Gazelle, Excellent Women, Jane and
Prudence, Less Than Angels, A Glass of Blessings, No Fond
Return of Love, The Sweet Dove Died, Quartet in Autumn,* and *A
Few Green Leaves.* In each of the subsequent six chapters Ackley
discusses a specific theme in Pym's work: the "ridiculous"
nature of relationships between men and women, friendships
between women, relationships between mothers and their adult
children, coping with isolation and loneliness, the passing of time

and anticipation of change, and connections between literature and life.

Cotsell's *Barbara Pym* (153 pages), a volume in Macmillan's Modern Novelists series, contains an introduction and six chapters. Cotsell's purpose is "to describe the main features of Pym's art." He discusses the novels in the order in which Pym wrote them, providing useful "biographical and historical context" and asking "questions about the relation of Pym's work to the historical developments of her time." Cotsell also discusses Pym's work "in relation to contemporary structuralist and poststructuralist accounts of language" as well as her "relations to modernist art" (6–7).

Liddell's *A Mind at Ease: Barbara Pym and Her Novels* (144 pages) is "intended as a critical survey" of the novels Pym herself prepared for publication. Liddell is careful to specify that his purpose in presenting Pym as a "worthwhile author" is "critical rather than scholarly." Including in his survey *Crampton Hodnet* and *An Unsuitable Attachment,* both of which he indicates Pym offered for publication but probably would "finally have rejected" (7), Liddell divides his book into three parts. Part One, "The Early Years," which describes the Bodleian Library and offers insights into Pym's friendship with Henry Harvey and Liddell, includes discussion of *Some Tame Gazelle* and *Crampton Hodnet.* Part Two, "The 'Canon'," discusses *Excellent Women, Jane and Prudence, Less Than Angels, A Glass of Blessings, No Fond Return of Love,* and *An Unsuitable Attachment,* which Liddell notes were written in "more hopeful years before the world was afflicted by inflation, the Churches by 'reforms,' and before Barbara herself was attacked by the illness that was to cause her death" (28). Part Three, "The Later Years," deals with the final three novels, *The Sweet Dove Died, Quartet in Autumn,* and *A Few Green Leaves.*

Mason Cooley's *The Comic Art of Barbara Pym* (New York: AMS) and Hazel Holt's *A Lot to Ask: A Life of Barbara Pym* (London: Macmillan; New York: Dutton) were both published in 1990. Cooley's thirteen chapters (292 pages) trace Pym's use of comic technique through eleven of the novels, including *Crampton Hodnet.* Holt's *A Lot to Ask: A Life of Barbara Pym* (308 pages) is, as the title indicates, a biography of Pym that attempts to "put Barbara into her own setting, to define the manners and mores of the social scene around her . . . , to describe her friends and colleagues, and to show how her books were moulded by her life, as well as the other way around'' (ix).

Published by G. K. Hall in 1991, Dale Salwak's *Barbara Pym: A Reference Guide* (162 pages), includes a brief preface that summarizes Pym's literary achievement, a list of published "Writings by Barbara Pym," and an annotated list of "Writings about Barbara Pym, 1950–1990." The listing of secondary material includes books, articles, and reviews arranged alphabetically by year of publication.

Annette Weld's *Barbara Pym and the Novel of Manners* (London: Macmillan; New York: St. Martin's) and Anne M. Wyatt-Brown's *Barbara Pym: A Critical Biography* (Columbia: University of Missouri Press) were both published in 1992.

In *Barbara Pym and the Novel of Manners* (224 pages), originally her 1989 University of Rochester Ph.D. dissertation, Weld explores Pym's novels within the tradition of the novel of manners. The book is in five chapters. Chapter one reviews the characteristics of the novel of manners and its relation to comedy. Chapter two, "The Early Works: Poems, Stories, Radio Plays," concentrates on Pym's experimentation with style in her early work. Chapter three moves on to the "The Early Novels"—*Some Tame Gazelle, Civil to Strangers,* and *Crampton Hodnet*— discussing Pym's technique as well as her concern with typical novel-of-manners topics such as food and clothing. Chapter four, "Something 'Very Barbara Pym,' " goes on to the novels of her middle period, *Excellent Women, A Glass of Blessings, Jane and Prudence,* and *No Fond Return of Love,* noting how her techniques relate to the novel of manners. Chapter five, "Rejection, Resurrection, Valediction," discusses several of the short stories and analyzes Pym's use of novel-of-manners techniques in *An Unsuitable Attachment, The Sweet Dove Died, Quartet in Autumn,* and *A Few Green Leaves.*

Wyatt-Brown's *Barbara Pym: A Critical Biography* (209 pages), brings a psychoanalytic approach to a study of Pym's life and work that emphasizes her creative process in the light of contemporary research into the writing process as well as the influence of her own aging and impending death. In her introduction Wyatt-Brown credits Pym's novels with contributing to "the understanding of gender specialists, gerontologists, writing and reading theorists, and psychoanalysts, as well as to any dispassionate person interested in the careers of talented women'' (2). The seven chapters that follow trace Pym's life and literary development from the juvenilia through the final novels, *Quartet in Autumn* and *A Few Green Leaves,* that reflect Pym's coming to terms with aging and impending death and her endorsement in *A Few Green Leaves* of her choice in becoming a novelist.

DISSERTATIONS

Pym's life and work have been the subject of more than a dozen Ph.D. dissertations. First was the 1978 doctoral thesis of Tullia Blundo, "La Narrativa di Barbara Pym" (tesi di laurea, University of Pisa), a copy of which is in the Pym collection at the Bodleian (Heberlein, *Communities of Imaginative Participation* 88). This was followed in 1984 by two dissertations, Glynn-Ellen Maria Fisichelli's *"The Trivial Round, the Common Task"*: *Barbara Pym: The Development of a Writer* (State University of New York at Stony Brook) and Kathleen Browder Heberlein's *Communities of Imaginative Participation: The Novels of Barbara Pym* (University of Washington). In 1987, Rhoda Irene Sherwood devoted a chapter to Pym and Alice Walker in her dissertation, *"A Special Kind of Double"*: *Sisters in British and American Fiction* (University of Wisconsin). Three dissertations were completed in 1988: Marlene San Miguel Groner's *The Novels of Barbara Pym* (St. John's University), Bruce Richard Jacobs's *Elements of Satire in the Novels of Barbara Pym* (Fordham University), and Patricia Mary Naulty's *"I Never Talk of Hunger"*: *Self-Starvation as Women's Language of Protest in Novels by Barbara Pym, Margaret Atwood, and Anne Tyler* (Ohio State University), the latter containing a chapter devoted to *Quartet in Autumn.* And another three were completed in 1989: Barbara Lee Bywaters's *"Re-Reading Jane"*: *Jane Austen's Legacy to Twentieth-Century Women Writers* (Bowling Green State University), which examines Austen's influence on Pym, Georgette Heyer, Stella Gibbons, and Anita Brookner; Laura Kathleen Johnson Roth's *Performance Considerations for the Adaptation of Selected Barbara Pym Novels for Chamber Theatre Production* (University of Texas at Austin); and Annette Forker

Weld's *Barbara Pym and the Novel of Manners* (University of
Rochester), subsequently published by St. Martin's and Macmillan (London). Isabel Ashe Bonnyman Stanley's *The Anglican
Clergy in the Novels of Barbara Pym* (University of Tennessee)
was completed in 1990; and Sun-Hee Lee's *Love, Marriage, and
Irony in Barbara Pym's Novels* (University of North Texas) and
Margaret Anne McDonald's *Alone Together: Gender and Alienation* (University of Saskatchewan), in 1991. Michelle Lynne
Jones's *Laughing Hags: The Comic Vision as Feminist* (University of Alberta), 1992, examines the feminist comedy in the novels
of Pym, Margaret Atwood, John Irving, and Muriel Spark.

TOPICS OF SCHOLARLY DISCUSSION

The topics treated in scholarly discussions of Pym's work,
including those contained in books, dissertations, articles in
scholarly journals, and in some cases substantive review articles,
fall into three general groups: those related to bibliography,
biography, and Pym's creative process; those that deal primarily
with themes in the novels; and those that focus on Pym's narrative
technique. Obviously there is substantial overlapping among the
categories, but for reasons of organization the following summary
generally adheres to these groupings.

Bibliography, Biography, and the Creative Process
In the first group, scholarly pieces related to bibliography,
biography, and Pym's creative process, some of the most helpful
to the Pym scholar are those that provide information about
unpublished work in the holdings in the Pym collection at the
Bodleian Library. Rossen's "The Pym Papers" provides an
"overview of the collection" at the Bodleian, summarizing the
contents and suggesting the "relative usefulness to scholars of its
various parts" (156). Rossen divides the contents into two main
groups: fiction, which includes unpublished novels and short
stories and early drafts of published work; and the diaries and
notebooks, including personal diaries, daily calendars, and little
notebooks. A complete listing of the contents, Rossen notes, is
contained in Tim Rogers's typescript catalog. Anthony Kaufman,
in "The Short Fiction of Barbara Pym," discusses thematic

elements of the short stories, mostly unpublished, naming more than a dozen separate stories and crediting Pym with "more than thirty pieces of short fiction" (50). Weld, in *Barbara Pym and the Novel of Manners,* discusses some of Pym's early unpublished work, including poems, stories, and radio plays. Wyatt-Brown's *Barbara Pym: A Critical Biography* contains a bibliography of unpublished materials, including "Juvenilia," "Poems Written at Oxford," "Post-Oxford Manuscripts," "Short Stories," "Radio Play," "Miscellaneous Notebooks," and "Talks," as well as discussion of unpublished manuscripts, particularly the juvenilia and short stories.

The intense interest in Pym's notebooks and diaries and in the events of her life is to be expected in view of the many parallels between her life and her work. Burkhart, *The Pleasure of Miss Pym,* Long, *Barbara Pym,* and Nardin, *Barbara Pym,* all offer an extended chronology in their books, focusing not only on Pym's life but on her publishing career; and Malloy, "The Quest for a Career," traces Pym's writing career from 1934 to her death in 1980. Ackley includes a summary of Pym's life and publishing history in *The Novels of Barbara Pym.* Holt's *A Lot to Ask: A Life of Barbara Pym* traces the events and relationships in Pym's life and notes many of the biographical parallels in her novels. Cotsell, whose *Barbara Pym* contains a brief biography and publishing history, devotes the first chapter of his book, "Oswestry and Oxford: Early Writings, Literary Influences, and *Some Tame Gazelle,*" to discussion of the events, friendships, and influences in Pym's life that shaped the nature of her novels, particularly her resistance to modernism. Wyatt-Brown, *Barbara Pym: A Critical Biography,* brings a psychoanalytic approach to her analysis of the influences of Pym's experiences on her creative process and literary accomplishments.

No doubt the most often-told story—in fact, few pieces manage to end without telling the story or at least alluding to it—is that of the sixteen years from 1961 to 1977 when Pym did not publish and of her "rediscovery" as a result of the January 21, 1977, *Times Literary Supplement* article "Reputations Revisited." Most of these pieces merely give an account of the rejection by Cape and other publishers and of Philip Larkin's and Lord David Cecil's mention in "Reputations Revisited" that led to Pym's return from "the wilderness." Some critics suggest, sometimes

citing Pym's own speculation, that her subject matter may not
have appealed to the reading public of the 1960s (Malloy, "Quest
for a Career" 10; Nardin 5). Also noted are Pym's "professional
ineptness" and Jonathan Cape's financial state and "outmoded"
marketing techniques (Wyatt-Brown, "Ellipsis, Eccentricity and
Evasion in the Diaries of Barbara Pym" 24–25).

Others criticize *An Unsuitable Attachment,* the novel that
marked the beginning of Pym's publishing eclipse, and offer some
rationale for Cape's rejection of it (Liddell, *Mind at Ease* 89–90).
Larkin, with whom Pym corresponded from 1961 until her death,
and whom she finally met in 1975, writes that the novel's "chief
failing is that the 'unsuitable attachment' between Ianthe Broome
. . . and the younger John Challow . . . is not sufficiently central to
the story and not fully 'done,' as Henry James would say."
Further, he notes, the book is "somewhat self-indulgent . . . full of
echoes" of characters from previous books. Inquiring into the
reasons for Cape's rejection of the novel, Larkin reports that the
chairman of Cape reported to him that it had received " 'unfa-
vourable reports,' " that one was " 'extremely negative' " and
the other, " 'fairly negative' " ("Foreword" 8–9). Weld, on the
other hand, points to the strengths of *An Unsuitable Attachment,*
noting that "it did not deserve to be the reason for her literary
excommunication" (*Barbara Pym and the Novel of Manners*
167).

The relationship between Pym's unrequited love experiences
and her treatment of male-female relationships, especially the
plight of spinsters, has drawn considerable attention from her
critics. The parallels most frequently discussed have to do with
her unrequited love for Henry Harvey during her Oxford years, her
relationships with Julian Amery in the late 1930s and Gordon
Glover in the early 1940s, and her relationship in the 1960s with
Richard Roberts (Cotsell; Holt, *Lot to Ask;* Long, *Barbara Pym;*
Malloy, "Quest for a Career"; Rossen, "Love in the Great
Libraries" and *World of Barbara Pym;* Wyatt-Brown, *Barbara
Pym: A Critical Biography* and "Ellipsis, Eccentricity and Eva-
sion in the Diaries of Barbara Pym"). Cotsell, Holt, and Wyatt-
Brown discuss at length Pym's relationship with Henry Harvey
and her unrequited love for Julian Amery, whom she met at
Oxford. Malloy points to the correspondence between Glover and
Fabian of *Jane and Prudence;* and Wyatt-Brown, noting the anger

and suffering that generated Pym's reflection of Glover in the character of Fabian, writes that Pym's style began to shift "outward to her audience" as a result of her affair with Glover (*Barbara Pym: A Critical Biography* 63). Rossen notes that Richard Roberts is reflected in the characters of both Ned and James of *The Sweet Dove Died* (*World of Barbara Pym* 68). In addition to Pym's relationships with Harvey and Roberts, Fisichelli, *"The Trivial Round, the Common Task,"* and Heberlein, *Communities of Imaginative Participation,* discuss her reflection of her romantic interest in Amery in some of her short stories. Wyatt-Brown includes in "Ellipsis, Eccentricity and Evasion in the Diaries of Barbara Pym" a psychological analysis that also takes into account Pym's relationship with her father as a means of explaining the male-female relationships reflected in her writing. Strauss-Noll is careful to point out that Pym suffered the pangs of unrequited love, yet her books are not the " 'spontaneous overflow of powerful feelings' "; instead, they are written with " 'calm of mind, all passion spent' " ("Love and Marriage in the Novels" 86).

Another topic of frequent discussion is Pym's use of her Oxford experience and of her nearly thirty years with the International African Institute in her writing about academics and the subject of anthropology. Academics and/or anthropologists appear in almost all of Pym's novels, but her most extended treatment of academics occurs in *Less Than Angels, Crampton Hodnet, Jane and Prudence,* and *An Academic Question,* with *Less Than Angels* focusing on anthropologists as academics. In "Love in the Great Libraries," Rossen points out that although Pym seldom uses Oxford as a setting in her novels, she "wrote intensely about Oxford feelings, relationships, and attitudes" (296). *Crampton Hodnet* is, however, set in Oxford, and a reflection of Oxford feelings and attitudes can be found in "Across a Crowded Room," *Jane and Prudence,* which "presents four academic generations" that "together suggest a wide spectrum of possibilities for Oxford-educated women" (289), and *No Fond Return of Love,* which reflects "the passion for contemporary 'research' " (294). Most frequently discussed in association with Pym's treatment of anthropology is her experience with the International African Institute that is reflected in both the subject matter and the technique of her novels (Holt, *Lot to Ask* and "The Novelist in the

Field: 1946–74''; Rossen, *World of Barbara Pym;* Burkhart,
Pleasure of Miss Pym). In "The Novelist in the Field," Holt gives
an account of her years working with Pym at the International
African Institute. In "The Novelist as Anthropologist," Schulz
writes that Pym's International African Institute experience provided her with comic and other raw material for her fiction. And
Nardin, *Barbara Pym,* and Fisichelli, "The Novelist as Anthropologist—Barbara Pym's Fiction: Fieldwork Done at Home,"
focus particularly on the parallels to be found in *Less Than
Angels,* which Fisichelli notes is a "full-scale satire" of anthropology (339).

Pym's critics frequently refer to her careful depiction of
English manners, and considerable attention has been given to the
parallels apparent between the social changes Pym experienced
and that are reflected in her notebooks and those portrayed in her
novels. Heberlein, *Communities of Imaginative Participation,*
traces the social change in the three novels "set in country
villages," *Some Tame Gazelle, Jane and Prudence,* and *A Few
Green Leaves,* and in the "London novels" (174). Fisichelli,
"The Trivial Round, the Common Task," discusses Pym's comments on the changing environment in her literary notebooks,
change that is depicted in the later novels, particularly *The Sweet
Dove Died* and *Quartet in Autumn.* And Nardin and Rossen point
specifically to Pym's treatment of social change in *The Sweet
Dove Died, Quartet in Autumn,* and *A Few Green Leaves.* Nardin
writes that Pym's last three novels reflect a changing view of
England, a world in which social science is replacing religion and
literature and where love and companionship are rarer and less
satisfactory (*Barbara Pym* 52). Rossen writes that *A Few Green
Leaves* "shows Pym in her element as a social satirist" (*World of
Barbara Pym* 154).

One important benefit the literary notebooks offer is the
opportunity to study Pym's creative process. Burkhart, Cotsell,
Fisichelli, and Heberlein discuss Pym's use of the literary notebooks as a repository for notes about her experiences and ideas
that eventually found a way into the novels. Burkhart notes the
importance of revision in Pym's writing process (*Pleasure of Miss
Pym* 5). Cotsell traces Pym's general writing process from a germ
in a notebook, to notebook entries recording ideas that "shaped

and altered her conception of characters and events, pondered titles and sketched scenes,'' to a first draft and at least a second draft before the final typescript (*Barbara Pym* 8). Fisichelli writes that the notebooks "provide a reliable guide to [Pym's] thoughts about writing" and that her notebook entries reveal her approach to writing the novels, including her personal concerns as she wrote, her attitude toward her characters, and her desire for audience response (*"The Trivial Round, the Common Task"* 34). In discussing Pym's notebook entries while she was writing *The Sweet Dove Died,* Fisichelli writes that Pym reflects "on the personality traits and motives of her characters,'' that the notebook entries helped her "to clarify the psychological subtleties of the relationships which she develops in the novel" (135). Heberlein also writes that the notebooks reveal Pym's "working methods in general as well as the composition process for each individual novel" (*Communities of Imaginative Participation* 27).

Wyatt-Brown studies the psychological conflicts that contributed to Pym's writing process. In "Ellipsis, Eccentricity and Evasion in the Diaries of Barbara Pym,'' she elaborates on Pym's lumber-room metaphor to explain Pym's process of distancing herself from her experiences so that she could incorporate them into detached, comic episodes in her novels. The lumber-room metaphor derives from an early Pym fragment titled "Beatrice Wyatt or the Lumber Room" in which the heroine compares memories of past loves to a storage room or attic—a lumber room—in which old pictures are stored. With the passing of time, as memory fades, it becomes safe to enter and inspect what was stored away in pain (45). In *Barbara Pym: A Critical Biography,* Wyatt-Brown extends her study of the psychological influences on Pym's creative process, employing the work of writing theorists and psychologists to show the effects of aging on her writing.

Themes in the Novels

The scholarly pieces that focus on the themes of Pym's novels treat a variety of topics that can be divided conveniently into two groups: topics concerning gender relationships and topics related to social issues and mutability. The most frequently discussed topic has to do with Pym's treatment of personal relationships based on issues associated with gender.

A number of scholarly pieces focus on the strengths and weaknesses of Pym's men and women. Benet, in *Something to Love: Barbara Pym's Novels,* offers the most extended treatment of this subject as she traces the evolution of Pym's male characters from an early state as ''emotional ciphers'' to becoming ''prominent citizens'' in Pym's universe. In the early novels Pym ''concentrates on the feminine point of view'' and ''radical differences separate women and men'' (15). The focus is on the emotional lives of women, for whom love is of great significance, but for men love is only one of many passions and of little significance. By the time she writes *Less Than Angels,* however, Pym's ''[m]en and women experience the same problems and confront the same choices; they have the same needs, are capable of the same strengths, and are subject to the same failings'' (63). Benet cites *Less Than Angels, A Glass of Blessings, No Fond Return of Love,* and *An Unsuitable Attachment*—novels of the middle period—as affirmative novels; in them ''women and men . . . find fulfillment that nourishes their emotional lives'' (64).

Other critics fail to see Pym's treatment of men and women in such an egalitarian light. Consensus among those who see differences in Pym's treatment of men and women is that Pym's women are the stronger lot. Ackley characterizes Pym's men as ''a shiftless, lazy lot whose inactivity is abetted by the constant attentions of women'' (*Novels of Barbara Pym* 49). Jacobs traces a progression in Pym's male characters from broad caricatures in the early works to darker, more complex portraits in the later novels. He cites John Challow of *An Unsuitable Attachment* as Pym's model for male behavior and writes that Pym's other males lack ''sensitivity towards the everyday world and towards the women who surround them'' (*Elements of Satire in the Novels of Barbara Pym* 47). Sanford Radner, ''Barbara Pym's People,'' points to a *seeming* inferiority among Pym's women. Radner notes Pym's repetition of the theme that when ''adult men and women come together in the rituals of contemporary life . . . they unconsciously play out one key fantasy: *a self-denying mother generously feeds her ungrateful baby son*'' and that her treatment of romantic relationships contributes to a ''basic ironic assumption'' of ''female inferiority'' (172–73). Isa Kapp, in ''Out of the

Swim with Barbara Pym,'' also sees Pym's world as a ''woman's world'' where ''men are the weaker sex'' (238). Anne Tyler writes that in Pym's novels women ''are in many ways far stronger than men can ever hope to be, although the women wouldn't dream of letting them find that out'' (''Foreword'' vi). And according to Nardin, who notes the emphasis Pym's men place on ''success and the realization of their own desires'' and her women's suppression of their own desires and devotion to caring for others, Pym suggests that ''men, rather than women, . . . are the main victims of sex-role differentiation'' in that women develop a ''heightened consciousness'' not usually attainable by men (*Barbara Pym* 39–40). Similarly, Marlene San Miguel Groner, in *The Novels of Barbara Pym,* emphasizes the power of the imagination for Pym's protagonists who, through their use of imagination, may either submit to self-destruction or isolation or alternatively triumph over limitations imposed by society.

Pym's women also tend to invite categorization. Snow, in *One Little Room an Everywhere,* casts Pym's spinsters into two classes: the '' 'excellent women,' who never tell their love, who devote themselves to the work of the parish, who make tea at moments of crisis in other people's lives, and who have few or no expectations for themselves'' (11), and ''those whom men select not for mere respect and esteem but for loving'' (15). Carol Wilkinson Whitney, noting the influence of the unbalanced female-male ratio in post-World War II Britain on society's perception of appropriate roles for women, points to two types of women who contribute to ''fear between the sexes'' in Pym's world: ''Terrifying women'' and ''formidable women.'' Whitney writes that the excellent woman, ''whose life usually centers on the church and who is quick to sort jumble, cook a joint, console the distressed, and . . . make tea,'' is not likely ''to strike panic in the hearts of men.'' But the terrifying woman, who ''single-mindedly'' seeks a husband, like Allegra Gray of *Excellent Women,* and the formidable woman, who confidently cultivates '' 'masculine' attitudes and interests, elicit both fear and respect from the opposite sex'' ('' 'Women Are So Terrifying These Days' '' 71). These two types of women contribute to the tension between the sexes in Pym's novels, a theme that prevails in Aylwin's fear, in *No Fond Return of Love,* of both terrifying and formidable women and in his preference for younger, seemingly

helpless women. Patricia Kane, "A Curious Eye: Barbara Pym's
Women," classifies Pym's women into three categories: "observers, manipulators, and typists." The three are linked by a "penchant for handsome men . . . and their crushes on these men often
cause the observation, manipulation, and typing. Whichever of
these activities the women choose, they achieve at least a limited
happiness" (50).

Halperin, in "Barbara Pym and the War of the Sexes," reviews
Pym's treatment of men and women in *Jane and Prudence, Less
Than Angels, A Glass of Blessings,* and *The Sweet Dove Died.*
Pym, he writes, portrays men as overbearing, egotistical, weak,
incompetent, and dependent upon women for survival, and
women as the victims of the selfishness and brutality of men. *Jane
and Prudence* he finds her "most sustained attack on men" (89).
Less Than Angels is "more even-handed" than *Jane and Prudence* in that although the women are stronger than the men, the
men use women to their advantage by "playing on their sympathies" (92–93). In *A Glass of Blessings,* Halperin sees the
"relation of the sexes" as bringing "out in some women a modest
sadism" (96). In *The Sweet Dove Died,* "women are more petty
than men" (99); nevertheless "the sexes remain at knife-edge,
with neither gaining a clear victory" (100). Similarly, Lynn
Veach Sadler points out that Pym upends sexual stereotypes and
that for Pym "people are their own worst enemies . . . . [B]ores
and boors can be male and female, and men can out-spinster
spinsters" ("Spinsters, Non-spinsters, and Men in the World of
Barbara Pym" 153).

Two essays deal specifically with Pym's treatment of male
homosexuality in the novels: Burkhart's "Glamorous Acolytes:
Homosexuality in Pym's World," and "Pym's Homosexuals" by
Merritt Moseley and Pamela Nickless. Burkhart traces the homosexual characters throughout Pym's novels, noting that her treatment of homosexuality reveals her "large-scale impartial tolerance" (95). Pym's straight men, Burkhart writes, are almost
always negative characters, but her homosexuals "are a solace,
though by no means a solution" (105). Moseley and Nickless also
survey Pym's homosexuals, noting that the homosexuals are
" 'excellent women' "—"considerate and caring," "interested
in food, clothing, and furniture," curious and interested in gossip,
while marrying men are "stolid, selfish, thick, and helpless" (7).

Homosexuals are ''an interesting sort of noncombatant or double agent in the war of the sexes''—their ''weakness'' becomes their strength (8).

Ackley, *The Novels of Barbara Pym,* Bywaters, *Rereading Jane: Jane Austen's Legacy to Twentieth-Century Women Writers,* and Sherwood, *''A Special Kind of Double''*: *Sisters in British and American Fiction,''* take a different approach to the treatment of male-female (and female-female) relationships by surveying Pym's treatment of mothers and sisters in the novels. Mothers, Ackley points out, are ''problematic for a large number of Pym's characters'' (96). The most problematic are elderly women who dominate and limit the lives of both their sons and daughters. The implications of mother-son relationships have some bearing on Pym's homosexual males in that ''single men who are still close to their mothers have problems with women'' (104).

Both Bywaters and Sherwood point to the positive emphasis that Pym accords to sister relationships. Comparing Pym's treatment of sisters with that of Jane Austen, Bywaters notes that six of Pym's novels deal with ''sister or sister-like relationships'' that provide ''companionship and emotional support'' and produce ''a sense of security, which functions as a form of continuity'' (30). Sherwood, concentrating on the relationship between Harriet and Belinda Bede in *Some Tame Gazelle,* posits that Pym's depiction of sisterhood spoofs romantic comedies by suggesting that spinster sisters who share fantasies about romance may be more blessed than wedded women.

This concern with the nature of male-female relationships at times leads to speculation about whether Pym is a feminist. Lee writes that for feminists women's strength derives from ''emotional and financial independence'' and from social commitment, but that Pym's women find strength in ''long-lasting love and quiet perseverance'' (*Love, Marriage, and Irony in Barbara Pym's Novels* 104). Sadler calls Pym a ''pre-Feminist Movement author,'' noting that she ''finds fault on both sides of the battle between the sexes,'' yet she is ''aware of the traditional limitations society imposes on women'' (''Spinsters, Non-spinsters, and Men in the World of Barbara Pym'' 145). Joseph Epstein, ''Miss Pym and Mr. Larkin,'' writes that Pym is a ''very feminine but very far from a conventionally feminist writer,'' that she ''partakes of . . . the superior feminism'' that finds men amusing

but "not quite to be taken seriously" (43). Burkhart holds that
Pym's feminism exists in her "dramatizations, not her explica-
tions." Her writing is, he says, a "show of the state of things, not
a shout against them" (*Pleasure of Miss Pym* 91). Barbara
Bowman, "Barbara Pym's Subversive Subtext," points out that
"Pym's heroines and narrators are not overtly feminist." They do
not attempt "to overthrow male domination"; however, "they do
dramatize the heroine's perception of the discrepancy between her
own and the dominant culture's assumptions" (85). Rossen,
"Love in the Great Libraries," noting that in *Jane and Prudence*
"[n]one of the available choices [for women] is wholly satisfactory" (289) and that in *No Fond Return of Love* the heroines are
literary women who show "the possible negative effect of
education" (293), holds that Pym does "create a wryly feminist
perspective on life for academic women" (279). Snow, *One Little
Room an Everywhere,* concludes that Pym's women are "latent
feminists." They are feminists in proving that they are stronger
and more intelligent than men, but they are not feminists in that
they all "play Eve to the men they love," conforming "outwardly
to the concept of women as the weaker sex" (64–65). Heberlein,
"Thankless Tasks or Labors of Love: Women's Work in Barbara
Pym's Novels," writes that because Pym's women "find work
meaningful in direct proportion to their feeling for the man with
whom or for whom it is done," Pym may not "seem to be making
a feminist statement," but that she is making a feminist statement
in showing how women's "need to be needed . . . opens them to
exploitation," and that she "might even be classified as a radical
feminist . . . because she portrays women as not only fundamentally different from men but also as superior" (3).

Related to Pym's treatment of gender issues, and noted repeatedly by critics, is her focus on the phenomenon of romantic love.
Romantic love, as the critics are quick to point out, does not fare
well in Pym's novels; in short, as Benet writes in *Something to
Love,* romantic love is treated unromantically. In the early novels,
Benet notes that love is of greater significance to women, who
must have something to dote on, than it is to men. Some of Pym's
men, she says, "consider love irrelevant or inappropriate to their
age"; others "desire not love but admiration" (58). Women
pursue men for love, but "[m]en pursue women, when they do, for
primarily practical reasons" (61). Also pointing to male-female

cross-purposes in the issue of romantic love is Jacobs, who notes that only during the marriage proposal do women's opinions really count in the male world and that the marriage proposal "reveals the gulf between the sexes," men seeking "sensible alliance," women wanting "something more than the promise of comfort and social respectability" and recognizing that "marriage will bring an end to romance" (125). To some extent this failure of communication about marriage comes about because women judge men by "romantic standards too lofty for" men's "work-bound temperaments" (43). Barbara Brothers, "Love, Marriage, and Manners in the Novels of Barbara Pym," takes the explanation a step further by noting that Pym's novels "demonstrate the absurdity of the Victorian *ideal* of the family" by "mocking romantic love and depicting the many forms that loving takes—platonic, love between men, friendship between women" (158). In another essay, "Women Victimized by Fiction," Brothers points out that Pym's novels make a statement about fiction. By contrasting "her characters and their lives with those which have been presented in literature" she mocks the idealized view of romantic love (62) and makes the point that "fiction should cease portraying an idealised version of love" (69).

Critics have noted that Pym offers few satisfactory male-female alliances in her novels, and as Burkhart points out in *The Pleasure of Miss Pym,* when they are satisfactory they usually involve older couples. Romantic love may offer an escape from isolation or, because of its illusory nature, it may actually inhibit meaningful communication. On the other hand, Pym's characters are sometimes incapable of achieving satisfactory romantic attachments because they fail to communicate. Kaufman, "The Short Fiction of Barbara Pym," discusses the treatment of "the need to love and the consequences of love's failure" in Pym's short fiction, noting how "memory and fantasy so often must take the place of actuality" (51). Long sees Pym's characters in *Jane and Prudence* and *Crampton Hodnet* attempting to "escape from their isolation through romance," yet failing when romance is undercut by romantic posturing and manipulation (*Barbara Pym* 82). Sometimes romance fails when narcissism and indifference prevent either gender from responding appropriately. Rossen writes that because of men's indifference, Pym's "women must develop emotional restraint in romantic love'' (*World of Barbara Pym* 69). And Benet points out that in *The Sweet Dove Died* and *Quartet in Autumn*, '' 'romance' can inhibit the expression of unifying love'' (*Something to Love* 159).

Critics note that although spinsterhood has its problems, the troubles associated with romantic love frequently lead Pym's characters to prefer spinsterhood. An interesting treatment of the subject of spinsterhood in the novels is Doan's "Pym's Singular Interest: The Self as Spinster," in which Doan sees Pym's treatment of spinsterhood as a means of coming to terms with her own unmarried state. Drawing primarily on *Crampton Hodnet,* which Doan sees as a "blueprint" for the other novels, she concludes that Pym uses her novels "to undermine traditional notions of the spinster and to create a positive self-identity." She presents spinsterhood as an "alternative life-style" through which women may take "an active role in society" (153).

Others who appreciate the positive attributes Pym assigns to spinsterhood include Burkhart, Graham, Rossen, Sadler, and Strauss-Noll. Burkhart, *The Pleasure of Miss Pym,* points out that marriage maneuvers occupy the novels but that marriage more often involves conflict or boredom than fulfillment and that women sometimes make other accommodations such as "excellent spinsterhood or . . . attempts at a career of liberated independence" (85). Graham, "Cumbered with Much Serving: Barbara Pym's 'Excellent Women,' '' writes that the observations of Pym's excellent women affirm spinsterhood and cast doubt upon marriage. Marriage, he points out, fails to offer mutuality of companionship because "men are inherently inferior" (146). Further, women are not permitted to assist in men's work except in menial ways. Marriage does not provide experiences necessary for a full life, tending instead to neutralize personalities and failing to provide love and contentment. Rossen, *The World of Barbara Pym,* also sees Pym's positive treatment of spinsters, noting that the "advantages of singleness . . . constitute a major subject" for Pym (42), that she provides "a survival manual for spinsters" (44). For Pym's heroines one of the greatest benefits is the solitary characteristic of the spinster's existence that provides opportunity for self-reflection. Sadler writes that Pym's world is full of spinsters because England is full of spinsters, but that "some of Pym's spinsters not only willfully choose their spinsterhood but use it deliberately to set their lives and the lives of others as they wish them to be'' (''Spinsters, Non-spinsters, and Men in the World of Barbara Pym'' 143). Strauss-Noll, in ''Love and Marriage in the Novels,'' also remarks on the ''ambivalence of the single women and the disillusionment of the married women . . . throughout all Pym's writings,'' but she holds that in *A Few Green Leaves* widowhood is presented as the ideal state (73).

Yet spinsterhood has its problems. Margaret Bradham, ''Barbara Pym's Women,'' points to the abundance of ''disappointment, despair, failure, and loneliness'' associated with ''spinsterhood and unmarriageability'' (31), and notes that the condition of the Pym women is that of ''lonely, restless, unhappy, and unfulfilled'' spinsters and of married women disillusioned by marriage (32). Rossen, *The World of Barbara Pym,* notes some of the frictions that result among women who live with women and that a theme of Pym's novels is the ''predicament of the spinster as she is type-cast in society'' and who must learn to deal with solitude and make do with limited resources (53). Pym is concerned, Rossen writes, with the issue of the spinster as a useless anachronism and with the problem of employment for women. Margaret Ezell, '' 'What Shall We Do with Our Old Maids?': Barbara Pym and the Woman Question,'' also sees the predicament of the spinster as an important theme in the novels, writing that Pym explores the paradox of the single woman ''trying to join the ranks of the married,'' while the community requires that she ''cultivate a type of behaviour that perpetuates her solitary state. . .'' (451).

Another gender-related topic brought to Pym criticism is the treatment of self-starvation as a means of protest in Pym's characterization of Marcia Ivory of *Quartet in Autumn.* Naulty, in *''I Never Talk of Hunger'': Self-Starvation as Women's Language of Protest in Novels by Barbara Pym, Margaret Atwood, and Anne Tyler,* applies feminist theory about women's language to Pym's novel. Drawing on the work of anthropologist Edward Ardener, Naulty explains women's frequent inability to articulate their experience as resulting from the inadequacy of the idioms of a male-dominant language and the differences in men's and women's perceptions of language. Accordingly, Marcia Ivory has to rely on the nonverbal language of self-starvation to protest her dissatisfaction with the limited space society allows to women and their needs. Naulty goes on to point out that critics have heretofore been unable to perceive this message in Pym's novels because as subscribers to the language of the dominant group they, too, have been unable to perceive Marcia's language of self-starvation.

In addition to gender-related themes, scholars often focus on Pym's treatment of issues related to social change. These issues include the shifting role of the Church of England and other social changes that have come about with the increasing emphasis on social science, particularly reflected in anthropology, as opposed to religion and literature. Pym's treatment of church-related topics has prompted Long to call Pym "the *great* satirical authority on the Church of England in modern times" (*Barbara Pym* 217).

Rossen, *The World of Barbara Pym,* points out that Pym treats the church not in theological but in social and historical terms. In Pym's novels, the Anglican Church serves as a "metaphor for England and as a container for the preservation of English culture" (81). Pym's objections to the church are reflected in the contempt for it shown by some of her anthropologists and in objections to its replacing the natives' religion. The Anglican church is threatened by elements of paganism, atheism, and aestheticism, and it is challenged by the Roman Catholic Church, yet it endures because it assimilates opposing factions and becomes a "repository for the past, as well as for history as it unfolds" (100). Burkhart, *The Pleasure of Miss Pym,* also points to Pym's affirmation of the church, but he notes that in her novels there is much about ecclesiastical ritual but little about spiritual experience, perhaps because the latter was "an area in which she did not jest" (108).

Jacobs, *Elements of Satire in the Novels of Barbara Pym,* also looks at Pym's treatment of the Anglican Church, concluding that although Pym implies that the Church's "unusual tolerance and the deliberate blandness of its service" may be partly responsible for the declining number of worshipers, her treatment of the church is not harshly satiric (178). Stanley, *The Anglican Clergy in the Novels of Barbara Pym,* examines both the evolution of the Anglican Church throughout Pym's novels, and Pym's use of clergyman types descended from the literary tradition of Austen, the Brontës and Trollope. Stanley traces Pym's treatment of the Church from her identification of it with the mid-nineteenth-century Church of England in the early novels, to connections between the clergy and anthropologists in her middle period, to the usurpation of the Church's role by the welfare state in the final novels. Stanley concludes that although Pym sees the shortcomings of the Anglican Church, she "loves 'that vast moth-eaten musical brocade' and realizes that it is necessary to her sense of reality" (131).

Benet, "The Language of Christianity in Pym's Novels," points out that in her novels Pym criticizes three "language-related problems" associated with the church: a "stock of pious words that has been devitalized, outmoded devotional forms that often do not appeal to the modern sensibility, and a clergy that has difficulty communicating the ancient faith to its contemporary flock" (505). Eleanor Wymard, "Barbara Pym on Organized Religion," discusses Pym's disappointment with the Church, noting that "liturgy practised by the church . . . is without social commitment, causing worship to be alienating and almost self-destructive" (319–20). Jill Rubenstein also sees Pym's novels as somewhat critical of the church. Yet, Rubenstein writes, in "Comedy and Consolation in the Novels of Barbara Pym," that where "the inability to admit the strange or the imaginative or even the unfamiliar into religious experience" prevents most of Pym's characters "from realizing their spirituality," a few of her characters find in "the very familiarity of their religion . . . true consolation" (183).

The church is an important factor in Pym's treatment of social change since the lack of commuunity and the loss of love and companionship that Pym's characters must deal with results in large part because social science is usurping the role of religion and literature. Nardin, in *Barbara Pym,* notes Pym's treatment of the church in relation to social change in *Quartet in Autumn* and *A Few Green Leaves. Quartet in Autumn* portrays "a London where the institutions that have traditionally related people to one another are no longer functioning, and where individuals find themselves isolated, unable to depend on others for companionship and aid" (124). *A Few Green Leaves* also reflects radical transformations in the "texture of rural English life" (134), including changes in daily life involving such matters as food, television, the welfare state, and the replacement of religion and literature by science.

Pym's treatment of academics is frequently discussed in relation to the shift away from literature and the church. Jacobs, *Elements of Satire in the Novels of Barbara Pym,* discusses the ways Pym deflates the academic world's "image of intellectual superiority and ever-advancing scholarship" (81). Her images of the library are frequently negative. It is not a place where one enjoys research; rather it is a place where her characters look up male acquaintances in *Who's Who* and *Crockford,* eat in the reading room, and dump unwanted milk bottles. The library heads are more concerned with modernizing the cloakroom and heating facilities than with improving collections.

Closely related to social change are resulting problems associated with aging. Rossen, *The World of Barbara Pym,* notes that the main subject of both *Quartet in Autumn* and *A Few Green Leaves* is aging and that *A Few Green Leaves* reflects Pym's "concern with the immediacy of death . . . and . . . with the judging of one's life in retrospect" (156–57). Ackley, *The Novels of Barbara Pym,* treats at length the subject of isolation and loneliness in Pym's novels, noting how the nature of modern life results in alienation. She includes a close study of the isolation of Marcia Ivory in *Quartet in Autumn,* noting in her concluding paragraph that many of Pym's characters "discover that autonomy is ample compensation for the drawbacks of solitude" and that those characters "who remain emotionally out of touch and therefore doomed to a permanent disassociation from any meaningful interaction, are those whose inner lives have withered" (142).

Wyatt-Brown has discussed Pym's treatment of aging in two essays, "From Fantasy to Pathology: Images of Aging in the Novels of Barbara Pym" and "Late Style in the Novels of Barbara Pym and Penelope Mortimer," and in *Barbara Pym: A Critical Biography,* noting that Pym's increasing understanding of the aging process in the later novels may be related to her own experiences with ill health. Pym, she writes, "makes an important contribution to our understanding of old age," providing a "realistically grim yet surprisingly optimistic view of the possibilities that older people have for change because of the new understanding they gain by suffering" ("From Fantasy to Pathology" 5). In *Barbara Pym: A Critical Biography,* Wyatt-Brown brings to a discussion of Letty's experiences in *Quartet in Autumn* current theories about retirement and concludes that instead of pitying Marcia, "Pym accepted her desire to die" (132).

In *From the Hearth to the Open Road: A Feminist Study of Aging in Contemporary Literature,* Barbara Frey Waxman devotes a section of one chapter to a study of Marcia and Letty and their attempts to "deal emotionally and physically with retirement" (105). Positing a new genre, which she names the *Reifsrungroman,* or "novel of ripening" as opposed to "the usual notion of deterioration in old age" (2), Waxman interprets Letty's statement about life's "infinite possibilities for change" at the end of *Quartet in Autumn* as a reflection of growth. Because Pym's quartet reject institutionalized life and the generalizations of social agencies about their needs and "how they should live," Waxman sees the novel as a "force for change in Anglo-American society" (119).

Narrative Technique

Among the most interesting studies of Pym's novels are those that focus on her narrative technique. In this group are scholarly pieces connecting Pym and her writing to other writers in terms of influence and of contrasts and similarities, and pieces that deal specifically with some aspect of Pym's subject matter or narrative style. Critics have linked Pym's name with more than thirty other writers who have either influenced her work or with whom her work can be compared. This number does not include the discussion of Pym's frequent quotations from and allusions to English literature. Sometimes the linking amounts to a brief mention, suggesting opportunities for further study; in some cases extended discussions of Pym's work as it relates to that of other prominent writers offer important insights to the novels.

The most frequently discussed connection is with Jane Austen. Long discusses at length the multiple aspects of the connection with Austen and summarizes some of the positions taken by other commentators in his concluding chapter of *Barbara Pym.* In addition, he discusses Pym's affinity with a number of other authors, including Anita Brookner, Philip Larkin, Angela Thirkell, Anthony Trollope, and Charlotte M. Yonge. Several critics, including Rossen, *The World of Barbara Pym,* and Fisichelli, *"The Trivial Round, the Common Task,"* have called attention to Pym's reverence for and study of Austen, and Rossen points to Pym's denial that she should be compared with Austen, pointing out that although Austen provided an example and a model, Pym may have rejected the comparisons because she felt they might diminish her own work. A reader, for example, looking for echoes of Austen might fail to discern Pym's own "unique style." In supporting her argument, Rossen points to the eagerness of Pym's characters, notably Prudence Bates in *Jane and Prudence,* Emma Howick in *A Few Green Leaves,* and Ianthe Broome in *An Unsuitable Attachment,* to disassociate themselves from Austen's fiction. By constantly evoking "ghosts of the past" in her novels, Pym "defines herself as someone different in the process" (15–16). Similarly, Fergus, discussing Pym's "highly sophisticated art of allusion" in *"A Glass of Blessings,* Jane Austen's *Emma,* and Barbara Pym's Art of Allusion," writes that Pym uses allusions to Austen "to insist on an immense distance—both social and aesthetic—between Austen's world and her own," thus undercutting "the notion of a resemblance to Austen" (110–11). Pym's friend Robert Liddell allows the comparison only in the sense that both writers possessed "[a] mind lively and at ease" that "can do with seeing nothing, and can see nothing that does not answer" (*Mind at Ease* 27).

Bruce Stovel, "Subjective to Objective: A Career Pattern in Jane Austen, George Eliot, and Contemporary Women Novelists," points to parallels between the careers of Austen and Pym. Noting that Pym's novels are filled with characters with Austen names, dialogues, and allusion, and that like Austen, "Pym writes comic novels which glance obliquely at the big questions rather than confronting them directly," Stovel writes that there is a "striking resemblance" in their writing careers in that "Pym's novels fall into two groups separated by a gap of more than ten years." In the novels of both Austen and Pym, there is a similar "shift in subject and form from the early to the late novels" (58).

Other comparisons have been drawn between subject and form in the novels of Austen and Pym. A. L. Rowse and Burkhart both note differences between the social scenes the two authors portray. "The difference," writes Burkhart, "is that Jane Austen spoke out of an assured and moral culture, while Barbara Pym is afloat in an ebb tide" (*Pleasure of Miss Pym* 14). Similarly, Rowse, "Miss Pym and Miss Austen," calls attention to the "successful governing-class" to which Austen belonged as opposed to Pym's participation in postwar England, England in a state of transformation (64). Rowse also notes a contrast in subject matter—marriage in Austen as opposed to the choice of a career in Pym—and Pym's wider experience, her time in the WRNS and her treatment of homosexuality. "Love, rather than marriage, is the crux of Barbara Pym's novels" (68). But both "have an adult view of life" (69), and both are "linked to the central spine of English life and tradition, and give an authentic and faithful depiction of it . . ." (71).

Others, too, find similarities in the work of Pym and Austen. Snow, *One Little Room an Everywhere,* writes that unlike Austen, Pym tells us little about the influence of family and education in the life of her characters (77); however, both authors bring "charm and strength" to their novels through "the maturity of the heroines" (81). Mason Cooley, *The Comic Art of Barbara Pym,* cites parallels of character and event in several of the novels and notes that *Crampton Hodnet* can be compared with Austen's novels written during the Napoleonic Wars but not about them—it "shows us a little world of gentlefolk pursuing their love affairs and their gossipy social rounds exempt from war, disease, aging, poverty, and the darker passions" (24).

Cotsell, commenting on some of the comparisons that have been drawn, writes that Pym's "novels of manners are in the Austen tradition" and that "her achievement can be compared to Austen's . . . though Austen is the greater writer" (143). Robert Smith, in "How Pleasant to Know Miss Pym," the first scholarly piece written on Pym's novels, cites Pym's "range and scope" as "considerably wider than those of Jane Austen," but notes that both have the "same woman's view, dealing sharply but on the whole good-humoredly with the closely-observed minutiae of middle-class daily life, always enlivened by the needle of wit" (63–64). Long, in *Barbara Pym,* notes similar parallels between Pym and Austen, similarities of classical form and subject matter, citing their realistic portrayal of the manners of the time "that is conspicuous for its wit, irony, and social observation" and their "woman's point of view" (201).

Benet, *Something to Love,* Heberlein, *Communities of Imaginative Participation,* Rossen, *The World of Barbara Pym,* and Bywaters, *Rereading Jane: Austen's Legacy to Twentieth-Century Writers,* cite similar parallels of subject matter and point

of view. Bywaters places Pym "squarely in the Austen tradition"
in her treatment of unmarried women, comic point of view, and
use of irony (9). Noting that Pym read Austen throughout her life,
Bywaters sees parallels in "the dynamics of the sister relationship" that "drives the narratives" of both novelists (30). Nardin,
Barbara Pym, points particularly to similarities of plot structure
between *Some Tame Gazelle* and the plot structure of Austen's
novels—the circle of women dealing with an intruder and the
absorption, expulsion, or change that ends in a celebratory
marriage. Nardin, however, sees in Pym's early novels "an ironic
reversal of the comic form" of Austen's novels (64). In Pym, the
"celebratory marriage that traditionally concludes comedy" cele-
brates singleness, not marriage (71).

Frederick Keener, "Barbara Pym Herself and Jane Austen,"
also notes both similarities and differences in subject and form.
Both Pym and Austen write about small groups of people,
focusing on a heroine or two. Both "work permutations on
recurrent character types," and both use "self-possessed" third-
person narrators. But Austen "stands more firmly in the tradition
of novelistic romance" than Pym, whose heroines at the end of
her novels are typically unmarried, unless married when the novel
began (91).

Barbara Bowman, "Barbara Pym's Subversive Subtext: Private Irony and Shared Detachment," sees similarities in the irony
of the two novelists. "The complexity of Austen's irony," she
writes, "resides in the narrator's voice as it collides with the
reader's recognition of the statement's untruth and its depiction of
a useful social facade." Pym uses some of the same assumptions:
"that the narrator and the reader's knowledge and points of view
correspond, and . . . that the heroine will be initiated into this
alignment of narrator and reader" (84).

Critics frequently point to Pym's allusions to and use of
Austen's novels in her work. Snow, "Literary Allusions in the
Novels," writes that Pym uses four of Austen's six novels (the
exceptions, *Northanger Abbey* and *Sense and Sensibility*) in five
of her own. Pym's allusions to and uses of *Emma* are discussed by
several critics. Snow cites specifically Pym's use of *Emma* "to
characterise Prudence and Jane" and her use of *Emma* in *A Few
Green Leaves* (139–40). In addition to parallels in the lives of
Pym and Austen and in the general subject matter of their novels,

Peter Graham, ''Emma's Three Sisters,'' points to specific parallels between *Emma* and *Some Tame Gazelle*. Both novels, he says, present a ''series of romantic attachments experienced by one woman, observed by the other, and making life interesting for them both'' (46). Heberlein, *Communities of Imaginative Participation*, and Long, *Barbara Pym*, cite Pym's use of *Emma* in *Jane and Prudence*, both noting the matchmaking of the heroines Jane Cleveland and Emma Woodhouse. Long says that both are misguided in their matchmaking. In *Emma*, he writes, ''moral order ultimately prevails''; however, ''in *Jane and Prudence*, what one finds, beneath its comic surfaces, is chiefly estrangement'' (90). Keener, ''Barbara Pym Herself and Jane Austen,'' contrasts Austen's Miss Bates and Prudence Bates of *Jane and Prudence*, but notes that Miss Bates is ''the closest thing in Austen to an Excellent Woman'' (92).

Wilmet Forsyth of *A Glass of Blessings* is also frequently compared with Austen's Emma Woodhouse. Nardin, *Barbara Pym*, writes that Hazel Holt, Pym's literary executor, told her that Pym herself sometimes compared *A Glass of Blessings* with *Emma* (108). Heberlein, *Communities of Imaginative Participation*, cites Wilmet's movement from egoism and self-absorption to ''self-discovery and sympathetic understanding of others'' as similar to the pattern of Emma Woodhouse's movement toward self-discovery (158). Long's comparison of the two characters is similar in that he discusses Wilmet's awakening and transformation (*Barbara Pym* 117–20). And Fergus, ''*A Glass of Blessings*, Jane Austen's *Emma* and Barbara Pym's Art of Allusion,'' sees parallels between sets of characters and other aspects of the two novels. She notes that *A Glass of Blessings* contains no overt allusions to Austen's novels, yet its ''covert references to *Emma* partially control both form and content so extensively that Pym can almost be said to have rewritten that novel'' (110). Nardin, *Barbara Pym*, discusses at length Pym's use of *Emma*, writing that Pym based the plot of *A Few Green Leaves* on *Emma*, thus making ''two points about literature: first, that it teaches us about individual people in a way that social science cannot rival, and second, that its material is forever new, no matter how many times it has been 'done' before'' (144).

In addition to parallels between *A Few Green Leaves* and *Emma*, Nardin also notes a possible borrowing in *A Few Green*

Leaves from *Mansfield Park* in the use of "a house as a symbol of English traditions," comparing the "competition for control of Mansfield Park" with the question in *A Few Green Leaves* of who is to live in "the Old Rectory" (145). Others have seen parallels between Pym's novels and *Mansfield Park,* including Keener, who calls attention to the garden images and events in *A Glass of Blessings* that recall "the garden at Sotherton" in *Mansfield Park* ("Barbara Pym Herself and Jane Austen" 108). Keener also sees parallels between Anne Elliott of *Persuasion* and Emma Howick of *A Few Green Leaves,* both concerned with regaining the affection of a suitor.

Other comparisons between individual novels include Saar's comparison, in "Irony from a Female Perspective," of Mildred in *Excellent Women* with Elizabeth in *Pride and Prejudice* and her discussion of a possible ironic allusion to *Northanger Abbey* in Mildred's declaration that she is nothing like Jane Eyre. Long, in *Barbara Pym,* sees affinities between *An Unsuitable Attachment* and *Pride and Prejudice* in that they share the qualities of the "comedy of errors, of misperception based on erroneous first impressions" (148).

Pym's allusions to *Jane Eyre* in *Excellent Women, Less Than Angels,* and *The Sweet Dove Died* have evoked response from several critics who comment on Pym's use of Brontë's work. Long's response to Mildred Lathbury's claim in *Excellent Women* that she is "not like Jane Eyre" is that the statement is ironic, that Lathbury is like Jane Eyre "in her plainness and marginality and even—though on a diminished scale—in the romantic impulse that beats within her" (*Barbara Pym* 57). Long also sees Catherine Oliphant of *Less Than Angels* as an ironic Jane Eyre. And Alaric Lydgate, whom Pym compares to Mr. Rochester several times in the novel, Long says, is like Rochester in the "thwarting of his psychic energies" and in the wearing of masks implying a "gothic inner life." Both Lydgate and Rochester "have blighted pasts" and are "redeemed by an unmarried woman who occupies a marginal place in society and is an 'outsider' " (106). Snow, *One Little Room an Everywhere,* credits Brontë with serving "as an aid to characterization in five of the novels" (51), noting the comparison of Mildred Lathbury and Catherine Oliphant to Jane Eyre and the use "with satiric intent" of the name Eyre in *The Sweet Dove Died* (52).

Two extended discussions of Pym and Brontë are found in articles by Rossen and Ezell. Rossen, "On Not Being Jane Eyre: The Romantic Heroine in Barbara Pym's Novels," finds that Pym "consciously modelled her work on Brontë's in order to mark her own identification with the frustrations which Brontë depicts as inherent in a woman's lot" (138). Pym transforms *Jane Eyre* "into a study of alternative renderings of the Jane Eyre story" in "Something to Remember," *Excellent Women,* and *The Sweet Dove Died* (137). Pym's heroines are like Jane Eyre in that they are " 'distressed gentlewomen' " and are of the "conviction that love is not to be expected for them." At the same time, they are not like Jane Eyre in that they "succeed in renouncing their love for the Rochester heroes" (138). In "Something to Remember," the heroine attempts to forget the hero years after a disappointment. In *Excellent Women,* Mildred renounces her love for Rocky and substitutes "Everard Bone [Brontë's St. John] and the work she can do for him" (147). In *The Sweet Dove Died,* Leonora rejects James's attempts to reinstate their "quasi-romantic relationship" (153). Ezell, "What Shall We Do with Our Old Maids?" focuses on Pym's affinity with Brontë in her treatment of the dilemma of the single woman, the " 'woman question,' " which Ezell sees as linking Pym to the "social protest novels of Charlotte Brontë" (450). Ezell concentrates on *An Unsuitable Attachment* and *Excellent Women,* noting that Pym's novels lack "the passionate denouncements of society" found in *The Professor* and *Shirley,* that Pym's protests are "done in an undertone, in quiet, unstressed asides" (461).

Pym's narrative technique and her treatment of English society have evoked several comparisons of her novels with the novels of Anthony Trollope. Heberlein, "Barbara Pym and Anthony Trollope: Communities of Imaginative Participation," provides an extended comparison of the two authors, citing both for opening the "traditional novel's closed form" and deflating its "romantic paradigms" (95). She notes that both use carryover characters to blur the boundaries of individual novels, both use allusions to "expand their imaginative communities," and both use multiple points of view to present "multiple moral perspectives concerning social behavior" (98). Both Pym and Trollope, she writes, "achieve a dual impression: multiple points of view but one narrative voice" (100). Nardin, who finds Pym "more cheerful in tone'' than Trollope, compares the two in "choosing to end" novels with "marriages or approaches to marriage, after having slyly undermined the value of marriage in the body of the book" (*Barbara Pym* 82). Rossen, *The World of Barbara Pym,* sees affinities with Trollope, noting that "[n]ot since Anthony Trollope's Barchester novels about Victorian England has the Anglican Church received such minute and detailed treatment in fiction" (77). Although both Pym and Trollope write about the inner workings of the church, their clerical worlds are fundamentally different in that Trollope's "assumes church allegiance as a matter of course," whereas Pym's does not (99). The church fails to attain omnipotence for Pym as it does for Trollope, and Pym's clergymen "exert little direct influence on society" (101).

Other writers with whom Pym has been linked more than once include Aldous Huxley, Ivy Compton-Burnett, Charlotte Yonge, Elizabeth Bowen, Margaret Drabble, Philip Larkin, Henry James, Virginia Woolf, and Denton Welch. Pym's mention of Huxley, whose *Crome Yellow* she credits in her diaries as having inspired her to write the unpublished first novel, "Young Men in Fancy Dress," has elicited comment from a number of critics.

Wyatt-Brown, Jacobs, and Cotsell offer substantial commentary on Huxley's influence. Wyatt-Brown discusses Huxley's influence in *Barbara Pym: A Critical Biography;* in "Ellipsis, Eccentricity and Evasion in the Diaries of Barbara Pym," she sees Huxley's influence as helping Pym develop a spirit of detachment, yet she notes that Pym's interest in romantic involvement precluded her from following "his example with complete success" (37). Jacobs, *Elements of Satire in the Novels of Barbara Pym,* furnishes an extended discussion of Huxley's influence, noting parallels in the authors' caricatures of the historian, the academic, and the clergyman; use of characters who as parallel lines fail to communicate; use of carryover characters; use of quotations and wordplay; settings and satiric tone; and their combination of "absurdist satire" with a " 'satisfying acceptant quality' " (20). Cotsell, *Barbara Pym,* quotes from "Young Men in Fancy Dress" to show parallels with *Crome Yellow* and to make the point that Pym was "establishing her own style and fictional world by a process of parody of a fictional influence" (12), that her work simultaneously imitated and rejected "the sophisticated, intellectual Huxley world," thus demonstrating "that the development of her fiction cannot be seen as flowing in an unbroken stream from the Victorian and Edwardian novel, unpolluted by an alien modernism" (13).

Ivy Compton-Burnett is also among the frequently named influences. In her diaries and letters, Pym alludes in various contexts to her reading of Compton-Burnett and specifically cites Compton-Burnett's influence when she was writing her early novels (VPE 100). Liddell, *A Mind at Ease,* cites the early influence of Compton-Burnett on *Crampton Hodnet* (22–23). Burkhart, *The Pleasure of Miss Pym,* offers examples of Pym's echoing of "Compton- Burnett syntax, the abstract, and . . . the insistent and elementary declarative statement" (12). Rossen, *The World of Barbara Pym,* sees a profound influence reflected in Pym's dialogue, noting Pym's technique of juxtaposing dialogue with her characters' unspoken thoughts, giving the unspoken "the same sparkle as dialogue" and thus "pointing up the irony between what the characters feel or perceive and how they are constrained to modify it out of politeness" (11).

Pym's references and allusions to Charlotte Yonge, Elizabeth Bowen, and Margaret Drabble in her novels and diaries have also elicited comment. Heberlein, *Communities of Imaginative Participation,* sees the influence of Yonge, as well as Trollope, in Pym's use of carryover characters. Wyatt-Brown, *Barbara Pym: A Critical Biography,* acknowledges the influence of Yonge in that Yonge's "conservatism reinforced Pym's sense of helplessness." Wyatt-Brown also attributes to Pym's affection for Yonge "the slightly dated air of [her] early novels" as well as her "fascination with Victorian village life" (39). Rossen, *The World of Barbara Pym,* mentions Pym's admiration of and allusions to Yonge's novels, as well as the influence of Bowen and Drabble. Pym's heroines "seem drawn to Bowen's work," and Prudence Bates and Wilmet "show affinities with Bowen's elegant, poised heroines" (10). Rossen sees Drabble as an influence in that she evoked Pym's self-doubts, citing Pym's writing in her diaries after reading *The Ice Age* and *Realms of Gold* that Drabble " 'gives one almost *too* much' . . . 'but I give too little' " (12). Sadler, "Drabbling in Pym's Garden of the Critics," finds parallels between the novels of Pym and Drabble, noting that both writers were discontent with the role of " 'woman's writer' " and expanded their canvas to larger issues, that both use a technique of remembering earlier novels, thus creating a bond between author and reader, and that both write for the middle classes and use literary allusion (1–2).

Pym is sometimes discussed in connection with Philip Larkin. Rossen, *The World of Barbara Pym,* compares the two in their presentation of the "lonely protagonist who compares himself with others, or who gauges his worth according to what he possesses" (165), specifically noting parallels in the characterization of Emma and Beatrix Howick and Daphne Dagnall of *A Few Green Leaves* and Larkin's poems "Mr. Bleaney" and "Dockery and Son." In *A Few Green Leaves,* Rossen finds a "series of Larkinesque soliloquies, filled with odd musings and haunted by disillusionment" (167). Joseph Epstein, "Miss Pym and Mr. Larkin," also compares Pym and Larkin, finding them both "quintessentially, untranslatably English" (16). Noting the friendship between them, their admiration for each other's writing, and Larkin's encouragement of Pym during the years when her novels were not being published, Epstein points out that their work "goes pretty thoroughly against the grain of much mainstream contemporary American writing." Both were "solidly middle class and quite without interest in the social climb"; neither Pym nor Larkin "taught or regularly lectured or otherwise attempted to live off the lustre of a literary career; both worked at middling cultural jobs"; both were extraordinary yet "prided themselves on living ordinary lives"; and both wrote about loneliness and middle age (10). Holt, whose discussion includes some of Larkin's comments and advice to Pym about her manuscripts, writes at length about Pym's friendship with Larkin, tracing the development of their relationship from their early correspondence in 1961 when he offered to review her next novel, to the later years when he visited her in Finstock (*Lot to Ask;* "Philip Larkin and Barbara Pym").

Several critics mention parallels between Pym and Henry James. Linking Pym with James and Forster, Isa Kapp sees Pym's work as "more than a comedy of manners"; instead "it is a drama of disposition, willpower, and ethics" ("Out of the Swim with Barbara Pym" 240). Halperin, "Barbara Pym and the War of the Sexes," sees Pym as more akin to James than Austen in that Pym's novels contain "virtually no relationship between the sexes which is entirely satisfactory." Ubiquitous in Pym's novels,

Halperin writes, is "James's 'vampire' theme—one human being living off and gaining sustenance from another, and depriving him or her of life in the process" (88–89). In discussing *Jane and Prudence* in his book, *Barbara Pym*, Long writes that Pym's use of symbolism is "often reminiscent of Henry James" (89). He compares Pym's "symbolism of perfection and flaw" in *The Sweet Dove Died* with James's use of symbolism in *The Wings of the Dove* and *The Golden Bowl* (170). Long also notes Pym's reference to *Washington Square* in *The Sweet Dove Died*, the parallel endings of the novels, and the resemblances and differences between Leonora Eyre and Catherine Sloper. Cooley, *The Comic Art of Barbara Pym*, sees similarities between Leonora's "distaste for sexual relations and disruptive emotion" and Isabel Archer, and between Leonora and the mother in James's *Spoils of Poynton*, who subordinates human relations to beautiful possessions (206).

Margaret Diane Stetz, "*Quartet in Autumn:* New Light on Barbara Pym as a Modernist," discusses Pym's narrative technique to show her kinship with Virginia Woolf, thus refuting critics who say Pym is " 'just like' " Jane Austen. Concentrating on *Quartet in Autumn* and *Mrs. Dalloway*, Stetz writes that instead of using traditional novel of manners techniques, Pym uses modernist methods of "simultaneity, association, imagery, memory, and dreams" to "convey a character's consciousness" (24). Stetz notes that in *Quartet in Autumn* successive scenes are not occurring consecutively but simultaneously and that Pym uses association of ideas to link the scenes. She also points to Pym's repetition of words, phrases, and imagery to provide unity in the novel and to Pym's portrayal of her characters' consciousness, as opposed to speech and gesture, as a means of characterization.

Judy Little, "Influential Anxieties: Woolf and Pym," sees evidence of Woolf's influence on Pym's narrative technique, specifically her use of "the designing narrator." Little also suggests that Pym was influenced by Woolf's "feminism and implicit social criticism" (5).

Wyatt-Brown, in *Barbara Pym: A Critical Biography*, also notes the influence of Woolf, whose themes Pym "skillfully borrowed" (89), as well as Pym's affinity with Denton Welch. Wyatt-Brown cites Pym's claim of having become " 'besotted with Denton Welch,' " her sympathy over his early death, her retracing of his "tours of country churches and graveyards," and similarities in their fact-finding techniques (97). Similarly, Weld notes that Pym borrowed her "method of observation" from Denton Welch (*Barbara Pym and the Novel of Manners* 55).

Pym's work with the International African Institute from 1945 to 1974 influenced her writing by providing subject matter for her novels and by influencing her technique as a novelist. Scholars have written about the International African Institute influence from several perspectives. Rossen, Muriel Schulz, and Burkhart discuss at length its influence on the subject matter and technique of Pym's novels. Rossen, *The World of Barbara Pym,* points to Pym's comic treatment of anthropologists, her increasing tolerance for other cultures, and the fact that the novels furnish an anthropological study of England. Rossen also finds that Pym's work with anthropologists influenced her writing style, which becomes "sharper and crisper" (108); her conception of the importance of fieldwork in the novelist's art, reflected in the heroines who perform fieldwork in writing fiction or narrating their own stories; her writing process, particularly in her use of notebooks to record her own observations before transposing them in the novels; her use of details "as signifiers and as concrete examples of underlying, meaningful structures" (110); and her use of anthropology as a technique for social satire. Rossen notes that Pym satirizes anthropologists in her novels, thus inviting the reader to observe those who observe others, and that she acts as a "social historian in her meticulous notation of detail and physical surface," so that her "portrayal of England is akin to the anthropologist's study of daily customs and rituals in his chosen culture" (106). Schulz, "The Novelist as Anthropologist," writes similarly about Pym's use of anthropology, in that it provided raw material for her novels and that Pym drew parallels between the techniques of the novelist and the anthropologist. *Less Than Angels, No Fond Return of Love,* and *A Few Green Leaves* Schulz sees as constituting an anthropological study of middle-class England—Pym's novels explore "the possibility that the novelist is a kind of anthropologist of her own culture" (108). On the same subject, Burkhart, "Barbara Pym and the Africans," writes that "[a]nthropology is everywhere in the novels" and it is "central in *Excellent Women, Less Than Angels, An Unsuitable Attachment,* and *A Few Green Leaves*" (47). "One of the great richnesses" of

Pym's "novels derives from the contrast between the rites of anthropological Africa and the ceremonies of the world her characters, and we ourselves, think of as civilized, a churchy world of flower festival and rummage sale" (48–49).

Others have pointed specifically to Pym's satire on anthropologists in *Less Than Angels.* Fisichelli, *"The Trivial Round, the Common Task"* and "The Novelist as Anthropologist," notes the influence of the International African Institute job on Pym's use of anthropology as a subject in the novels and on her conception of her role as a realistic novelist. *Less Than Angels,* focuses attention on the "institution of anthropology—its academic and bureaucratic trappings, the in-fighting among scholars and the dramatic intrigue set off by the availability of research funds." It comments on anthropology "as a profession, a romantic quest, and an anomaly to people outside the discipline" ("Novelist as Anthropologist" 439–40). Nardin, *Barbara Pym,* Long, *The Pleasure of Miss Pym,* and Benet, *Something to Love,* also discuss Pym's treatment of anthropology in *Less Than Angels,* noting the isolation of the anthropologists, parallels between the methods of observation used by both novelist and anthropologist, and Pym's anthropological detachment in describing the rituals of English society. Cotsell, *Barbara Pym,* sees the use of anthropology in *Less Than Angels* as indicative of Pym's modernist tendencies, pointing out that Pym "sets against professional anthropology what might be called literary anthropology," indicating the possible influence of Sir James Frazer's *The Golden Bough* and T. S. Eliot (68). Anthropology, Cotsell writes, becomes a "metaphor of a male need to make relationship on the basis of separateness, assured identity, and knowledge" (72).

Also citing Pym's application of anthropological techniques in writing her novels are Dobie, Schofield, Rubenstein, and Daniel Schmidt. Dobie, "The World of Barbara Pym: Novelist as Anthropologist," notes Pym's power of observation and her research techniques and that she catalogs the rituals of her own society. Clothing in Pym's novels, Dobie says, "suggests temperament, social standing, and self image" (15). Food, "its selection, preparation, appearance, and taste," reflects "the most meaningful daily ritual in the lives of Pym's characters" (16) and "becomes a metaphor for life itself" (17). Schofield, "Well-Fed or Well-Loved?—Patterns of Cooking and Eating in the Novels of

Barbara Pym,'' sees parallels between the focus on food and eating in Pym's novels and Claude Levi-Strauss's ideas on food preparation as an indication of the civilizing process. Pym's ''novels become, then, almost anthropological studies of the civilizing process of man, his eating habits, and the culturing power of certain foods'' (2). Rubenstein, '' 'For the Ovaltine Had Loosened Her Tongue': Failures of Speech in Barbara Pym's *Less Than Angels*,'' uses the speech-act theory of Austin and Searle to show the failure of communication in *Less Than Angels*, noting that the novel is to a great extent ''about language itself and the comic, sad, and occasionally liberating misfires of language'' (576). Schmidt, ''Excellent Women and the Code of Suitability,'' draws on Roland Barthes's concept of myth as depoliticized speech to posit that in her exposure of myths and codes of British society Pym is a mythologist. In *Excellent Women* and *An Unsuitable Attachment* Pym exposes the code of the excellent woman by calling attention to the cliché and thus making the myth visible.

Overlapping with the discussions of the influence of anthropology on Pym's technique as a novelist and her affinities with other writers are the discussions of other elements of her narrative technique. Topics treated include Pym's technique and its relation to traditional form in the novel. These studies focus on Pym's novel-of-manners technique and her uses of comedy and satire as well as the placing of her work in its historical context. Other studies focus on specific elements of narrative technique including her use of literary allusion and quotation, her use of carryover characters, and her use of a dual-voiced narrative.

As can be expected from the frequent affinities noted between Pym and Austen, critics have studied Pym's work in the tradition of the novel of manners. Brothers, ''Love, Marriage, and Manners in the Novels of Barbara Pym,'' finds that the pervasive treatment of romantic love in Pym's novels ''places them in the tradition of the novel of manners'' but that they do not ''hold forth the promise of fulfillment through mutual love and sharing'' found in the ''courtship novels of the nineteenth century'' (155). Pym uses irony and comedy to expose the artificiality of manners and the ''gap between human desire and fulfillment'' (160). Focusing her study on *Jane and Prudence*, Brothers writes that Pym's characters ''must do battle with the windmills of their imaginations'' and that happy endings occur because her characters accept "the rightness of their feelings over the correctness of social expectations" (161).

The most extended treatment of Pym's work in the tradition of the novel of manners is Weld's *Barbara Pym and the Novel of Manners*. Weld holds that Pym "simultaneously continues the tradition of her predecessors and adds an [sic] uniquely feminine and personal perspective" (6). Tracing Pym's use of novel-of-manners technique throughout her literary career, Weld concludes that Pym's contribution "lies in her unarticulated feminism, delivered from the perspective of a solitary female who measures the moral basis of her world with clear-eyed generosity" (203–04).

Others point to Pym's treatment of commonplace matters. Ackley, *The Novels of Barbara Pym,* discusses Pym's theory about the novel, noting her focus on the trivial and her use of recurring devices, including "references to seasons, nature and church events that provide a framework useful for moving the story forward" and that "become metaphors for conditions of the heart" (14); and "detailed descriptions of food, clothes, and color as those things reflect character" (15). Other aspects of Pym's narrative technique discussed by Ackley include her Austen-like "command of the humorous scene and her wry detached observations" (12); the seeming plotlessness, yet classical structure of the novels, and their indefinite conclusions; the use of an intruder who temporarily alters routine; and "her skill at comic juxtapositions" (23).

Rossen, who devotes a chapter of *The World of Barbara Pym* to Pym's writing style noting influences and Pym's uses of literary tradition, writes that Pym's characteristic style is one that "trivializes life" and "diminishes grand passions" (17–18). Discussing Pym's use of details and repetition that reflects her concern with ritual, Rossen writes that Pym's "books are a novelistic version of heroic couplets in poetry; neatly dovetailed and self-contained, the small pieces each link together into a coherent whole" (18).

Pym's use of the quotidian is also noted by Rosemary de Paolo, "You Are What You Drink," who observes that what Pym's "characters choose to drink, when, and how much are central issues in the definition of character and of class" (1). Tea, for example, confirms national as well as personal identity, and alcohol, which is associated with men and with women who have a greater "sense of personal worth," implies dissolution (4). Alcohol is not suitable for excellent women in that it implies "freedom, danger, sex" (5). Graham, who describes aspects of Pym's narrative manner and examines key elements of her technique in "The Narrative Sense of Barbara Pym," cites Pym's "special poetic sensibility including delight in the common-place and in the potential of colloquial speech" (149) and her "extraordinary powers of observation" (151). Snow, *One Little Room an Everywhere,* writes that Pym "chronicles with poignant comedy the drama of minutiae, 'the trivial round, the common task' " (21). Edith Larson, "The Celebration of the Ordinary in Barbara Pym's Novels," writes that the "power of the ordinary to offer sustenance in the face of indefiniteness, sadness, and even terror of life, is the most important theme of Barbara Pym's novels" (17). Nardin, *Barbara Pym,* defends Pym's treatment of the ordinary, writing that she uses "innovatively understated approaches" to "make her readers understand that ordinary lives, when closely and sympathetically scrutinized, may turn out not to be so ordinary after all" (34). And Joan Gordon, "Cozy Heroines: Quotidian Bravery in Barbara Pym's Novels," discusses Pym's use of the quotidian, focusing on her middle-class London settings, muted style, gentle irony, and point of view, to "simultaneously disguise and illustrate . . . a vision which recognizes at both a cultural and a spiritual level the values of humility, community, and the ordinary miracle" (224).

Several critics have discussed Pym's comic technique at length. Cooley's *The Comic Art of Barbara Pym,* the most extensive treatment of comedy in the novels, offers a reading of eleven of the novels to show how Pym plies her comic art. Cooley observes that Pym's "detachment" results from looking at her subject from a "perspective of literary tradition and convention" that illuminates the "clash between literary convention" and "common experience," or between "stock character types" and "reality" (8–9). Pym patterns her excellent women on the stock character type of the old maid and alters the happy ending of romantic comedy, evoking a rule and then reversing it. Pym mixes "witty observations and the strained proprieties" with "zaniness and farce, satire and burlesque" (12). Cooley notes Pym's debt to *Don Quixote* in *Some Tame Gazelle* and *Jane and Prudence* and sees her affinity with Aristophanes and Rabelais in her "references to excretion as a way of deflating The Ideal" in *Some Tame Gazelle* (62). *The Sweet Dove Died,* he writes, adapts the "erotic merry-go-round of Viennese bedroom farce . . . to the more restrained conditions of British high comedy" (211), and the "Ned-James-Leonora episode . . . has a heartless brilliance, wit, and perversity that suggest Restoration comedy . . ." (215). Cooley cites the "unobtrusive but powerful ironic poetry of images"—noting in particular the images of hair—that "fuse comic and tragic" in *Quartet in Autumn* (229). The mood of *A Few Green Leaves* "is that of a pastoral valedictory, an extended farewell to a vanishing world" (244). Cooley devotes a large part of his final chapter to a discussion of Pym's style, which he says is "a modern version of the plain style of Swift and Defoe, with no hint of modernist experiment or virtuoso flights of sensibility in the manner of Virginia Woolf" (270).

Burkhart and Nardin also discuss Pym's comic technique in some detail. Burkhart, *The Pleasure of Miss Pym,* credits Pym with using "a double voice, one above that presents and one beneath that comments. The distance between the two is the distance of irony" (72). Pym achieves her comedy through the use of "[i]ncongruity, irrelevance, inconsequence, and enlargement" or sudden amplification of the trivial, and the absurd (73–74). Burkhart cites her use of character types, scatology, epigram, and simile, the latter preserved from ostentation by her humor. Nardin, *Barbara Pym,* also discusses the quality and sources of Pym's humor, which lie in her "characteristically muted" treatment of "[s]ocial pretension, selfishness disguised as humility, and the discrepancy between thought and expression" (27).

Others link Pym's comic art to the tradition of the English novel and to classical tradition. Heberlein, "Barbara Pym and Anthony Trollope," sees Pym's novels as "classically comic" in that "the main character moves from a position of relative exclusion or isolation to one of integration in a community" (96), and Fisichelli, "*The Trivial Round, the Common Task,*" cites Pym's frequent parodies of the conventions of romance fiction (108). Also related to Pym's comic art is Barbara Griffin's observation in "Order and Disruption in *Some Tame Gazelle*" that Henry Hoccleve, as well as Nicholas Parnell, Mr. Mold, and the Bishop of Mbawawa, is a primary disrupting influence in *Some Tame Gazelle,* a "primary threat to Belinda and Harriet's orderly and contented existence" (2). And Saar, "Irony from a Female Perspective," cites Pym's inversion of the "conventions of the sentimental novel form" to "heighten its gentle humor and create a series of 'event' ironies" (68–69).

Long, *Barbara Pym,* writes that *Some Tame Gazelle* "combines conventions of the pastoral with various kinds of comedy" in a form that is "distinctly classical" with strict symmetries of character relationships and plots (31). Pym uses "the conventions of the Victorian courtship novel in *Some Tame Gazelle* to create an ironic modern version of courtship" (38). Long also notes the precise symmetry of the courtships in *An Unsuitable Attachment* and the "comedy of errors" quality of *No Fond Return of Love* (132). Weld, *Barbara Pym and the Novel of Manners,* also cites the "formal comic characteristics" of *No Fond Return of Love,* its combination of comic dialogue and the commonplace that echoes the tradition of early farce, and its "convoluted comic plot" based on "a principle of tripling" (136).

Jacobs, in *Elements of Satire in the Novels of Barbara Pym,* offers a thorough treatment of Pym's use of satire and comedy in the novels. Linking Pym's satire with the first- and fourth-phase satire of Northrop Frye's spectrum, Jacobs cites among the satiric techniques operating in Pym's prose "the undercutting of lofty characters and situations through the use of absurdly low language, and the deliberate elevation of trivialities through high diction" (36). He also notes her use of caricature, wordplay, and surprises that include "the indirection of irony, the occasional descent into farcical humor and an unerring flow of wit" (303). Her "fiction is satiric because it is possible to isolate specific targets of attack . . . that are deliberately distorted to show their weaknesses and expose them to ridicule" (150). In her last four novels, *The Sweet Dove Died, An Academic Question, Quartet in Autumn,* and *A Few Green Leaves,* Pym moves toward Frye's fourth phase of satire—"away from comedy towards 'the ironic aspect of tragedy' " (250). She creates "a darker, more disturbing social vision" inhabited by "stunted, severely repressed characters" in a "bleak setting with autumnal images of sterility and decay," with "a narrative tone that is often mournful and bitter in describing the rapid deterioration of human relations in modern society" (295–96).

Concentrating on Pym's use of irony is Lee's *Love, Marriage, and Irony in Barbara Pym's Novels*. Lee cites Pym's use of "irony of dilemma" to show that while "love is not complete without marriage," marriage "inevitably brings romantic love to an end," and her use of "irony of situation" in which "excellent but plain-looking women who have an irresistible longing for love tend to remain unmarried in spite of—or because of—their self-effacing goodness" (199).

Two recent dissertations study the ironic aspects of Pym's humor. Michelle Lynne Jones applies feminist critical theory to Pym's novels in *Laughing Hags: The Comic Vision as Feminist*. Examining the novels of Margaret Atwood, John Irving, Muriel Sparks, and Pym, Jones discusses Pym's mockery of the ideological structures of the academy, the church, and the coherent self. Margaret Anne McDonald, in *Alone Together: Gender and Alienation in the Novels of Barbara Pym*, writes that Pym subverts the "romance/marriage plot," presenting an "ironic perception of a gender-determined society" (10); yet discernible throughout the novels is a belief "in the idea of community" (21).

Also significant in that it offers insight into Pym's place in English literary history is Cotsell's *Barbara Pym*. Cotsell seeks not only to trace the general writing process of the novels but to see Pym's work in relation to the "historical developments of her time." Further, he discusses her work "in relation to contemporary structuralist and post-structuralist accounts of language" (7), noting her resistance to modernism as well as indications of modernist elements in her novels. Similarly, Marlene San Miguel Groner, *The Novels of Barbara Pym*, notes the modernist nature of Pym's characters whose imaginations permit them to "see themselves as characters in their own lives and actively participate in the shaping and reshaping of the reality they perceive" (3).

Other characteristics of Pym's narrative technique that have drawn attention include her use of patterning, her characteristic narrator's point of view, her use of literary allusion and quotation, and her carryover of characters from one novel to another.

Nardin, Graham, Fisichelli, Roth, and Weld comment explicitly on the structure of Pym's narrative. Nardin, *Barbara Pym*, discusses Pym's technique of tantalizing her reader by "refusing to complete the patterning of her details" as a "basic strategy in dealing with theme" (29). This technique, along with her "distinctive endings'' that lack conclusions, contributes to a sense of the "irresolvable complexity" of life (33). Graham, "The Narrative Sense of Barbara Pym," cites Pym's conscious crafting of her fiction. She achieves her characteristic effect by the "layering of small details," by constructing "tiers of *background* information." "[I]deas repeated in diverse forms through book after book" and "repeated key words and phrases" that "build cumulatively," the use of "deliberately arranged white spaces," the gradual uncovering of information, and the tentativeness achieved through her use of qualifying words so as to underscore impermanence all contribute to her narrative manner (147–49). Fisichelli, "*The Trivial Round, the Common Task,*" notes the care with which Pym constructed her narratives, pointing out how in *The Sweet Dove Died* "the events of Leonora's day in one chapter" contrast "with the related activities of James or his uncle in the next" so as to underscore the "irony of each character's limited perspective, while providing the reader with an overview" (140). Fisichelli also points to Pym's use of concealment in *Quartet in Autumn* to stress the anonymity of her characters' lives, her "interweaving of four separate motifs" to achieve "one unified melody" (156), and her use of stream-of-consciousness technique as the characters age.

Laura Roth, *Performance Considerations for the Adaptation of Selected Barbara Pym Novels for Chamber Theatre Production,* uses her adaptations to investigate Pym's narrative form in *Excellent Women, An Unsuitable Attachment,* and *Quartet in Autumn.* In *Excellent Women,* Roth notes Pym's pattern of complicating incident, rising action, minor climax, and resolution that in turn leads to a new complication and a new cycle. In *An Unsuitable Attachment,* Pym varies the "classic dramatistic structure" of *Excellent Women* by using associational clusters to treat the three major relationships (126). In *Quartet in Autumn,* Roth points to Pym's increased use of narration as well as her more rhythmic narrative (173). Weld, *Barbara Pym and the Novel of Manners,* also cites the complexity of Pym's narrative in spite of the "disarming simplicity" of her style, noting her "deceptively simple sentence structure," her use of dashes and "static nouns with few verbs," and her frequent use of qualifying language (100–01).

An interesting approach that deals with Pym's narrative patterning is Bixler's "Female Narrative Structure in Barbara Pym's *Excellent Women.*" Bixler sees a link between Pym's failure to publish from 1961 to 1977 and her publishers' "inability to read and value novels cast in female narrative form." Drawing on Winnett's "Coming Unstrung: Women, Men, Narrative, and Principles of Pleasure" (*PMLA* 105 [1990]: 505–18), which compares the two forms of narrative structure—the male based on sexual experience with its pattern of tension and resolution, and the female based on childbirth and breastfeeding, a "dynamic narrative that is '*pro*spective' rather than 'detumescent,' " that ends not in sleep, but in " 'beginning itself' " (2)—Bixler looks at the various types of cycles in *Excellent Women* as demonstrative of Winnett's ideas. For Pym the "positive state of being unmarried is an alternative cycle" (3), and "the endless cycle of daily events and human needs is integral to understanding the pleasure principle as it relates to female experience" (5).

Others have commented on Pym's use of point of view in her novels. Benet, *Something to Love,* cites Pym's "shifting point of view" in her third-person narratives, pointing out that there is a primary point of view but that the additional points of view provide detachment and objectivity and that Pym frequently uses a detached narrator to comment on the action (6). Bowman, "Barbara Pym's Subversive Subtext: Private Irony and Shared Detachment," discusses the manner in which Pym's narrators "adopt points of view resembling those of her heroines" (82); in addition, she points out that in *Excellent Women* Pym uses "characteristic linguistic patterns" to reflect a distance between the narrator and heroine that permits the reader to share with the narrator "an irony of which Mildred is unaware" (83). Graham, "The Narrative Sense of Barbara Pym," also discusses Pym's use of a "detached observer," a "central intelligence" who "knows more than other characters about matters at hand" (144).

Doan, "Text and the Single Man: The Bachelor in Pym's Dual-Voiced Narrative," writes that Pym uses a dual-voiced narrative to present her spinsters and other heroines, a technique she suspends for bachelors and other characters with whom she is not sympathetic. In a later essay, "Pym's Singular Interest: The Self as Spinster," Doan carries her thesis further, writing that Pym's "dual-voiced narrative" allows "two attitudes toward the single woman to emerge simultaneously from the text: the voice of the patriarchy and the voice challenging that authority'' (152).

Also concerned with voice in Pym's narrative is Barbara Griffin, whose "Private Space and Self-Definition in Barbara Pym's *Excellent Women*'' points to Mildred's use of "three distinct narrative voices'': one "dutiful and deprecating,'' a second "more resistant,'' and a "third and more resistant voice that affords her a measure of freedom'' (133). Griffin draws on the work of Jean Baker Miller, Nancy Chodorow, Jessica Benjamin, and Carol Gilligan, pointing out Mildred's (and Pym's) understanding of the central paradox of women's lives, that women are encouraged "to value themselves only in terms of affiliations in which, as those affiliations are traditionally structured, they may lose themselves'' (142).

One characteristic of Pym's novels that has attracted considerable attention is her use of names and other forms of literary allusion and quotation. The most extended treatment of Pym's use of literary allusion and quotation is Snow's "Literary Allusions in the Novels.'' Snow catalogs the quotations and allusions throughout the novels to show Pym's "range of knowledge and her preferences among the English poets and novelists'' (121), concluding that her survey reveals Pym's familiarity with the English poets as well as an "especial kinship with Matthew Arnold'' and a "preference for the Metaphysicals, particularly Donne'' (141). Groner, "Barbara Pym's Allusions to Seventeenth-Century Poets,'' lists instances of Pym's allusions to and use of quotations in her novels to show that "Pym's characters are most familiar with and most fond of the poetry of the greater and lesser seventeenth-century poets'' (5), who "provide a way to express without artifice or self-consciousness hopes, longings, and perceptions both of life and of those around them'' (7).

Rossen, *The World of Barbara Pym,* discusses Pym's use of literary allusion and quotation throughout the novels. She finds, for instance, that the poetry quotations in *Some Tame Gazelle* parody the "Oxford University pride in learning,'' and that in Pym's later work, the quotations "outwardly pay deference'' to literary tradition, yet "undercut it and assert her own individuality'' (13). Pym uses literary tradition "as a point of comparison for her own work, alternately reinforcing it so as to lend a learned and authoritative cast to her fiction, and also to provide something she can parody'' (14). Pym's ''quotations can embody a particular kind of communication'' for characters who would find it difficult to ''say for themselves that they are lonely or melancholy.'' For some characters, poetry provides a ''starting point for further creativity and flights of fancy'' (16). Ackley, *The Novels of Barbara Pym,* also points to Pym's use of literature, noting that in Pym's novels literature ''gives consolation and pain, it helps people 'connect' with one another, it can liberate the spirit, and it ultimately makes those with knowledge of it more compassionate humans'' (206).

The allusive quality of Pym's fiction adds irony and comedy and gives insights into her characters. Saar, ''Irony from a Female Perspective,'' points to the irony resulting from the juxtapositon of Pym's world against the ''world inhabited by the great characters of English literature'' (71). Brothers, ''Women Victimized by Fiction: Living and Loving in the Novels of Barbara Pym,'' sees Pym's use of literary allusion as a means of mocking ''the idealised view of the romantic paradigm'' and of emphasizing that ''her tales present the truth of the matter'' (62). Weld, *Barbara Pym and the Novel of Manners,* also notes the comic and ironic function of the literary allusion and quotation, including Pym's use of ''literary parody to initiate comic reverberations, creating a unifying gag from a single reference'' (71).

Heberlein, *Communities of Imaginative Participation,* sees the allusion and quotation from quite another perspective. In addition to using it to develop characters, Pym uses it to expand her imaginative communities, providing ''a validation of present experience in relation to the past'' (108). Pym's allusion demonstrates her ''desire to link her novels to the larger corpus of English literature,'' creating ''communities of imaginative participation between reader, characters, and writers since the reader's learning upon which it depends is treated as a communal possession'' (267).

Pym's use of the same characters from one novel to another also functions, Heberlein believes, ''to stress within the texts an imaginative participation'' (271). Heberlein, ''Pym's Carry-Over Characters,'' finds more than thirty carryover characters in the novels and notes that Pym's use of the technique serves to create ''a community of readers who recognize carryover characters and catch intra-textual allusions,'' ''underscores the value of love and

marriage," and has a mimetic function in that it "equates her
fiction with the real world" (2).

Benet, *Something to Love,* points to the cohesive effect
achieved by the carryover characters in creating "the sense of a
whole society." These characters satisfy the reader's "curiosity
about the fate of certain characters" from earlier novels, and they
help to "create a sense of perspective" (4). Frances Bachelder,
"The Importance of Connecting," notes the connection the
technique creates between the novels, comparing the novels to
cars on a train with communicating doors. Ackley, *The Novels of
Barbara Pym,* sees the reappearance of characters as lending "a
kind of fictional reality" by establishing their "continuity," thus
implying "a larger world populated by people who do not cease to
exist at the end of the novel in which they are introduced" (22).
Jean Caffey Lyles, "Pym's Cup: Anglicans and Anthropologists," finds that the carryover characters give Pym's "whole
body of fiction a special texture—rather like the kinship tables to
which her anthropologists are so devoted" (521). Philip Larkin,
with whom Pym discussed the technique in her letters, remarks on
their effect of creating a sense of an oeuvre of Pym's novels ("The
World of Barbara Pym" 260). Similarly, Fisichelli, *"The Trivial
Round, the Common Task,"* writes that Pym's use of the same
characters and themes in the novels and some of her short stories
creates "a fictional repertory company of characters" and fosters
our appreciation of her "fiction as a unified body of work"
(97–98).

The most extensive treatment of Pym's carryover characters is
Snow's *One Little Room an Everywhere.* Snow catalogs the
characters, noting that they are "fully developed in the novels in
which they first appear" (68) and that in only one instance
characters make "more than a cameo appearance in a later
novel" (73). This occurs with Miss Morrow and Miss Doggett,
who first appear in *Crampton Hodnet* and then reappear in *Jane
and Prudence.* Snow explores Pym's motives in using the carryover characters, including Pym's discussion on the subject with
Larkin, and concludes that regardless of her motive Pym creates
"of London and its environs her own Yoknaptawpha County"
and that this "revivalist impulse enabled her to make of her
oeuvre a unified whole, a world distinctly recognizable as Barbara
Pym's" (76).

Several critics have ventured overall assessments of Pym's novels. The earliest comes from Robert Smith, who, in his 1971 article "How Pleasant to Know Miss Pym," intended in part to persuade her publishers to publish more of her novels and refers to her novels as "miniatures, exquisitely, nearly perfectly done" (67). Larkin, "The World of Barbara Pym," regarded her novels as "miniatures" that "will not diminish" (260). In summing up her strengths and limitations, Long, *Barbara Pym*, calls her "a writer of first-rate talents, and one of the most original comic novelists to have written in England in the last thirty years" (211–12). Snow, *One Little Room an Everywhere*, ranks the novels, citing *Quartet in Autumn* as the "most flawless in unity of tone and structure" (83), the "most classically perfect" of the novels; *Some Tame Gazelle* and *Excellent Women* as the "most representative" (96); and *Excellent Women* as the "most popular" of the novels (91). Ackley, *The Novels of Barbara Pym*, also calls *Quartet in Autumn* "a masterpiece" (30); and Liddell, *A Mind at Ease*, calls it "darker and sadder than any other" of her novels, but her "strongest, finest work" (122). Moseley, "Barbara Pym's Dark Novels," points to *Quartet in Autumn* and *The Sweet Dove Died* as "dark novels, or problem novels"—the "odd novels in her canon" (3). Cooley, *The Comic Art of Barbara Pym*, sees *The Sweet Dove Died* as "the most brilliant success" of her career (205). Rossen, *The World of Barbara Pym*, offers as her final assessment that Pym's "fiction will probably fall ultimately into the category of 'minor, but elegant,' " that "her scope is too narrow to exalt her to the category of major novelist" (178). Cotsell, however, writes that Pym "is now generally recognised as one of the leading British novelists in the period since the Second World War" (*Barbara Pym* 2).

How Pym will endure, time and the interests and enthusiasm of her readers and critics will tell. Clearly she has generated a creative, scholarly response among those who have read her that has in turn opened additional avenues for the study of her novels. One area relates to Pym's affinities with other writers, a topic approached by a number of critics but seldom developed at length. Comparisons and/or discussions of influence involving Pym and Ivy Compton-Burnett, Angela Thirkell, Elizabeth Taylor, Anita Brookner, and Anne Tyler are only a few of the possibilities for further study.

Pym's phenomenal success in holding our interest as readers and as scholars points to a need for further study of her narrative technique. Possibilities here include studies that focus on the narrative technique of individual novels. A particularly promising area is Pym's use of literary allusion in individual novels. Several critics have mentioned her use of literary allusion in general and have noted instances in particular novels, and Snow has cataloged the use of it throughout the novels. But insights could be sharpened by studies of the ways Pym uses it to achieve comic effect and to expand the scope of individual novels.

John Bayley, "Where, Exactly, Is the Pym World," has remarked on the difficulty of criticizing Pym's novels, noting that the difficulty rests in part in our involvement in the novels no matter how many times we have read them. The result is that "we can never fix our gaze" on her technique (51). We read without understanding why we read, challenged to understand and to articulate our fascination. Pym's novels warrant study that will further illuminate their complexity of theme and technique.

PART FOUR—BARBARA PYM BIBLIOGRAPHY: A COMPREHENSIVE LISTING OF PRIMARY AND SECONDARY PUBLISHED MATERIALS

Primary

BOOKS

An Academic Question. Ed. Hazel Holt. London: Macmillan; New York: Dutton, 1986.

Civil to Strangers and Other Writings. Ed. Hazel Holt. London: Macmillan, 1987; New York: Dutton, 1988.

Crampton Hodnet. Ed. Hazel Holt. London: Macmillan; New York: Dutton, 1985.

Excellent Women. 1952. London: Jonathan Cape; New York: Dutton, 1978.

A Few Green Leaves. London: Macmillan; New York: Dutton, 1980.

A Glass of Blessings. 1958. London: Jonathan Cape, 1977; New York: Dutton, 1980.

Jane and Prudence. 1953. London: Jonathan Cape, 1978; New York: Dutton, 1981.

Less Than Angels. 1955. London: Jonathan Cape, 1978; New York: Vanguard, 1957; Dutton, 1980.

No Fond Return of Love. 1961. London: Jonathan Cape, 1979; New York: Dutton, 1982.

thel

Quartet in Autumn. London: Macmillan, 1977; New York: Dutton, 1978.

Some Tame Gazelle. 1950. London: Jonathan Cape, 1978; New York: Dutton, 1983.

The Sweet Dove Died. London: Macmillan, 1978; New York: Dutton, 1979.

An Unsuitable Attachment. Ed. Hazel Holt. London: Macmillan; New York: Dutton, 1982.

A Very Private Eye: An Autobiography in Diaries and Letters. Ed. Hazel Holt and Hilary Pym, London: Macmillan; New York: Dutton, 1984.

SHORT STORIES AND MISCELLANEOUS PIECES

"Across a Crowded Room." Short story. *New Yorker* 16 July 1979: 34–39. Rpt. in *Civil to Strangers and Other Writings.* Ed. Hazel Holt. London: Macmillan, 1987; New York: Dutton, 1988. 367–80.

"The Christmas Visit." Short story. *Church Times* 1979. Rpt. in *Civil to Strangers and Other Writings.* Ed. Hazel Holt. London: Macmillan, 1987; New York: Dutton, 1988. 357–66.

"Finding a Voice: A Radio Talk." Broadcast BBC Radio 3, 4 Apr. 1978. *Civil to Strangers and Other Writings.* Ed. Hazel Holt. London: Macmillan, 1987; New York: Dutton, 1988. 381–88.

"Gervase and Flora." Novel fragment. *Civil to Strangers and Other Writings.* Ed. Hazel Holt. London: Macmillan, 1987; New York: Dutton, 1988. 173–215.

"Goodbye Balkan Capital." Short story. *Civil to Strangers and Other Writings.* Ed. Hazel Holt. London: Macmillan, 1987; New York: Dutton, 1988. 343–55.

"Home Front Novel." Novel fragment. *Civil to Strangers and Other Writings.* Ed. Hazel Holt. London: Macmillan, 1987; New York: Dutton, 1988. 217–69.

"In Defence of the Novel: Why You Shouldn't Have to Wait until the Afternoon." *Times* [London] 22 Feb. 1978: 18.

"So, Some Tempestuous Morn." Short story. *Civil to Strangers and Other Writings.* Ed. Hazel Holt. London: Macmillan, 1987; New York: Dutton, 1988. 329–42.

"So Very Secret." Novel fragment. *Civil to Strangers and Other Writings.* Ed. Hazel Holt. London: Macmillan, 1987; New York: Dutton, 1988. 271–324.

"The State of Fiction—A Symposium." *New Review* 5.1 (1978): 58–59.

"The White Elephant." Short story. *Women and Beauty* 1949. (Wyatt-Brown, *Barbara Pym: A Critical Biography* 191.)

"A Year in West Oxfordshire." *Places: An Anthology of Britain.* Ed. Ronald Blythe. Oxford: Oxford UP, 1981. 119–25.

Secondary

BOOKS ABOUT BARBARA PYM AND HER WORK

Ackley, Katherine Anne. *The Novels of Barbara Pym.* New York: Garland, 1989.

Benet, Diana. *Something to Love: Barbara Pym's Novels.* Literary Frontiers Edition 27. Columbia: University of Missouri Press, 1986.

Burkhart, Charles. *The Pleasure of Miss Pym.* Austin: University of Texas Press, 1987.

Cooley, Mason. *The Comic Art of Barbara Pym.* New York: AMS, 1990.

Cotsell, Michael. *Barbara Pym.* Macmillan Modern Novelists. London: Macmillan; New York: St. Martin's, 1989.

Holt, Hazel. *A Lot to Ask: A Life of Barbara Pym.* London: Macmillan, 1990; New York: Dutton, 1991.

Liddell, Robert. *A Mind at Ease: Barbara Pym and Her Novels.* London: Peter Owen, 1989.

Long, Robert Emmet. *Barbara Pym.* New York: Ungar, 1986.

Nardin, Jane. *Barbara Pym.* Twayne's English Author Series 406. Boston: Twayne, 1985.

Pym, Hilary, and Honor Wyatt. *The Barbara Pym Cookbook.* New York: Dutton, 1988.

Rossen, Janice, ed. *Independent Women: The Function of Gender in the Novels of Barbara Pym.* Brighton: Harvester; New York: St. Martin's, 1988.

―――. *The World of Barbara Pym.* London: Macmillan; New York: St. Martin's, 1987.

Salwak, Dale. *Barbara Pym: A Reference Guide.* Boston: G. K. Hall, 1991.

―――, ed. *The Life and Work of Barbara Pym.* London: Macmillan; Iowa City: University of Iowa Press, 1987.

Snow, Lotus. *One Little Room an Everywhere: The Novels of Barbara Pym.* Orono, ME: Puckerbrush, 1987.

Weld, Annette. *Barbara Pym and the Novel of Manners.* New York: St Martin's, 1992.

Wyatt-Brown, Anne M. *Barbara Pym: A Critical Biography.* Columbia: University of Missouri Press, 1992.

DISSERTATIONS ABOUT BARBARA PYM AND HER WORK

Blundo, Tullia. La Narrativa di Barbara Pym. First doctoral thesis on Pym. 1978. *tesi di laurea,* University of Pisa. Copy at Bodleian, MS 174 (Heberlein, *Communities of Imaginative Participation* 88).

Bywaters, Barbara Lee. *"Rereading Jane"*: *Jane Austen's Legacy to Twentieth-Century Women Writers.* Diss. Bowling Green State University, 1989. Ann Arbor, MI: UMI, 1990. 9011607.

Fisichelli, Glynn-Ellen Maria. *"The Trivial Round, the Common Task,"* *Barbara Pym: the Development of a Writer.* Diss. State University of

New York at Stony Brook, 1984. Ann Arbor, MI: UMI, 1984. 8416639.

Groner, Marlene San Miguel. *The Novels of Barbara Pym.* Diss. St. John's University, 1988. Ann Arbor, MI: UMI, 1989. 8900580.

Heberlein, Kathleen Browder. *Communities of Imaginative Participation: The Novels of Barbara Pym.* Diss. University of Washington, 1984. Ann Arbor, MI: UMI, 1984. 8419147.

Jacobs, Bruce Richard. *Elements of Satire in the Novels of Barbara Pym.* Diss. Fordham University, 1988. Ann Arbor, MI: UMI, 1988. 8809473.

Jones, Michelle Lynne. *Laughing Hags: The Comic Vision as Feminist.* Diss. University of Alberta, 1992. Ann Arbor, MI: UMI, 1992. DANN73080.

Lee, Sun-Hee. *Love, Marriage, and Irony in Barbara Pym's Novels.* Diss. University of North Texas, 1991. Ann Arbor, MI: UMI, 1991. 9128713.

McDonald, Margaret Anne. *Alone Together: Gender and Alienation in the Novels of Barbara Pym.* Diss. University of Saskatchewan, 1991. Ann Arbor, MI: UMI, 1991. DANN68227.

Naulty, Patricia M. *"I Never Talk of Hunger": Self-Starvation as Women's Language of Protest in Novels by Barbara Pym, Margaret Atwood, and Anne Tyler.* Diss. Ohio State University, 1988. Ann Arbor, MI: UMI, 1989. 8907274.

Roth, Laura Kathleen Johnson. *Performance Considerations for the Adaptation of Selected Barbara Pym Novels for Chamber Theatre Production.* Diss. University of Texas at Austin, 1989. Ann Arbor, MI: UMI, 1989. 8920829.

Sherwood, Rhoda Irene. *"A Special Kind of Double": Sisters in British and American Fiction.* Diss. University of Wisconsin, 1987. Ann Arbor, MI: UMI, 1987. 8725284.

Stanley, Isabel Ashe Bonnyman. *The Anglican Clergy in the Novels of Barbara Pym.* Diss. University of Tennessee, 1990. Ann Arbor, MI: UMI, 1991. 9121756.

Weld, Annette Forker. *Barbara Pym and the Novel of Manners.* Diss. University of Rochester, 1989. Ann Arbor, MI: UMI, 1989. 8926064.

ARTICLES IN PERIODICALS AND COLLECTIONS, AND CHAPTERS IN BOOKS

Ackley, Katherine Anne. "But What Does It Lead To?" *Barbara Pym Newsletter* 3.2 (1988): 3–5.

———. "Proving One's Worth: The Importance of Marriage in the World of Barbara Pym." *Joinings and Disjoinings: The Significance of Marital Status in Literature.* Ed. JoAnne Stephens Mink and Janet Doubler Ward. Bowling Green, OH: Bowling Green State University Popular Press, 1991. 132–44.

Adamson, Lesley. "Guardian Women." *Guardian* [Manchester] 14 Sept. 1977: 11.

Bachelder, Frances H. "The Importance of Connecting." *The Life and Work of Barbara Pym.* Ed. Dale Salwak. London: Macmillan; Iowa City: University of Iowa Press, 1987. 185–92.

Bayley, John. "Where, Exactly, Is the Pym World?" *The Life and Work of Barbara Pym.* Ed. Dale Salwak. London: Macmillan; Iowa City: University of Iowa Press, 1987. 50–57.

Beiswenger, Eleanor. "Teaching Barbara Pym in Britain." *Barbara Pym Newsletter* 4.2 (1989): 8–10.

Bell, Hazel K. "The Image of the Indexer?" *Indexer* 14 (1985): 202–203.

———."Indexers in Fiction." *Indexer* 13 (1983): 197–98.

———. "A Pymian Occasion." *Indexer* 15 (1986): 66.

Benet, Diana. "The Language of Christianity in Pym's Novels." *Thought* 59 (1984): 504–13.

Berndt, Judy. "Barbara Pym: A Supplementary List of Secondary Sources." *Bulletin of Bibliography* 43 (1986): 76–80.

Bixler, Frances. "Female Narrative Structure in Barbara Pym's *Excellent Women.*" *Barbara Pym Newsletter* 5.2 (1991): 2–6.

Bowman, Barbara. "Barbara Pym's Subversive Subtext: Private Irony and Shared Detachment." *Independent Women: The Function of*

Gender in the Novels of Barbara Pym. Ed. Janice Rossen. Sussex: Harvester; New York: St. Martin's, 1988. 82–94.

Bradham, Margaret C. "Barbara Pym's Women." *World Literature Today* 61 (1987): 31–37.

Brothers, Barbara. "Love, Marriage, and Manners in the Novels of Barbara Pym." *Reading and Writing Women's Lives: A Study of the Novel of Manners.* Ed. Bege K. Bowers and Barbara Brothers. Ann Arbor, MI: UMI, 1990. 153–70.

———. "Women Victimized by Fiction: Living and Loving in the Novels of Barbara Pym." *Twentieth-Century Women Novelists.* Ed. Thomas F. Staley. Totowa: Barnes & Noble, 1982. 61–80.

Burkhart, Charles. "Barbara Pym and the Africans." *Twentieth-Century Literature* 29 (1983): 45–53. Rpt. as "Miss Pym and the Africans." *The Pleasure of Miss Pym.* By Burkhart. Austin: University of Texas Press, 1987. 60–69.

———. "Glamorous Acolytes: Homosexuality in Pym's World." *Independent Women: The Function of Gender in the Novels of Barbara Pym.* Ed. Janice Rossen. Sussex: Harvester; New York: St. Martin's, 1988. 95–105.

Calisher, Hortense. "Enclosures: Barbara Pym." *New Criterion* 1 (1982): 53–56.

Campbell, Jenny. "Jenny Campbell Joins the Barbara Pym Groupies." *Sunday Times* [London] 27 July 1986: 44.

Cooley, Mason. "*The Sweet Dove Died:* The Sexual Politics of Narcissism." *Twentieth-Century Literature* 32 (1986): 40–49.

Crosland, Margaret. "Resurrecting." *Beyond the Lighthouse: English Women Novelists in the Twentieth Century.* New York: Taplinger, 1981. 172–85. (Chapter on Jean Rhys, Christina Stead, and Barbara Pym)

De Paolo, Rosemary. "You Are What You Drink." *Barbara Pym Newsletter* 2.2 (1987): 1–5.

Doan, Laura L. Introduction. *Old Maids to Radical Spinsters: Unmar-*

ried Women in the Twentieth-Century Novel. Ed. by Doan. Urbana: University of Illinois Press, 1991. 1–16.

―――. "Pym's Singular Interest: The Self as Spinster." *Old Maids to Radical Spinsters: Unmarried Women in the Twentieth-Century Novel.* Ed. by Doan. Urbana: University of Illinois Press, 1991. 139–54.

―――. "Text and the Single Man: The Bachelor in Pym's Dual-Voiced Narrative." *Independent Women: The Function of Gender in the Novels of Barbara Pym.* Ed. Janice Rossen. Brighton: Harvester; New York: St. Martin's, 1988. 63–81.

Dobie, Ann B. "The World of Barbara Pym: Novelist as Anthropologist." *Arizona Quarterly* 44 (1988): 5–18.

Duffy, Martha. "In Praise of Excellent Women." *Time* 26 Sept. 1983: 70.

Edgecombe, Rodney Stenning. "Barbara Pym's Arraigning Adverbials." *Barbara Pym Newsletter* 6.1,2 (1992): 1–3.

Epstein, Joseph. "Miss Pym and Mr. Larkin." *Commentary* July 1986: 38–46. Rpt. in *Quadrant* Dec. 1986: 9–17.

―――. "What's Left to Shock When Anything Goes." *New York Times Book Review* 5 Feb. 1984: 14.

Ezell, Margaret J. M. " 'What Shall We Do with Our Old Maids?': Barbara Pym and the 'Woman Question.' " *International Journal of Women's Studies* 7 (1984): 450–65.

Fergus, Jan. "*A Glass of Blessings,* Jane Austen's *Emma* and Barbara Pym's Art of Allusion." *Independent Women: The Function of Gender in the Novels of Barbara Pym.* Ed. Janice Rossen. Brighton: Harvester; New York: St. Martin's, 1988. 109–36.

Finlayson, Iain. "An Interview with Barbara Pym." *Literary Review* 23 Feb. 1980: 2–5.

Fisichelli, Glynn-Ellen. "The Novelist as Anthropologist—Barbara Pym's Fiction: Fieldwork Done at Home." *Papers on Language and Literature* 24 (1988): 436–45.

Godwin, Gail. "Years of Neglect." *The Life and Work of Barbara Pym.*
Ed. Dale Salwak. London: Macmillan; Iowa City: University of Iowa
Press, 1987. 193.

Goldstein, William. "A Novel, A Biography, A Play: A Peek Inside the
Pym Estate." *Publishers Weekly* 4 Oct. 1985: 43.

Gordon, Joan. "Cozy Heroines: Quotidian Bravery in Barbara Pym's
Novels." *Essays in Literature* [Macomb, IL] 16 (1989): 224–33.

Graham, Peter W. "Emma's Three Sisters." *Arizona Quarterly* 43
(1987): 39–52.

Graham, Robert J. "Cumbered with Much Serving: Barbara Pym's
'Excellent Women.' " *Mosaic* 17 (1984): 141–60. Rpt. in *"For Better
or Worse"*: *Attitudes Toward Marriage in Literature.* Ed. Evelyn J.
Hinz. Winnipeg: University of Manitoba, 1985. 141–60.

———. "The Narrative Sense of Barbara Pym." *The Life and Work of
Barbara Pym.* Ed. Dale Salwak. London: Macmillan; Iowa City:
University of Iowa Press, 1987. 142–55.

Greenway, William. " 'The Trivial Round, the Common Task': Barbara
Pym's Working Girls." *Barbara Pym Newsletter* 6.1,2 (1992): 4–6.

Griffin, Barbara. "Order and Disruption in *Some Tame Gazelle.*"
Barbara Pym Newsletter 5.1 (1990): 2–4.

———. "Private Space and Self-Definition in Barbara Pym's *Excellent
Women. Essays in Literature* [Macomb, IL] 19 (1992): 132–43.

Groner, Marlene San Miguel. "Barbara Pym's Allusions to Seventeenth-Century Poets." *Cross-Bias: Newsletter of the Friends of
Bemerton.* 11 (1987): 5–7.

Halperin, John. "Barbara Pym and the War of the Sexes." *The Life and
Work of Barbara Pym.* Ed. Dale Salwak. London: Macmillan; Iowa
City: University of Iowa Press, 1987. 88–100.

Hazzard, Shirley. "Excellent Women." *The Life and Work of Barbara
Pym.* Ed. Dale Salwak. London: Macmillan; Iowa City: University of
Iowa Press, 1987. 3.

Heberlein, Kate Browder. "Barbara Pym and Anthony Trollope: Communities of Imaginative Participation." *Pacific Coast Philology* 19 (1984): 95–100.

———. "Pym's Carry-Over Characters." *Barbara Pym Newsletter* 1.1 (1986): 1–2.

———. "Thankless Tasks or Labors of Love: Women's Work in Barbara Pym's Novels." *Barbara Pym Newsletter* 2.1 (1987): 1–5.

Hills, C. A. R. "The Bubble, Reputation: The Decline and Rise of Barbara Pym." *Encounter* May 1987: 33–38.

Holt, Hazel. "The Home Front: Barbara Pym in Oswestry, 1939–41." *Independent Women: The Function of Gender in the Novels of Barbara Pym.* Ed. Janice Rossen. Brighton: Harvester; New York: St. Martin's, 1988. 50–59.

———. "No Thankless Task: Barbara Pym as Indexer." *Indexer* 15 (1987): 236–37.

———. "The Novelist in the Field: 1946–74." *The Life and Work of Barbara Pym.* Ed. Dale Salwak. London: Macmillan; Iowa City: University of Iowa Press, 1987. 22–33.

———. "Philip Larkin and Barbara Pym: Two Quiet People." *Philip Larkin: The Man and His Work.* Ed. Dale Salwak. London: Macmillan; Iowa City: University of Iowa Press, 1989. 59–68.

Kane, Patricia. "A Curious Eye: Barbara Pym's Women." *South Dakota Review* 24.2 (1986): 50–59.

Kapp, Isa. "Out of the Swim with Barbara Pym." *American Scholar* 52 (1983): 237–42.

Kaufman, Anthony. "Barbara Pym (1913–1980)." *Essays on the Contemporary British Novel.* Ed. Hedwig Book and Albert Wertheim. Munchen: Max Hueber, 1985. 119–35.

———. "Barbara Pym, *Some Tame Gazelle,* and the Nazis." *Barbara Pym Newsletter* 4.1 (1989): 3–5.

———. "Petrified Mimosa." *Barbara Pym Newsletter* 3.2 (1988): 1–3.

————. "The Short Fiction of Barbara Pym." *Twentieth-Century Literature* 32 (1986): 50–77.

Keener, Frederick M. "Barbara Pym Herself and Jane Austen." *Twentieth-Century Literature* 31 (1985): 89–110.

Knuth, Deborah J. "Teaching Barbara Pym." *Barbara Pym Newletter* 4.1 (1989): 1–2, 6–8.

Larkin, Philip. Foreword. *An Unsuitable Attachment*. By Barbara Pym. London: Macmillan; New York: Dutton, 1982. 5–10. Rpt. as "The Rejection of Barbara Pym." *The Life and Work of Barbara Pym*. Ed Dale Salwak. London: Macmillan; Iowa City: University of Iowa Press, 1987. 171–75.

————. "The World of Barbara Pym." *Times Literary Supplement* 11 Mar. 1977: 260. Rpt. in *Required Writing: Miscellaneous Pieces 1955–1982*. By Larkin. London: Faber, 1983; New York: Farrar, 1984. 240–44.

Larson, Edith S. "The Celebration of the Ordinary in Barbara Pym's Novels."*San Jose Studies* 9.2 (1983): 17–22.

Liddell, Robert. "A Success Story." *The Life and Work of Barbara Pym*. Ed. Dale Salwak. London: Macmillan; Iowa City: University of Iowa Press, 1987. 176–84.

————. "Two Friends: Barbara Pym and Ivy Compton-Burnett." *London Magazine* Aug./Sept. 1984: 59–69.

Little, Judy. "Humoring the Sentence: Women's Dialogic Comedy." *Women's Comic Vision*. Ed. June Sochen. Detroit: Wayne State University Press, 1991. 19–32.

————. "Influential Anxieties: Woolf and Pym." *Virginia Woolf Miscellany* 39 (Fall 1992): 5–6.

Lively, Penelope. "The World of Barbara Pym." *Literary Review* 1 (1980): 8–9. Rpt. in *The Life and Work of Barbara Pym*. Ed. Dale Salwak. London: Macmillan; Iowa City: University of Iowa Press, 1987. 45–49.

Lobrano, Alexander. "Pym's Cup Now Overflows." *Gentleman's Quarterly* May 1983: 48.

Lyles, Jean Caffey. "Pym's Cup: Anglicans and Anthropologists." *Christian Century* 21–28 May 1986: 519–22.

Maitre, Doreen. "Quartet in Autumn." *Literature and Possible Worlds.* London: Pembridge; Hamden, CT: Shoe String Press, 1983. 92–95.

Malloy, Constance. "The Quest for a Career." *The Life and Work of Barbara Pym.* Ed. Dale Salwak. London: Macmillan; Iowa City: University of Iowa Press, 1987. 4–21.

———. "A Very Public Eye." *Barbara Pym Newsletter* 1.1 (1986): 5–6.

Moorehead, Caroline. "How Barbara Pym Was Rediscovered After Sixteen Years Out in the Cold." *Times* [London] 14 Sept. 1977: 11.

Moseley, Merritt. "Barbara Pym's Dark Novels." *Barbara Pym Newsletter* 1.1 (1986): 3–4.

———. "The State of Letters: A Few Words about Barbara Pym." *Sewanee Review* 98 (1990): 75–87.

Moseley, Merritt, and Pamela J. Nickless. "Pym's Homosexuals." *Barbara Pym Newsletter* 5.1 (1990): 5–8.

Myers, Mary H. "Barbara Pym: A Further List of Secondary Sources." *Bulletin of Bibliography* 48 (1991): 25–26.

———. "Barbara Pym: A Supplement to a Further List of Secondary Sources." *Bulletin of Bibliography* 49 (1992): 81–82.

"Notebook." *New Republic* 27 Aug. 1984: 10.

Oates, Joyce Carol. "Barbara Pym's Novelistic Genius." *The Life and Work of Barbara Pym.* Ed. Dale Salwak. London: Macmillan; Iowa City: University of Iowa Press, 1987. 43–44.

Peterson, Lorna. "Barbara Pym: A Checklist, 1950–1984." *Bulletin of Bibliography* 41 (1984): 201–06.

Phelps, Gilbert. "Fellow Writers in a Cotswold Village." *The Life and Work of Barbara Pym.* Ed. Dale Salwak. London: Macmillan; Iowa City: University of Iowa Press, 1987. 34–39.

Pilgrim, Anne C. "Teaching the Novels of Barbara Pym and Jane Austen." *Barbara Pym Newsletter* 4.2 (1989): 12.

Radner, Sanford. "Barbara Pym's People." *Western Humanities Review* 39 (1985): 172–77.

Richard, Linda. "The Importance of Being Trivial: Barbara Pym's Excellent Woman." *Etudes Briianniques Contemporaines: Revue de la Societe d'Etudes Anglaises Contemporaines* Apr. 1992: 11–21.

Rossen, Janice. "Love in the Great Libraries: Oxford in the Work of Barbara Pym." *Journal of Modern Literature* 12 (1985): 277–96.

———. "On Not Being Jane Eyre: The Romantic Heroine in Barbara Pym's Novels." *Independent Women: The Function of Gender in the Novels of Barbara Pym.* Ed. by Rossen. Brighton: Harvester; New York: St. Martin's, 1988. 137–56.

———. "The Pym Papers." *The Life and Work of Barbara Pym.* Ed. Dale Salwak. London: Macmillan; Iowa City: University of Iowa Press, 1987. 156–67.

Rowse, A. L. "Miss Pym and Miss Austen." *The Life and Work of Barbara Pym.* Ed. Dale Salwak. London: Macmillan; Iowa City: University of Iowa Press, 1987. 64–71.

Rubenstein, Jill. "Comedy and Consolation in the Novels of Barbara Pym." *Renascence* 42 (1990): 173–83.

———. " 'For the Ovaltine Had Loosened Her Tongue': Failures of Speech in Barbara Pym's *Less Than Angels.*" *Modern Fiction Studies* 32 (1986): 573–80.

Saar, Doreen Alvarez. "Irony from a Female Perspective: A Study of the Early Novels of Barbara Pym." *West Virginia University Philological Papers* 33 (1987): 68–75.

Sadler, Lynn Veach. "The Pathos of Everyday Living in the Novels of Barbara Pym." *West Virginia University Philological Papers* 31 (1986): 82–90.

———. "Spinsters, Non-spinsters, and Men in the World of Barbara Pym." *Critique* 26 (1985): 141–54.

Salwak, Dale. "Survey of Scholarship." *Barbara Pym Newsletter* 1.1 (1986): 6–7.

———. "Survey of Scholarship." *Barbara Pym Newsletter* 2.1 (1987): 6.

———. "Survey of Scholarship." *Barbara Pym Newsletter* 4.1 (1989): 6.

Schmidt, Daniel W. "Excellent Women and the Code of Suitability." *Barbara Pym Newsletter* 6.1,2 (1992): 7–9.

Schofield, Mary Anne. "Well-Fed or Well-Loved?—Patterns of Cooking and Eating in the Novels of Barbara Pym." *University of Windsor Review* 18.2 (1985): 1–8.

Schulz, Muriel. "The Novelist as Anthropologist." *The Life and Work of Barbara Pym.* Ed. Dale Salwak. London: Macmillan; Iowa City: University of Iowa Press, 1987. 101–19.

Shapiro, Anna. "The Resurrection of Barbara Pym." *Saturday Review* July/Aug. 1983: 29–31.

Smith, Robert. "How Pleasant to Know Miss Pym." *Ariel: A Review of International English Literature* 2.4 (1971): 63–68. Rpt. in *The Life and Work of Barbara Pym.* Ed. Dale Salwak. London: Macmillan; Iowa City: University of Iowa Press, 1987. 58–63.

———. "Remembering Barbara Pym." *Independent Women: The Function of Gender in the Novels of Barbara Pym.* Ed. Janice Rossen. Brighton: Harvester; New York: St. Martin's, 1988. 159–63.

Snow, Lotus. "Literary Allusions in the Novels." *The Life and Work of Barbara Pym.* Ed. Dale Salwak. London: Macmillan; Iowa City: University of Iowa Press, 1987. 120–41. Rpt. as " 'Some Sweet Smattering of Culture': Literary Allusions in the Novels." *One Little Room an Everywhere: The Novels of Barbara Pym.* By Snow. Orono, ME: Puckerbrush, 1987. 31–54.

———. "The Trivial Round, the Common Task: Barbara Pym's Novels." *Research Studies* [Pullman, WA] 48 (1980): 83–93. Rpt. as "The Trivial Round, the Common Task: The Subject of the Novels."

One Little Room an Everywhere: The Novels of Barbara Pym. By Snow. Orono, ME: Puckerbrush, 1987. 9–21.

Stetz, Margaret Diane. "*Quartet in Autumn:* New Light on Barbara Pym as a Modernist." *Arizona Quarterly* 41 (1985): 24–37.

Stovel, Bruce. "Subjective to Objective: A Career Pattern in Jane Austen, George Eliot, and Contemporary Women Novelists." *Ariel* 18 (1987): 55–61.

Strauss-Noll, Mary. "Love and Marriage in the Novels." *The Life and Work of Barbara Pym.* Ed. Dale Salwak. London: Macmillan; Iowa City: University of Iowa Press, 1987. 72–87.

Strauss-Noll, Mary Therese. "Barbara Pym's Favorites." *Barbara Pym Newsletter* 5.1 (1990): 9–13.

Tilden, Lola S. "A Very Special Kinship." *Barbara Pym Newsletter* 2.2 (1987): 6–7.

Till, Roger. "Coincidence in a Bookshop." *Independent Women: The Function of Gender in the Novels of Barbara Pym.* Ed. Janice Rossen. Brighton: Harvester; New York: St. Martin's, 1988. 164–68.

Tyler, Anne. Foreword. *Excellent Women, Jane and Prudence, An Unsuitable Attachment.* By Barbara Pym. New York: Quality Paperback Book Club, 1984. v-xviii.

Waxman, Barbara Frey. "Barbara Pym's Retired Women: Intoxicating Choices and Spinsterly Love." *From the Hearth to the Open Road: A Feminist Study of Aging in Contemporary Literature.* Contributions in Women's Studies 113. By Waxman. New York: Greenwood, 1990. 105–19.

West, Martha Ullman. "Profile: Barbara Pym." *San Francisco Review of Books* Mar./Apr. 1983: 21–22.

Whitney, Carol Wilkinson. " 'Women Are So Terrifying These Days': Fear Between the Sexes in the World of Barbara Pym." *Essays in Literature* 16 (1989): 71–84.

Wyatt-Brown, Anne M. "Ellipsis, Eccentricity, and Evasion in the Diaries of Barbara Pym." *Independent Women: The Function of*

Gender in the Novels of Barbara Pym. Ed. Janice Rossen. Sussex: Harvester; New York: St. Martin's, 1988. 21–49.

————. "From Fantasy to Pathology: Images of Aging in the Novels of Barbara Pym." *Human Values and Aging Newsletter* Jan./Feb. 1985: 5–7.

————. "Late Style in the Novels of Barbara Pym and Penelope Mortimer." *Gerontologist* 28 (1988): 835–39.

Wymard, Eleanor B. "Barbara Pym on Organized Religion: A Case of Folly." *Month* Aug./Sept. 1987: 318–20.

————. "Characters in Search of Order and Ceremony: Secular Faith of Barbara Pym." *Commonweal* 13 Jan. 1984: 19–21.

REVIEWS

An Academic Question

Barr, Charles. "The 'Miracle' of Rediscovery." *Listener* 31 July 1986: 24.

Bayley, John. "Ladies." *London Review of Books* 4 Sept. 1986: 20.

British Book News Dec. 1987: 841.

Burkhart, Charles. "An Unpolished Novel by Pym." *Philadelphia Inquirer* 2 Nov. 1986: P6.

Byatt, A. S. "Marginal Lives." *Times Literary Supplement* 8 Aug. 1986: 862. Rpt. as "Barbara Pym." *Passions of the Mind: Selected Writings.* By Byatt. London: Chatto and Windus, 1991; New York: Random House, 1992. 241–44.

Clayton, Sylvia. "Pym's No. 1." *Punch* 13 Aug. 1986: 44–45.

Daniel, Margaret. "More Excellent Women." *Church Times* [London] 22 Aug. 1986: 10.

Digilio, Alice. "Barbara Pym's Faculty Party." *Washington Post Book World* 28 Sept. 1986: 9.

Donahue, Deirdre. " 'Question' is Lesser, but Pleasurable, Pym.'' *USA Today* 23 Dec. 1986: 4D.

Donavin, Denise P. *Booklist* Aug. 1986: 1663.

Dorris, Michael. *Los Angeles Times Book Review* 14 Sept. 1986: 6.

Fuller, Edmund. "Tale No. 12: Essentially Pym." *Wall Street Journal* 9 Sept. 1986: 26.

Gilman, Jayne. "Novels from Oxfordshire." *Oxford Mail Weekender* 2 Aug 1986: 2.

Goff, Martyn. "Vital Vignettes." *Daily Telegraph* [London] 1 Aug. 1986: 13.

Harvey, Anne. "In a Minor Key." *Tablet* 13 Sept. 1986: 959–60.

Horan, David. "Aces in the Lively Pack." *Oxford Times* 5 Sept. 1986: 14.

Ingrams, Lucy. "A Thoroughly Modern Couple." *Literary Review* Sept. 1986: 7–8.

Keates, Jonathan. "Out of Her Depth." *Observer* 3 Aug. 1986: 23.

Kemp, Peter. "Disappointments and Dashed Hopes." *Sunday Times* [London] 27 July 1986: 50.

Kempf, Andrea Caron. *Library Journal* Aug. 1986: 172.

King, Francis. "Not Quietly Desperate but Defiantly Humorous." *Spectator* 2 Aug. 1986: 23–24.

Kirkus Reviews 1 July 1986: 968–69.

Laski, Marghanita. "Pastel Palettes." *Country Life* 11 Sept. 1986: 790.

Lopez, Ruth. "Encore for Fans of Pym." *Chicago Tribune Tempo* 26 Aug 1986: sect. 5, 3.

New Yorker 3 Nov. 1986: 165.

O'Brien, Robert. "What Message Comes Across?" *Standard* [London] 30 July 1986: 11.

Observer 14 Feb. 1988: 27.

Parente, Elizabeth. *Best Sellers* Nov. 1986: 290.

Pritchard, William H. "Fictional Places." *Hudson Review* 39 (1989): 654–55.

Pulsifer, Gary. *British Book News* Oct. 1986: 601.

Raphael, Isabel. "Cool Pym's Number Seven." *Times* [London] 31 July 1986: 11.

Rubin, Merle. "A Cooler, Tougher Woman." *New York Times Book Review* 7 Sept. 1986: 25.

Sackville-West, Sarah. "Sipping Gently at the Latest Pym." *Catholic Herald* [London] 15 Aug. 1986: 9.

Satchell, Tim. "From Beyond." *Books and Bookmen* Aug. 1986: 4.

Shapiro, Laura. *Newsweek* 10 Nov. 1986: 84.

Shrapnel, Norman. "Making Victims." *Guardian* [Manchester] 1 Aug. 1986: 19.

Steinberg, Sybil. *Publishers Weekly* 11 July 1986: 53–54.

Waugh, Harriet. "Promoting the Pym Industry." *Illustrated London News* Oct. 1986: 80–81.

Wilce, Gillian. "Ghost Story." *New Statesman* 15 Aug. 1986: 31.

Civil to Strangers and Other Writings

Bailey, Hilary. "Other Worlds and Ours." *Guardian* [London] 27 Nov. 1987: 24.

Booklist 1 Dec. 1987: 602.

British Book News Sept. 1987: 608.

Cavaliero, Glen. "Pym Again." *Country Life* 24 Dec. 1987: 72.

Dorris, Michael. "Posthumous Pym." *Chicago Tribune* 3 Jan. 1988: sect 14, 4.

Kirkus Reviews 1 Nov. 1987: 1537.

Knapp, Mona. *World Literature Today* 63 (1989): 101.

Lively, Penelope. "Unpublished Pym." *Books* Nov. 1987: 21–22.

Marsh, Pamela. "Pym's World—the Sweetness Has a Touch of Lemon." *Christian Science Monitor* 10 May 1988: 20.

New Yorker 22 Feb. 1988: 117.

New York Times Book Review 12 Mar. 1989: 34.

O'Conner, Patricia T. "Romance Comes to Up Callow." *New York Times Book Review* 17 Jan 1988: sect. 7, 29.

Prokop, Mary K. *Library Journal* 15 Nov. 1987: 91.

Raphael, Isabel. "Wild Shore of Love." *Times* [London] 5 Nov. 1987: 17.

Rubin, Merle. "The Luck of the English." *Los Angeles Times Book Review* 7 Feb. 1988: 6.

Schofield, Mary Anne. *Barbara Pym Newsletter* 3.1 (1988): 10.

Shulman, Nicola. "To Marry or to Smoulder Gently." *Times Literary Supplement* 25 Dec. 1987: 1420.

Simmons, James. "Excess and Reticence." *Spectator* 2 Jan. 1988: 24–25.

Slung, Michele. "Barbara Pym: The Quiet Pleasure of Her Company." *Washington Post Book World* 17 Jan 1988: 3, 13.

Steinberg, Sybil. *Publishers Weekly* 20 Nov. 1987: 61.

Time 29 Feb. 1988: 100.

Tomalin, Claire. "Wife Support System." *Observer* 15 Nov. 1987: 26.

Wall, Stephen. "Being Splendid." *London Review of Books* 3 Mar. 1988: 10–11.

Washington Post Book World 12 Feb. 1989: 12.

Crampton Hodnet

Atlantic June 1985: 104.

Bailey, Paul. "Period Hoot." *Observer* 30 June 1985: 23.

Becker, Alida. "For Barbara Pym Addicts." *St. Petersburg Times* 9 June 1985: 6D.

Booklist 1 Apr. 1985: 1082.

Brookner, Anita. "The Loneliness of Miss Pym." *Sunday Times* [London] 23 June 1985: 45.

Burkhart, Charles. "An Early Novel by Pym Is Rescued for Her Fans." *Philadelphia Inquirer* 4 Aug. 1985: P6.

"*Crampton Hodnet* by Barbara Pym." *Book-of-the-Month Club News* 1 Sept 1985: 15.

Daniel, Margaret. "Early Pym." *Church Times* [London] 26 July 1985: 6.

Digilio, Alice. "Teatime at Oxford." *Washington Post Book World* 9 June 1985: 9.

Dorris, Michael. *New York Times Book Review* 1 Sept. 1985: 14.

Duffy, Martha. "Blue Velvet." *Time* 24 June 1985: 81.

Dyer, Richard. "Brimming with Pymlichkeit." *Boston Globe* 14 May 1985: 72.

East, Vickie Kilgore. " 'New' Barbara Pym Novel Gift from Past." [Nashville] *Tennessean* 26 May 1985: 8D.

Fenton, James. "A Team of Those Old Oxford Blues." *Times* [London] 20 June 1985: 11.

Fuller, Edmund. "High Farce in North Oxford." *Wall Street Journal* 28 May 1985: 28.

Gardham, Jane. "Limp Lovers." *Books and Bookmen* June 1985: 29–30.

Gerard, Alice E. *Best Sellers* Aug. 1985: 170.

Gilman, Jayne. "A Long-Lost Oxford Novel Brings the Thirties Back to Life." *Oxford Mail* 2 July 1985: 18.

Goldstein, William. *Publishers Weekly* 12 Oct. 1984: 27.

Henderson, Heather. "Vain Affairs of the Heart." *Macleans* 24 June 1985: 62.

Hill, Rosemary. "Consoling Humour." *Country Life* 8 Aug. 1985: 400–01.

Ingrams, Richard. *Spectator* 7 Dec. 1985: 37.

Johnson, Greg. "Pym Novel Gives Farcical View of English Society." *Atlanta Journal* 1 Sept. 1985: 9J.

Kemp, Peter. "Oxford Beginnings." *Listener* 27 June 1985: 31.

Kendall, Elaine. "More Pym's People, Not Quite Doing What's Just Not Done." *Los Angeles Times* 23 July 1985: V4.

———. *Los Angeles Times Book Review* 4 Aug. 1985: 8.

King, Francis. "Frequent Smiles at Pym's No. 1." *Spectator* 29 June 1985: 28.

Kirkus Reviews 1 May 1985: 389–90.

Long, Robert Emmet. *America* 2 Nov. 1985: 285–86.

Kempf, Andrea Caron. *Library Journal* Aug. 1986: 172.

King, Francis. "Not Quietly Desperate but Defiantly Humorous." *Spectator* 2 Aug. 1986: 23–24.

Kirkus Reviews 1 July 1986: 968–69.

Laski, Marghanita. "Pastel Palettes." *Country Life* 11 Sept. 1986: 790.

Lopez, Ruth. "Encore for Fans of Pym." *Chicago Tribune Tempo* 26 Aug. 1986: sect. 5, 3.

New Yorker 3 Nov. 1986: 165.

O'Brien, Robert. "What Message Comes Across?" *Standard* [London] 30 July 1986: 11.

Observer 14 Feb. 1988: 27.

Parente, Elizabeth. *Best Sellers* Nov. 1986: 290.

Pritchard, William H. "Fictional Places." *Hudson Review* 39 (1989): 654–55.

Pulsifer, Gary. *British Book News* Oct. 1986: 601.

Raphael, Isabel. "Cool Pym's Number Seven." *Times* [London] 31 July 1986: 11.

Rubin, Merle. "A Cooler, Tougher Woman." *New York Times Book Review* 7 Sept. 1986: 25.

Sackville-West, Sarah. "Sipping Gently at the Latest Pym." *Catholic Herald* [London] 15 Aug. 1986: 9.

Satchell, Tim. "From Beyond." *Books and Bookmen* Aug. 1986: 4.

Shapiro, Laura. *Newsweek* 10 Nov. 1986: 84.

Shrapnel, Norman. "Making Victims." *Guardian* [Manchester] 1 Aug. 1986: 19.

Steinberg, Sybil. *Publishers Weekly* 11 July 1986: 53–54.

Waugh, Harriet. "Promoting the Pym Industry." *Illustrated London News* Oct. 1986: 80–81.

Wilce, Gillian. "Ghost Story." *New Statesman* 15 Aug. 1986: 31.

Civil to Strangers and Other Writings

Bailey, Hilary. "Other Worlds and Ours." *Guardian* [London] 27 Nov. 1987: 24.

Booklist 1 Dec. 1987: 602.

British Book News Sept. 1987: 608.

Cavaliero, Glen. "Pym Again." *Country Life* 24 Dec. 1987: 72.

Dorris, Michael. "Posthumous Pym." *Chicago Tribune* 3 Jan. 1988: sect. 14, 4.

Kirkus Reviews 1 Nov. 1987: 1537.

Knapp, Mona. *World Literature Today* 63 (1989): 101.

Lively, Penelope. "Unpublished Pym." *Books* Nov. 1987: 21–22.

Marsh, Pamela. "Pym's World—the Sweetness Has a Touch of Lemon." *Christian Science Monitor* 10 May 1988: 20.

New Yorker 22 Feb. 1988: 117.

New York Times Book Review 12 Mar. 1989: 34.

O'Conner, Patricia T. "Romance Comes to Up Callow." *New York Times Book Review* 17 Jan 1988: sect. 7, 29.

Prokop, Mary K. *Library Journal* 15 Nov. 1987: 91.

Raphael, Isabel. "Wild Shore of Love." *Times* [London] 5 Nov. 1987: 17.

Rubin, Merle. "The Luck of the English." *Los Angeles Times Book Review* 7 Feb. 1988: 6.

Schofield, Mary Anne. *Barbara Pym Newsletter* 3.1 (1988): 10.

Shulman, Nicola. "To Marry or to Smoulder Gently." *Times Literary Supplement* 25 Dec. 1987: 1420.

Simmons, James. "Excess and Reticence." *Spectator* 2 Jan. 1988: 24–25.

Slung, Michele. "Barbara Pym: The Quiet Pleasure of Her Company." *Washington Post Book World* 17 Jan 1988: 3, 13.

Steinberg, Sybil. *Publishers Weekly* 20 Nov. 1987: 61.

Time 29 Feb. 1988: 100.

Tomalin, Claire. "Wife Support System." *Observer* 15 Nov. 1987: 26.

Wall, Stephen. "Being Splendid." *London Review of Books* 3 Mar. 1988: 10–11.

Washington Post Book World 12 Feb. 1989: 12.

Crampton Hodnet

Atlantic June 1985: 104.

Bailey, Paul. "Period Hoot." *Observer* 30 June 1985: 23.

Becker, Alida. "For Barbara Pym Addicts." *St. Petersburg Times* 9 June 1985: 6D.

Booklist 1 Apr. 1985: 1082.

Brookner, Anita. "The Loneliness of Miss Pym." *Sunday Times* [London] 23 June 1985: 45.

Burkhart, Charles. "An Early Novel by Pym Is Rescued for Her Fans." *Philadelphia Inquirer* 4 Aug. 1985: P6.

"*Crampton Hodnet* by Barbara Pym." *Book-of-the-Month Club News* 1 Sept. 1985: 15.

Daniel, Margaret. "Early Pym." *Church Times* [London] 26 July 1985: 6.

Digilio, Alice. "Teatime at Oxford." *Washington Post Book World* 9 June 1985: 9.

Dorris, Michael. *New York Times Book Review* 1 Sept. 1985: 14.

Duffy, Martha. "Blue Velvet." *Time* 24 June 1985: 81.

Dyer, Richard. "Brimming with Pymlichkeit." *Boston Globe* 14 May 1985: 72.

East, Vickie Kilgore. " 'New' Barbara Pym Novel Gift from Past." [Nashville] *Tennessean* 26 May 1985: 8D.

Fenton, James. "A Team of Those Old Oxford Blues." *Times* [London] 20 June 1985: 11.

Fuller, Edmund. "High Farce in North Oxford." *Wall Street Journal* 28 May 1985: 28.

Gardham, Jane. "Limp Lovers." *Books and Bookmen* June 1985: 29–30.

Gerard, Alice E. *Best Sellers* Aug. 1985: 170.

Gilman, Jayne. "A Long-Lost Oxford Novel Brings the Thirties Back to Life." *Oxford Mail* 2 July 1985: 18.

Goldstein, William. *Publishers Weekly* 12 Oct. 1984: 27.

Henderson, Heather. "Vain Affairs of the Heart." *Macleans* 24 June 1985: 62.

Hill, Rosemary. "Consoling Humor." *Country Life* 8 Aug. 1985: 400–01.

Ingrams, Richard. *Spectator* 7 Dec. 1985: 37.

Johnson, Greg. "Pym Novel Gives Farcical View of English Society." *Atlanta Journal* 1 Sept. 1985: 9J.

Kemp, Peter. "Oxford Beginnings." *Listener* 27 June 1985: 31.

Kendall, Elaine. "More Pym's People, Not Quite Doing What's Just Not Done." *Los Angeles Times* 23 July 1985: V4.

————. *Los Angeles Times Book Review* 4 Aug. 1985: 8.

King, Francis. "Frequent Smiles at Pym's No. 1." *Spectator* 29 June 1985: 28.

Kirkus Reviews 1 May 1985: 389–90.

Long, Robert Emmet. *America* 2 Nov. 1985: 285–86.

Marsh, Pamela. "Early Pym Unsettling, Comforting." *Christian Science Monitor* 7 June 1985: B2.

McClurg, Jocelyn. "Posthumous Pym: Less Than Others." *Hartford* [CT] *Courant* 22 Sept. 1985: G3.

McGurn, William. *American Spectator* Nov. 1985: 46.

Murphy, Marese. "Life Work." *Irish Times* 29 June 1985: 11.

New Yorker 29 July 1985: 76–77.

New York Times Book Review 29 June 1986: 38.

New York Times Book Review 7 Dec. 1986: 82.

Observer 21 July 1985: 22.

Phelan, Nancy. "Early Pym and a Late Wesley." *Sydney Morning Herald* 19 Oct. 1985: 28.

Porter, Dorothy. "Cause for Laughter in the Bodleian." *Glasgow Herald* 22 June 1985: 11.

Quigly, Isabel. "Period Piece." *Tablet* 10 Aug. 1985: 836–37.

Quill and Quire Aug. 1985: 49.

Regan, Jennifer. "Pym Novel Is Great; 'Saratoga, Hot' Is Not." *Buffalo* [NY] *News* 28 July 1985: F8.

Ryan, Alan. "A Real Treat for Fans of Pym." *The Plain Dealer* [Cleveland] 9 June 1985: 22.

Seymour, Miranda. "Spinsters in Their Prime." *Times Literary Supplement* 28 June 1985: 720.

Seymour-Smith, Martin. "Cambridge Blue Stocking and Northern Grit." *Financial Times* [London] 22 June 1985: xvi.

Spice, Nicholas. "Costa del Pym." *London Review of Books* 4 July 1985: 10.

Steinberg, Sybil. *Publishers Weekly* 19 Apr. 1985: 69.

Sutton, Judith. *Library Journal* 1 May 1985: 80.

Taylor, D. J. "Artefacts and Art: Recent Fiction." *Encounter* June 1986: 53–54.

Toepfer, Susan. "A Perfect, Posthumous Pym." [New York] *Daily News Leisure* 26 May 1985: 7.

Tomkins, Pat. "A Vintage Pym Novel of Oxford." *San Francisco Examiner Review* 28 Apr. 1985: 5.

Trease, Geoffrey. *British Book News* Sept. 1985: 555.

Virginia Quarterly Review Winter 1986: 23.

Washington Post Book World 8 June 1986: 16.

Wilce, Gillian. *New Statesman* 5 July 1985: 30.

Wilson, A. N. "Daffodil Yellow and Coral Pink." *Literary Review* June 1985: 43–44.

Excellent Women

Bailey, Paul. "A Novelist Rediscovered." *Observer Review* 25 Sept. 1977: 25.

Baird, Michelle. "Pym Offers Intimate Look at Some Real-Life People." *Atlanta Constitution* 8 Oct. 1978: 5E.

Bannon, Barbara A. *Publishers Weekly* 24 July 1978: 80.

Baum, Joan. "Excellence Rediscovered." *Newsday* 1 Oct. 1978: 20.

Berkley, Miriam. "A 'Lost' Writer Restored." *Chicago Sun Times* 24 Dec 1978: 44.

Booklist 15 Oct. 1978: 355.

Brodie, Polly. *Library Journal* 15 Oct. 1978: 2135–36.

Church Times [London] 16 May 1952: 11.

Cohen, Carolyn Benson. "Narrow Compass." *New Directions for Women*. Mar./Apr. 1981: 13.

Coleman, Alan B. "People Getting Involved." *Kansas City Star* 8 Oct. 1978: 14E.

Daniel, Margaret. "St. Luke's Summer." *Church Times* [London] 25 Nov. 1977: 14.

"Divided Loyalties." *Times Literary Supplement* 28 Mar. 1952: 217.

Dowling, Ellen. "Pym: A Twentieth Century Jane Austen." *Houston Chronicle Zest* 5 Nov. 1978: 19.

Duchêne, Anne. "Brave Are the Lonely." *Times Literary Supplement* 30 Sept. 1977: 1096.

Engber, Diane. "Very British and Very Good." *Cincinnati Enquirer* 15 Oct 1978: G9.

Fried, Ethel F. "Undiscovered and Unpretentious—Barbara Pym." *Goodtimes* [West Hartford, CT] 23 Nov. 1978: 6.

Fuller, Edmund. "Finding a Lifetime Friend in a Writer's Work." *Wall Street Journal* 20 Oct. 1980: 26.

Glendinning, Victoria. "The Best High Comedy." *New York Times Book Review* 24 Dec.1978: 8.

Gold, Edith. "Fiction: Old-Fashioned and Terrific." *Miami Herald* 3 Sept 1978: 7E.

Hospital, Janette T. "Gallery of Eccentrics Is Deliciously Funny." *Boston Globe* 8 Oct. 1978: 68.

Irish Times 15 Mar. 1952: 6.

Jones, Richard. "Happy Rediscovery—Barbara Pym." *Virginian-Pilot* Oct. 1978: C6.

King, Francis. "Barbara Pym's Sunlit Garden." *Books and Bookmen* July 1978: 8–9.

Kirkus Reviews 1 Aug. 1978: 837.

Kirsch, Robert. "Barbara Pym: Our Cup of Tea." *Los Angeles Times* 16 Oct 1978: part 4, 4–5.

Laski, Marghanita. "New Novels." *Observer* [London] 9 Mar. 1952.

Laws, Frederick. *News Chronicle* [London] 7 Mar. 1952: 6.

Leighton, Betty. "Out of Obscurity, Two Unerringly Beautiful Novels." *Winston-Salem* [NC] *Journal* 17 Sept. 1978: C4.

Lenhart, Maria. "Quiet Novels Earn Belated Applause." *Christian Science Monitor* 8 Nov. 1978: 18.

McMurtry, Larry. "Two Books of Barbara Pym—and Where's She Been?" *Washington Star* 2 Oct. 1978: D2.

Meagher, Cyndi. "Pym's Novels: Showcases of Style." *Detroit News* 5 Nov 1978: 4F.

Miller, Karl. "Ladies in Distress." *New York Review of Books* 9 Nov. 1978: 24–25.

New York Times Book Review 31 Aug. 1980: 19.

Overmyer, Janet. " 'Sensible People' Shine in Barbara Pym Novels." *Columbus Dispatch* 1 Apr. 1979: 21.

Parini, Jay. "Writers Reading." *Horizon* Oct. 1987: 63.

Pool, Gail. "Doses of Reality." *New Boston Review* June/July 1980: 15–16.

Rosenstein, Harriet. "Have You Discovered Barbara Pym Yet?" *Ms.* May 1979: 33–35.

Rowse, A. L. "Austen mini?" *Punch* 19 Oct. 1977: 732–34.   \

Shrapnel, Norman. "Tea and Sympathy." *Guardian* [London] 15 Sept. 1977: 18.

Staley, Thomas F. "The Inside Story." *Tulsa Home and Garden* Mar. 1979: 76–77.

Toomey, Philippa. *Times* [London] 15 Sept. 1977: 18.

Updike, John. "Lem and Pym." *New Yorker* 26 Feb. 1979: 116–21. Rpt. in *Hugging the Shore: Essays and Criticism.* By Updike. New York: Knopf, 1983. 516–25.

USA Today 5 Feb. 1987: 4D.

Wade, Rosalind. "Quarterly Fiction Review." *Contemporary Review* 232 (1978): 45–47.

Washington Post Book World 25 Jan. 1987: 12.

Wax, Judith. "Two British Novelists Who Travel Well." *Chicago Tribune Book World* 1 Oct. 1978: sect. 7, 3.

Wyndham, Francis. "The Gentle Power of Barbara Pym." *Sunday Times* [London] 18 Sept. 1977: 41.

A Few Green Leaves

Auchincloss, Eve. "Surprises of Comedy and Sadness. *New York Times Book Review* 1 Feb. 1981: 9, 25–26.

Bailey, Paul. "The Art of the Ordinary." *Observer* 27 July 1980: 29.

———. "A Novelist Rediscovered." *Observer* 25 Sept. 1977: 25.

Bannon, Barbara A. *Publishers Weekly* 29 Aug. 1980: 355.

Benet, Diana. "Barbara Pym and the Novel of Manners." *Cross Currents* 33 (1983–84): 499–501.

Billington, Rachel. "Spinster Spy." *Financial Times* [London] 2 Aug. 1980: 6.

Braine, John. "Truth for Writing's Sake." *Sunday Telegraph* [London] 3 Aug. 1980: 10.

Brunsdale, Mitzi. "Pleasure from a Much Underrated British Author." *Houston Post* 9 Nov. 1980: 14AA.

Butcher, Maryvonne. "Ironies and Crises." *Tablet* 16 Aug. 1980: 512.

Clark, Anne. "Posthumous Disappointment from Pym." *Los Angeles Times Book Review* 12 Oct. 1980: 13.

Cole, Thomas. "Barbara Pym's Last Novel: A Kind of Summing Up." [Baltimore] *Sun* 21 Sept. 1980: D5.

Cook, Bruce. "The Art of Making Routine Lives Absorbing." *Detroit News* 21 Sept. 1980: 2E.

Donavin, Denise P. *Booklist* 15 Sept. 1980: 100.

Fagg, Martin. "Village Life." *Church Times* [London] 25 July 1980: 8.

Feinstein, Elaine. *Times* [London] 17 July 1980: D11.

Fitzgerald, Penelope. "A Secret Richness." *London Review of Books* 20 Nov.–3 Dec. 1980: 19.

Fuller, Edmund. "Finding a Lifetime Friend in a Writer's Work." *Wall Street Journal* 20 Oct. 1980: 26.

Gilman, Jayne. "The Private Life of an Oxfordshire Village." *Oxford Mail* 24 July 1980: 4.

Gold, Edith. "A Talented Writer's Last Book." *Miami Herald* 28 Sept 1980: 6E.

Higgens, Alison. "The Last Book by One of the Best." *Sacramento Bee* 19 Oct. 1980: F4.

Hughes-Onslow, James. *Spectator* 5 Dec. 1981: 23.

Kemp, Peter. "Grave Comedy." *Listener* 17 July 1980: 89.

King, Francis. "Fairly Excellent Woman." *Spectator* 19 July 1980: 21–22.

King, Nina. "Barbara Pym: Middle-Class Wry." *Newsday* 8 Feb. 1981: 20–21.

Kirkus Reviews 15 July 1980: 933.

Leighton, Betty. "A Splendid New Beginning Is Aborted by Fate." *Winston-Salem* [N.C.] *Journal* 26 Oct. 1980: C4.

Levin, Bernard. "Middles Marches. . . ." *Sunday Times* [London] 27 July 1980: 40.

Lodico, Michael. "Quiet Yet Powerful Barbara Pym." *Greensboro* [NC] *Daily News Record* 17 May 1981: G5.

Massie, Allan. "To Be Read with Muffins." *Scotsman* [Edinburgh] 2 Aug 1980: 1.

McLeod, Kirsty. *Country Life* 25 Sept. 1980: 1085.

Modert, Jo. "Rediscovering the Delights of Pymland." *St. Louis Post-Dispatch* 26 Feb. 1984: 13.

Murphy, Marese. "Women Only?" *Irish Times* [Dublin] 19 July 1980: 12.

Paley, Maggie. "What Makes the World Tick." *50 Plus* Jan. 1981: 60.

Phillips, Robert. "Narrow, Splendid Work." *Commonweal* 8 May 1981: 284–85.

Raksin, Alex. *Los Angeles Times Book Review* 16 Nov. 1986: 14.

Rowse, A. L. *Spectator* 18 Dec. 1982: 45.

Seymour-Smith, Martin. "The British Novel 1976–1980." *British Book News* June 1981: 325.

Shrimpton, Nicholas. "Bucolic Bones." *New Statesman* 15 Aug. 1980: 17–18.

Slung, Michele. "Pym's Last Cup." *Washington Post Book World* 12 Oct 1980: 6.

Stewart, Ian. "Recent Fiction." *Illustrated London News* Oct. 1980: 99.

Thornton, John. "Not So Small Change of Village Life." *Glasgow Herald* 23 Aug. 1980: 8.

Trease, Geoffrey. *British Book News* Dec. 1980: 761.

Tuck, Sherrie. *Library Journal* 1 Oct. 1980: 2108.

Virginia Quarterly Review Spring 1981: 59–60.

Washington Post Book World 26 Oct. 1986: 12.

Wilson, A. N. "Thinking of Being Them." *Times Literary Supplement* 18 July 1980: 799. Rpt. in "Barbara Pym." *Pen Friends from Porlock.* By Wilson. London: Hamish Hamilton, 1988. 112–20.

Wright, Helen. *Best Sellers* Dec. 1980: 314–15.

A Glass of Blessings

Baird, Michelle Ross. "Writer Barbara Pym Knew That Real Life Is Enough." *Atlanta Journal* 11 May 1980: E5.

Bargreen, Melinda. "Underrated Novelist." *Seattle Times Magazine* 22 June 1980: 14.

Brodie, Polly. *Library Journal* 15 June 1980: 1410.

Browne, Joseph. *Philadelphia Inquirer* 24 Aug. 1980: 13H.

Buckmaster, Henrietta. "High Comedy—Deftly Hidden." *Christian Science Monitor* 12 May 1980: B7.

Chicago Tribune Book World 3 Aug. 1980: sect. 7, 2.

Clemons, Walter. "An Unnoticed World." *Newsweek* 14 Apr. 1980: 96.

Daniel, Margaret. "St. Luke's Summer." *Church Times* [London] 25 Nov. 1977: 14.

Duchêne, Anne. "Brave Are the Lonely." *Times Literary Supplement* 30 Sept 1977: 1096.

Fairbanks, Ellen. *Ms.* July 1980: 30–31.

Fuller, Edmund. "Finding a Lifetime Friend in a Writer's Work." *Wall Street Journal* 20 Oct. 1980: 26.

Hooper, William Bradley. *Booklist* 1 Apr. 1980: 1109.

King, Francis. "Barbara Pym's Sunlit Garden." *Books and Bookmen* July 1978: 8–9.

Kirkus Reviews 15 Feb. 1980: 249.

Kubal, David. "Fiction Chronicle." *Hudson Review* 33 (1980): 437–39.

Miller, Karl. "Ladies in Distress." *New York Review of Books* 9 Nov. 1978: 24–25.

Oates, Joyce Carol. "One of the Most Undervalued Writers." *Mademoiselle* Sept. 1980: 62, 65.

Overmyer, Janet. "Pym Novel Will Delight." *Columbus Dispatch* 22 June 1980: J8.

Pinkham, Penny. "Pym's Cup Full." *Boston Sunday Globe* 11 May 1980: A8, A10.

Pool, Gail. "Doses of Reality." *New Boston Review* June/July 1980: 15–16.

Rowse, A. L. "Austen mini?" *Punch* 19 Oct. 1977: 732–34.

Seton, Cynthia Propper. "Tea and Titillation in the Rectory." *Washington Post Book World* 6 Apr. 1980: 5.

Shrapnel, Norman. "Tea and Sympathy." *Guardian* [London] 15 Sept. 1977: 18.

"Tinkle of Teacups." *Church Times* [London] 13 June 1958: 5.

Toomey, Philippa. *Times* [London] 15 Sept. 1977: 18.

Wade, Rosalind. "Quarterly Fiction Review." *Contemporary Review* 232 (1978): 45–46.

Washington Post Book World 25 Jan. 1987: 12.

"Ways of Women." *Times Literary Supplement* 23 May 1958: 281.

White, Edward M. "Pym's Newest Cup and an American Marriage." *Los Angeles Times Book Review* 8 June 1980: 12.

Wyndham, Francis. "The Gentle Power of Barbara Pym." *Sunday Times* [London] 18 Sept. 1977: 41.

Jane and Prudence

Bannon, Barbara A. *Publishers Weekly* 11 Sept. 1981: 59.

Bargreen, Melinda. "Pym Deftly Captures Human Foibles and Follies." *Seattle Times* 21 Feb. 1982: F9.

Bellasis, M. "Ladies and Gentlemen." *Tablet* 24 Oct. 1953: 405.

Bloomfield, Paul. "New Novels." *Guardian* [Manchester] 18 Sept. 1953: 4.

Broyard, Anatole. "Overflowing Her Situation." *New York Times Book Review* 15 Aug. 1982: 27.

Donavin, Denise P. *Booklist* 1 Oct. 1981: 179.

Dyer, Richard. "The Action Runs Beneath the Surface." *Boston Globe* 27 Oct. 1981: 16.

"Family Failings." *Times Literary Supplement* 2 Oct. 1953: 625.

Fuller, Edmund. "An Anthropologist of the English Middle Class." *Wall Street Journal* 25 May 1982: 30.

Gibbons, James. "Pym: A Magellan of the Everyday." *Houston Chronicle Zest* 20 Dec. 1981: 21.

H., E. *Observer* [London] 20 Sept. 1953: 11.

Harvey, Stephen. *Village Voice* 2 Dec. 1981: 56.

Johnston, Marguerite. "Glimpses of a Pym and Proper World." *Houston Post* 23 Jan. 1983: 24F.

New Yorker 2 Nov. 1981: 188.

Sutton, Judith. *Library Journal* 1 Nov. 1981: 2154.

Less Than Angels

Antioch Review 39 (1981): 519–20.

Auchincloss, Eve. "Surprises of Comedy and Sadness." *New York Times Book Review* 1 Feb. 1981: 9, 25–26.

Bannon, Barbara A. *Publishers Weekly* 5 Dec. 1980: 43.

Catholic World Sept. 1957: 473.

Chicago Tribune Book World 14 June 1981: sect. 7, 13.

Fuller, Edmund. "Stylish High Comedy and Astute Perception." *Wall Street Journal* 2 Mar. 1981: 16.

Holloway, David. "With Rod and Gun in Far Suburbia: New Novels." *News Chronicle* [London] 3 Nov. 1955: 6.

Hooper, William Bradley. *Booklist* 1 Jan. 1981: 615.

Kennedy, Joseph Patrick. "Pym: Studying the Anthropologists." *Houston Chronicle Zest* 25 Jan. 1981: 18.

Kessler, Julia Braun. "Reprinting Pym's Prim and Not-So-Proper Characters." *Los Angeles Times Book Review* 24 May 1981: 10.

King, Nina. "Barbara Pym: Middle-Class Wry." *Newsday* 8 Feb. 1981: 20–21.

Kirkus Reviews 1 Dec. 1980: 1544.

Kubal, David. "Fiction Chronicle." *Hudson Review* 34 (1981): 462–63.

Leighton, Betty. "Pym Explores Foibles and Vanities of Us All." *Winston-Salem* [NC] *Journal* 15 Feb. 1981: C4.

Mansten, S. P. *Saturday Review* 1 June 1957: 14.

McAleer, John. *Best Sellers* Mar. 1981: 428.

Nyren, Dorothy. *Library Journal* 15 Apr. 1957: 1068.

Overmyer, Janet. "Recent and Readable." *Columbus Dispatch* 15 Mar. 1981: 12.

Pippett, Aileen. "Observers Observed." *New York Times Book Review* 31 Mar 1957: 33.

Quinn, Miriam. *Best Sellers* 15 May 1957: 70.

San Francisco Chronicle 28 Apr. 1957: 23.

Silver, Adele Z. "Modest but Witty World of Barbara Pym." *The Plain Dealer* [Cleveland] 7 June 1981: 17C.

Strouse, Jean. "Elegant Surgery." *Newsweek* 19 Jan. 1981: 84.

"Trouble Brewing." *Times Literary Supplement* 18 Nov. 1955: 685.

Virginia Kirkus Service Bulletin 1 Feb. 1957: 96.

Wickenden, Dan. "Fun Among Anthropologists." *New York Herald Tribune Book Review* 5 May 1957: 3.

Zuckerman, Amy. "Making the Ordinary Fascinating." *Worcester* [MA] *Sunday Telegram* 1 Mar. 1981: 17.

No Fond Return of Love

Bannon, Barbara A. *Publishers Weekly* 15 Oct. 1982: 47.

Bitker, Marjorie. "A Tea-Time Treat from Pym." *Milwaukee Journal* 9 Jan 1983: 11.

Broyard, Anatole. "A Funnier Jane Austen." *New York Times* 1 Jan. 1983: 10.

Chicago Tribune Book World 1 May 1983: sect. 7, 2.

Donahue, Deirdre. "More Social Comedy from Barbara Pym." *The Plain Dealer* [Cleveland] 13 Feb. 1983: 18C.

Dyer, Richard. "The Sharply Observant Barbara Pym." *Boston Globe* 21 Dec 1982: 34.

Epstein, Joseph. "Sex and the Single Novel." *Hudson Review* 36 (1983): 185–86.

Fuller, Edmund. "Two Remaining Works of a Novelist of the Ordinary." *Wall Street Journal* 18 July 1983: 18.

Gold, Edith. "Pym's Cup Runneth Over." *Miami Herald* 27 Feb. 1983: 7E.

Gordon, Cecilia. *Indexer* 12 (1980): 108–109.

Halio, Jay L. "Fiction and Reality." *Southern Review* 21 (1985): 210.

Hooper, William Bradley. *Booklist* 1 Dec. 1982: 484.

Iyer, Pico. "Tricks of Self-Consciousness." *Partisan Review* 52 (1985): 288–91.

Johnston, Marguerite. "Glimpses of a Pym and Proper World." *Houston Post* 23 Jan. 1983: 24F.

Kapp, Isa. "One Woman's Virtue." *Washington Post* 14 Jan. 1983: D4.

Kirkus Reviews 1 Nov. 1982: 1216.

Leighton, Betty. "Ah, What Pym Can Do with a Meager Plot." *Winston-Salem* [NC] *Journal* 20 Feb. 1983: C4.

Marsh, Pamela. "Pym—Subtle and Accomplished." *Christian Science Monitor* 29 Dec. 1982: 15.

"The Milieus of Love." *Times Literary Supplement* 17 Feb. 1961: 108.

New Yorker 17 Jan. 1983: 112–13.

New York Times Book Review 12 June 1983: 36.

Niemtzow, Annette. "Pym: Old-Fashioned and Sweet but Not an Equal of Jane Austen." *Philadelphia Inquirer* 6 Feb. 1983: 7.

Rochmis, Dorothy H. *West Coast Review of Books* Jan./Feb. 1983: 29.

Sorensen, Robert. "Index This One Under 'D'—for 'Delightful.' " *Minneapolis Tribune* 16 Jan. 1983: 13G.

Strouse, Jean. "Tempest in a Teacup." *Newsweek* 24 Jan. 1983: 68–69.

Sutton, Judith. *Library Journal* 15 Dec. 1982: 2353.

Tyler, Anne. "From England to Brooklyn to West Virginia." *New York Times Book Review* 13 Feb. 1983: 1, 22.

Washington Post Book World 17 June 1984: 12.

Quartet in Autumn

Bailey, Paul. "A Novelist Rediscovered." *Observer Review* 25 Sept. 1977: 25.

Bainbridge, Beryl. *Observer* [London] 18 Dec. 1977: 21.

Baird, Michelle. "Pym Offers Intimate Look at Some Real-Life People." *Atlanta Constitution* 8 Oct. 1978: 5E.

Bannon, Barbara A. *Publishers Weekly* 24 July 1978: 78.

Baum, Joan. "Excellence Rediscovered." *Newsday* 1 Oct. 1978: 20.

Berkley, Miriam. "A 'Lost' Writer Restored." *Chicago Sun Times* 24 Dec 1978: 44.

Bitker, Marjorie. "Four in Old Age." *Milwaukee Journal* 24 Sept. 1978: part 5, 5.

Boeth, Richard. "Brief Lives." *Newsweek* 23 Oct. 1978: 121, 125.

Booklist 15 Oct. 1978: 355.

Brodie, Polly. *Library Journal* 15 Oct. 1978: 2135–36.

Chesman, Andrea. "A Quartet of 'Nobodies' Brought to Life in Novel." *Rocky Mountain News* 5 Nov. 1978.

Cohen, Carolyn Benson. "Narrow Compass." *New Directions for Women* Mar./Apr. 1981: 13.

Cooper, Jilly. *Sunday Times* [London] 4 Dec. 1977: 33.

Cooper, William. "Ending Up." *Daily Telegraph* [London] 6 Oct. 1977: 14.

Daniel, Margaret. "St. Luke's Summer." *Church Times* [London] 25 Nov. 1977: 14.

Dowling, Ellen. "Pym: A Twentieth Century Jane Austen." *Houston Chronicle Zest* 5 Nov. 1978: 19.

Duchêne, Anne. "Brave Are the Lonely." *Times Literary Supplement* 30 Sept 1977: 1096.

Firth, Brian. "Art of the Surface." *Tablet* 5 Nov. 1977: 1062.

Fried, Ethel F. "Undiscovered and Unpretentious—Barbara Pym." *Goodtimes* [West Hartford, CT] 23 Nov. 1978: 6.

Fuller, Edmund. "Finding a Lifetime Friend in a Writer's Work." *Wall Street Journal* 20 Oct. 1980: 26.

Glendinning, Victoria. "The Best High Comedy." *New York Times Book Review* 24 Dec.1978: 8.

Gold, Edith. "Fiction: Old-Fashioned and Terrific." *Miami Herald* 3 Sept 1978: 7E.

Hospital, Janette T. "Gallery of Eccentrics Is Deliciously Funny." *Boston Globe* 8 Oct. 1978: 68.

Hughes, David. "A Personal Best of 1977." *Times Christmas Books* [London] 25 Nov. 1977: xxxi.

Irish Press 22 Dec. 1977: 6.

Jones, Richard. "Happy Rediscovery—Barbara Pym." *Virginian-Pilot* Oct. 1978: C6.

King, Francis. "Barbara Pym's Sunlit Garden." *Books and Bookmen* July 1978: 8–9.

Kirkus Reviews 15 July 1978: 773–74.

Kirsch, Robert. "Barbara Pym: Our Cup of Tea." *Los Angeles Times* 16 Oct 1978: part 4, 4–5.

Larkin, Philip. *Observer* 18 Dec. 1977: 21.

Leighton, Betty. "Out of Obscurity, Two Unerringly Beautiful Novels." *Winston-Salem* [NC] *Journal* 17 Sept. 1978: C4.

Lenhart, Maria. "Quiet Novels Earn Belated Applause." *Christian Science Monitor* 8 Nov. 1978: 18.

Long, Grady. "The Long View." *Chattanooga Times* 11 Mar 1979: 13.

Maddocks, Melvin. " 'I Don't Need Anybody,' and Other Illusions." *Christian Science Monitor* 5 Mar. 1979: 27.

McMurtry, Larry. "Two Books of Barbara Pym—and Where's She Been?" *Washington Star* 2 Oct. 1978: D2.

Meagher, Cyndi. "Pym's Novels: Showcases of Style." *Detroit News* 5 Nov 1978: 4F.

Mellors, John. "Mixed Foursomes." *Listener* 27 Oct. 1977: 550.

Miller, Karl. "Ladies in Distress." *New York Review of Books* 9 Nov. 1978: 24–25.

Mowbray, S. M. *British Book News* Feb. 1978: 155–56.

Murray, Isobel. "Lonely Hearts." *Financial Times* [London] 22 Sept. 1977: 4.

New York Times Book Review 31 Aug. 1980: 19.

Overmyer, Janet. " 'Sensible People' Shine in Barbara Pym Novels."
Columbus Dispatch 1 Apr. 1979: 21.

Parini, Jay. "Writers Reading." *Horizon* Oct. 1987: 63.

Paulin, Tom. "Talkative Transparencies—Recent Fiction." *Encounter*
Jan 1978: 72.

Pool, Gail. "Doses of Reality." *New Boston Review* June/July 1980:
15–16.

Quigley, Pat. " 'Quartet in Autumn' a Touching Story of Four Single
Women [sic]." *Denver Post* 29 Oct. 1978: 27.

Raksin, Alex. *Los Angeles Times Book Review* 16 Nov. 1986: 14.

Rosenstein, Harriet. "Have You Discovered Barbara Pym Yet?" *Ms.*
May 1979: 33–35.

Shrapnel, Norman. "Tea and Sympathy." *Guardian* [London] 15 Sept.
1977: 18.

Spray, Campbell. "Dulling the Senses through Middle-Age." *Yorkshire
Post* 22 Sept. 1977: 14.

Staley, Thomas F. "The Inside Story." *Tulsa Home and Garden* Dec.
1978: 96.

Stewart, Ian. "Recent Fiction." *Illustrated London News* Nov. 1977:
103.

Sykes, Peter. "Professional Mr. Fowles." *Oxford Times* 7 Oct. 1977: 16.

Time 9 Oct. 1978: 114–15.

Toomey, Philippa. *Times* [London] 15 Sept. 1977: 18.

Treglown, Jeremy. "Puff Puff Puff." *New Statesman* 23 Sept. 1977:
418.

Updike, John. "Lem and Pym." *New Yorker* 26 Feb. 1979: 116–21. Rpt.

in *Hugging the Shore: Essays and Criticism.* By Updike. New York: Knopf, 1983. 516–25.

Wade, Rosalind. "Quarterly Fiction Review." *Contemporary Review* 232 (1978): 45–46.

Washington Post Book World 26 Oct. 1986: 12.

Wax, Judith. "Two British Novelists Who Travel Well." *Chicago Tribune Book World* 1 Oct. 1978: sect. 7, 3.

Wyndham, Francis. "The Gentle Power of Barbara Pym." *Sunday Times* [London] 18 Sept. 1977: 41.

Some Tame Gazelle

Bannon, Barbara A. *Publishers Weekly* 10 June 1983: 55–56.

Burkhart, Charles. "A First Novel Highlights the Revival of an Author's Work." *Philadelphia Inquirer Books/Leisure* 7 Aug. 1983: 2.

Caldwell, Margaret. "Some News of Our Country Cousins from Barbara Pym." *The Plain Dealer* [Cleveland] 28 Aug. 1983: 28C.

Casey, Constance. "Very British, Very Charming." *USA Today* 22 July 1983: 3D.

Dyer, Richard. "Pym's Comedic Skill Makes Quiet Happenings Reverberate." *Boston Sunday Globe* 31 July 1983: A9.

Ezell, Margaret. "Pym: An 'Excellent Woman.' " *Houston Chronicle Zest* 9 Oct. 1983: 22.

Fuller, Edmund. "Two Remaining Works of a Novelist of the Ordinary." *Wall Street Journal* 18 July 1983: 18.

Gold, Edith. *Miami Herald* 27 Nov. 1983: E7.

Gorra, Michael. "Restraint is the Point." *New York Times Book Review* 31 July 1983: 12, 18.

Hale, Lionel. "New Novels." *Observer* [London] 14 May 1950: 24.

Hooper, William Bradley. *Booklist* 15 May 1983: 1166.

Jenkins, Elizabeth. "New Novels." *Guardian* [Manchester] 26 May 1950: 4.

Johnston, Marguerite. "More Pym, Proper Humor." *Houston Post* 11 Sept 1983: 12F.

Jones, Susan Curvin. "If You Don't Know Barbara Pym. . . ." *Minneapolis Tribune* 25 Sept. 1983: 15G.

Kakutani, Michiko. "Books of the Times." *New York Times* 5 Aug. 1983: C22.

King, Nina. "Humorous and Gentle Country Loves." *Newsday* 27 July 1983: sect. 2, 52.

Kirkus Reviews 1 June 1983: 634–35.

Kissel, Howard. *Women's Wear Daily* 27 July 1983: 44.

Marsh, Pamela. "Pym's First Novel Is Finally in Print Stateside." *Christian Science Monitor* 7 Oct. 1983: B9.

Modert, Jo. "Rediscovering the Delights of Pymland." *St. Louis Post-Dispatch* 26 Feb. 1984.

New Yorker 5 Sept. 1983: 112.

Nichols, Thelma. *West Coast Review of Books* Jan./Feb. 1984: 39.

Overmyer, Janet. "Pym's First Novel Fine." *Columbus Sunday Dispatch* 28 Aug. 1983: 13.

Owings, Alison. "Bridled Passions in an English Village." *San Francisco Chronicle Review* 21 Aug. 1983: 1, 10.

Peyton, Georgina. "Main Street, England." *San Diego Union* 24 July 1983: E6.

Quinn, Mary Ellen. *Library Journal* July 1983: 1383.

Rubin, Merle. "For Anglophiles, Pym's Number One." *Los Angeles Herald-Examiner* 28 Aug. 1983: F5-F6.

See, Carolyn. "Romance: Does It Last or Does It Lust?" *Los Angeles Times* 16 Aug. 1983: V6.

Smith, F. Seymour. *What Shall I Read Next? A Personal Selection of Twentieth Century English Books.* Cambridge: Cambridge University Press, 1953. 98.

Stewart, Susan. "Passion vs. Poetry in Pym's 'Gazelle.' " *Dallas Times Herald* 2 Oct. 1983: 9.

Taliafero, Frances. *Harpers* Aug. 1983: 74–75.

Vogel, Christine B. "A Sip of Pym's Number One." *Washington Post Book World* 21 Aug. 1983: 1, 14.

Washington Post Book World 17 June 1984: 12.

Washington Post Book World 22 June 1986: 12.

White, Antonia. "New Novels." *New Statesman and Nation* 1 July 1950: 21–22.

"Women of Character." *Times Literary Supplement* 7 July 1950: 417.

Zuckerman, Amy. "Vintage First Novel." *Worcester* [MA] *Telegram* 25 Sept 1983: 17.

The Sweet Dove Died

Ableman, Paul. "Genteelism." *Spectator* 8 July 1978: 26.

Ackroyd, Peter. "Minor Passions at a Good Address." *Sunday Times* [London] 16 July 1978: 41.

Bannon, Barbara A. *Publishers Weekly* 12 Mar. 1979: 65–66.

Blum, J. M., and L. R. Leans. "Current Literature, 1978." *English Studies* 60 (1979): 628.

Brodie, Polly. *Library Journal* 15 Mar. 1979: 754.

Butcher, Maryvonne. "Sympathies." *Tablet* 2 Sept. 1978: 848–49.

Butscher, Eugene. *Booklist* 15 Apr. 1979: 1275.

Chicago Tribune Book World 13 Jan. 1980: sect. 7, 5.

Clapp, Susannah. "Genteel Reminders." *Times Literary Supplement* 7 July 1978: 757.

Clemons, Walter. "The Pleasures of Miss Pym." *Newsweek* 16 Apr. 1979: 91–92.

Cohen, Carolyn Benson. "Narrow Compass." *New Directions for Women* Mar./Apr. 1981: 13.

Cole, Thomas. "A Pym's Cup That Runneth Over with Wit and Satire." [Baltimore] *Sun* 26 Aug. 1979: D4.

Cosh, Mary. "Dramatic Finale to an Oxford Quintet." *Glasgow Herald* 6 July 1978: 8.

Dowling, Ellen. "Pym: Silence Well Used." *Houston Chronicle Zest* 17 June 1979: 20.

Dulac, Alicia. *Best Sellers* July 1979: 121.

Fuller, Edmund. "Finding a Lifetime Friend in a Writer's Work." *Wall Street Journal* 20 Oct. 1980: 26.

Hinerfield, Susan Slocum. "A Case of Possessions." *St. Louis Globe-Democrat* 19–20 May 1979: 4E.

Howard, Philip. *Times* [London] 6 July 1978: 14.

Kenyon, John. *Observer* 17 Dec. 1978: 33.

King, Francis. "Barbara Pym's Sunlit Garden." *Books and Bookmen* July 1978: 8–9.

Kirkus Reviews 1 Jan. 1979: 31.

Leighton, Betty. "Stead and Pym's Revival Is a Cause for Rejoicing." *Winston-Salem* [NC] *Journal* 13 May 1979: C4.

Massie, Allan. "Worlds of Spiritual Perversion." *Scotsman* [Edinburgh] 29 July 1978: 15.

McMurtry, Larry. "Lucid Fiction: An Artistic Return for Barbara Pym." *Washington Star* 27 May 1979: 26.

Meagher, Cyndi. "Pym's Wicked Wit Carves Another Gem." *Detroit News* 15 Apr. 1979: F2.

Mellors, John. "Bad Trips." *Listener* 17 Aug. 1978: 223.

Mesher, David. "The Parakeats." *Jerusalem Post* 4 Aug. 1978: 13.

Modert, Jo. *St. Louis Post-Dispatch* 1 May 1979: 13.

New York Times Book Review 31 Aug. 1980: 19.

Oates, Quentin. "Critics Crowner." *Bookseller* 15 July 1978: 266.

Observer 23 July 1978: 21.

Pinkham, Penny. "Pym's Latest Missing Something." *Boston Globe* 24 June 1979: 91.

Pool, Gail. "Doses of Reality." *New Boston Review* June/July 1980: 15–16.

Rosenstein, Harriet. "Have You Discovered Barbara Pym Yet?" *Ms.* May 1979: 33–35.

Seymour-Smith, Martin. "The British Novel 1976–1980." *British Book News* June 1981: 325.

Seymour-Smith, Martin. "Small Is Good." *Financial Times* [London] 6 July 1978: 37.

Somerville-Large, Gillian. "The Poon Show." *Irish Times* 15 July 1978: 11.

Stewart, Ian. "Recent Fiction." *Illustrated London News* Sept. 1978: 103.

Sullivan, Mary. "Woman of Exquisite Taste." *Sunday Telegraph* [London] 9 June 1978: 16.

Tehan, Arline B. "Artistic." *Hartford* [CT] *Courant,* 29 Apr. 1979: 8G.

Thwaite, Anthony. "Delicate Manoeuvers." *Observer* 9 July 1978: 25.

Toulson, Shirley. *British Book News* Oct. 1978: 843.

Treglown, Jeremy. "Snob Story." *New Statesman* 7 July 1978: 27.

Washington Post Book World 25 Jan. 1987: 12.

An Unsuitable Attachment

Ackroyd, Peter. "Survival of the Faithful." *Sunday Times* [London] 21 Feb. 1982: 43.

Alabaster, Carol. " 'Twentieth Century Jane Austen' Sheds Light on England." *Arizona Republic* 25 July 1982: 13.

Allen, Bruce. "Droll Matchmaking from Pym." *Christian Science Monitor* 7 July 1982: 17.

———. "Summer's Buried Treasures: 'The Winter People' and Other Neglected Fiction." *Chicago Tribune Book World* 1 Aug. 1982: sect. 7, 1.

Bannon, Barbara A. *Publishers Weekly* 2 Apr. 1982: 69.

Becker, Alida. " 'Lost' Novel Well Worth Discovering." *Philadelphia Inquirer* 1 Aug. 1982: N6.

Butcher, Maryvonne. "Period Piece." *Tablet* 13 Mar. 1982: 22.

Butler, Marilyn. "Keeping Up with Jane Austen." *London Review of Books* 6–19 May 1982: 16–17.

Campbell, James. "Kitchen Window." *New Statesman* 19 Feb. 1982: 25.

Cantwell, Mary. "Books of the Times." *New York Times* 10 May 1982: C15.

Carlo, Michele. *Best Sellers* Aug. 1982: 175.

Craig, Patricia. *Times Literary Supplement* 1 July 1983: 711.

Cullinan, Elizabeth. *Commonweal* 3 Dec. 1982: 658–59.

Cunningham, Valentine. "A World of Ordinary Gentlefolk." *Observer* 21 Feb 1982: 32.

Daniel, Margaret. "Period Piece." *Church Times* [London] 19 Feb. 1982: 7.

Donahue, Deirdre. "The Lost Novel of a Latter-Day Jane Austen." *Washington Post Book World* 20 June 1982: 6.

Donavin, Denise P. *Booklist* 15 Apr. 1982: 1042.

Duchêne, Anne. "Handing on Loneliness." *Times Literary Supplement* 26 Feb 1982: 214.

Dyer, Richard. "Rediscovering Barbara Pym." *Boston Globe* 25 May 1982: 62.

Elliott, Janice. "Thunder of Teacups." *Sunday Telegraph* [London] 21 Feb. 1982: 12.

Fuller, Edmund. "An Anthropologist of the English Middle Class." *Wall Street Journal* 25 May 1982: 30.

Gold, Edith. "Pym's Novel Finds Deserved Home." *Miami Herald* 15 July 1982: 6C.

Hendricks, David. " 'Lost' Novel Resurrects British Author's Work." [San Antonio] *Express-News* 26 Sept. 1982.

Kemp, Peter. "Pym's No. Seven." *Listener* 18 Feb. 1982: 24.

Kirkus Reviews 15 Mar. 1982: 367.

Leighton, Betty. "A Good Novel Was Rejected, a Career Blighted." *Winston-Salem* [NC] *Journal* 30 May 1982: C4.

Levine, Suzanne. *Ms.* June 1982: 18.

Lively, Penelope. *Encounter* Apr. 1982: 76–78.

Mars-Jones, Adam. ''Pym's Number Two.'' *Financial Times* [London] 27 Feb 1982: 27.

McLeod, Kirsty. ''Women of the Cloth.'' *Yorkshire Post* 4 Mar. 1982: 10.

Miller, Roger. ''Underrated, Overrated, It's Pure Pym.'' *Milwaukee Journal* 13 June 1982: 13.

Milton, Edith. ''Worlds in Miniature.'' *New York Times Book Review* 20 June 1982: 11.

New Yorker 24 May 1982: 133–34.

New York Times Book Review 5 Dec. 1982: 48.

New York Times Book Review 4 Sept. 1983: 19.

Oates, Quentin. ''Critics Crowner.'' *Bookseller* 27 Feb. 1982: 801–803.

Observer 10 Apr. 1983: 31.

Overmyer, Janet. ''Late Author's Tale Scores Anew.'' *Columbus Sunday Dispatch* 18 July 1982: H11.

Phillips, Robert. ''Posthumous Pym.'' *Ontario Review* Fall/Winter 1982: 114–15.

Raksin, Alex. *Los Angeles Times Book Review* 16 Nov. 1986: 14.

Redmond, Lucile. ''Pym's Number Seven.'' *Irish Times* 6 Mar. 1982: 12.

Reefer, Mary M. ''A Tender Irony Enlightens Lives of Lonely Gentility.'' *Kansas City* [MO] *Star* 13 June 1982: 1K, 10K.

Seymour, Miranda. *Times* [London] 18 Feb. 1982: 10.

Silver, Adele Z. ''More Quiet Pleasure from Barbara Pym.'' *The Plain Dealer* [Cleveland] 11 July 1982: 24C.

Sutton, Judith. *Library Journal* 15 May 1982: 1012.

Toulson, Shirley. *British Book News* June 1982: 385.

Virginia Quarterly Review Winter 1983: 18, 20.

Washington Post Book World 26 Oct. 1986: 12.

Willison, Marilyn Murray. "Amour of Lady to the Mannerly Born." *Los Angeles Times Book Review* 22 July 1982: 26.

Wilson, A. N. "St. Barbara-in-the-Precinct." *Spectator* 20 Feb. 1982: 22–23. Rpt. in "Barbara Pym." *Pen Friends from Porlock.* By Wilson. London: Hamish Hamilton, 1988. 112–20.

Wilson, John. "An Unsuitable Attachment." *Magill's Literary Annual 1983.* Vol. 2. Ed. Frank N. Magill. Englewood Cliffs: NJ, 1983. 855–59.

A Very Private Eye: An Autobiography in Diaries and Letters

Abel, Betty. "Barbara Pym Novelist and Diarist." *Contemporary Review* 245 (1984): 278–79.

Abley, Mark. "A Writer's Resurrection." *Macleans* 27 Aug. 1984: 50.

Ackroyd, Peter. "Manufacturing Miss Pym." *Times Literary Supplement* 3 Aug. 1984: 861.

Antioch Review 42 (1984): 507.

Bailey, Paul. "Smiling Through." *Observer* 22 July 1984: 20.

Bargreen, Melinda. "British Author Had Creative, Turbulent Life." *Seattle Times* 5 Aug. 1984: G7.

Bayley, John. "Barbara Pym: Sharp Clarity and Cosy Obscurity." *Harpers Queen* July 1984: 142.

Bell, Hazel K. " 'Thankless Task' Accomplished for Pym." *Indexer* 14 (1985): 189.

Billington, Rachel. "Spinster Eye." *Financial Times* [London] 21 July 1984: 23.

Broyard, Anatole. "Books of the Times." *New York Times* 14 June 1984: C21.

Bunke, Joan. "Miss Pym to the Life" *Des Moines* [IA] *Register* 19 Aug 1984: 18.

Carey, John. "Pym's Little Ironies." *Sunday Times* [London] 22 July 1984: 41.

Chicago Tribune 12 Aug. 1984: sect. 14, 39.

Clemons, Walter. "A Quiet Life Full of Surprises." *Newsweek* 23 July 1984: 64.

Cole, Thomas. "Pym, the Heart-on-Sleeve Spinster." *Evening Sun* [Baltimore] 20 Aug. 1984: 17.

Colegate, Isabel. "Tea and Sympathy: Philip Larkin and Barbara Pym." *Washington Post Book World* 1 July 1984: 1, 5.

Corrigan, Maureen. "Pym Agonistes." *Village Voice* 31 July 1984: 45–46.

Dahlin, Robert. "How Could I Have Waited So Long, Miss Pym?" *Christian Science Monitor* 7 Dec. 1984: B2.

Daniel, Margaret. "Excellent Women." *Church Times* [London] 3 Aug. 1984: 6.

Danto, Arthur C. *Nation* 22 Dec. 1984: 688.

Dick, Kay. "The Reluctant Spinster." *Spectator* 18 Aug. 1984: 23.

Dinnage, Rosemary. "Comic, Sad, Indefinite." *New York Review of Books* 16 Aug. 1984: 15–16.

Dixler, Elsa. *Nation* 22 Dec. 1984: 686.

Donavin, Denise P. *Booklist* 1 June 1984: 1373.

Dutka, J. *Canadian Catholic Review* Apr. 1985: 33–34.

Dyer, Richard. "The 'Real' Barbara Pym." *Boston Globe* 3 July 1984: 11.

East, Vickie Kilgore. "Diaries Reveal a Different Barbara Pym." [Nashville] *Tennessean* 22 Sept. 1985: 9F.

Espey, John. "Barbara Pym in Her Own Words." *Los Angeles Examiner* 26 Aug. 1984: F5-F6.

Everett, Barbara. "The Pleasures of Poverty." *London Review of Books* 6–19 Sept. 1984: 5–6. Rpt. in *Independent Women: The Function of Gender in the Novels of Barbara Pym.* Ed. Janice Rossen. Sussex: Harvester; New York: St. Martin's, 1988. 9–20.

Fenton, James. "The Passionate Spinster Who Found Humour." *Times* [London] 19 July 1984: 10.

Finlayson, Iain. "Portrait of a Born-Again Novelist." *Glasgow Herald* 1 Sept. 1984: 11.

Fullbrook, Kate. *British Book News* Oct. 1984: 628.

Fuller, Edmund. "An Excellent Woman." *Wall Street Journal* 3 July 1984: 22.

Gill, Penny. "Getting to Know an Unknown Writer." *Gazette* [Montreal] 4 Aug. 1984: I3.

Glendinning, Victoria. "Spontaneous Obsessions, Imposed Restraint." *New York Times Book Review* 8 July 1984: 3.

Guimaraes, Dona. "The Most Private Eye." *Vogue* July 1984: 120, 122.

Gunn, H. D. "A Writer Rescued from Oblivion." *Philadelphia Inquirer* 15 July 1984: 3.

Halperin, John. *Modern Fiction Studies* 30 (1984): 780–82.

Harnett, Lynn. "Barbara Pym's Diaries and Letters Readable and Revealing." *Portsmouth* [NH] *Herald* 22 July 1984: 5E.

Heberlein, Kate Browder. "Barbara Pym." *Contemporary Literature* 26 (1985): 368–71.

————. "Myopia: A Look at Pym's Autobiography." *Northwest Review of Books* 1 (1985): 9.

Heller, Karen. " 'Private Eye': Pym Remains Undercover." *USA Today* 20 July 1984: 3D.

Hildebrand, Holly. "The Other Side of Pym and Proper Life." *Houston Post* 22 July 1984: 11F.

Howe, Pamela. "The 'Cruelly Perceptive Eye' of a Born Novelist." *Listener* 5 July 1984: 14–15.

"In Print." *Inquiry* July 1984: 32.

Kaufmann, James. *Christian Science Monitor* 2 Aug. 1985: B7.

Kemp, Peter. "The Private Barbara Pym." *Listener* 2 Aug. 1984: 23–24.

Kendall, Elaine. "Bits and Pieces for Posterity." *Los Angeles Times Book Review* 5 Aug.1984: 1, 10.

Kirkus Reviews 15 May 1984: 486–87.

Kiser, Thelma Scott. "New Biographies Feature Literary Lights." *Sunday Independent* [Ashland, KY] 22 July 1984: 41–42.

Larkin, Philip. *Observer* 2 Dec. 1984: 19.

Lively, Penelope. "Pym's Aren't What You Thought They Were." *Books and Bookmen* June 1984: 8–9.

Long, Robert Emmet. *America* 24 Nov. 1984: 348.

Lopez, Ruth. "Pym's Diaries Show Inspiration for Her Comic World." *Detroit Free Press* 5 Aug. 1984: 5B.

Lucy, Margaret. "Whispers of Wit but Unlucky in Love." *Catholic Herald* 15 Mar. 1985: 8.

Maher, Bernard. "An Excellent Woman?" *Irish Times* 21 July 1984: 13.

Meade, Marion. *Ms.* July 1984: 21.

Mernit, Susan. ''Spinster of the Parish.'' *Women's Review of Books* Jan. 1985: 5.

Meyers, Valerie. *Modern Fiction Studies* 30 (1984): 783–85.

Milan, Karen. ''Her Life Also Attained No Fond Return of Love.'' *Ft. Worth Star-Telegraph Books* 16 Sept. 1984: 1.

Moose, Ruth. ''Barbara Pym: The Ordinary Made Special.'' *Charlotte* [NC] *Observer* 23 Sept. 1984: 5F.

New Directions for Women Nov./Dec. 1984: 20.

New Yorker 16 July 1984: 91–92.

Oates, Quentin. ''Critics Crowner.'' *Bookseller* 28 July 1984: 429–30.

Paul, Barbara. '' 'Very Private Eye' Life of Barbara Pym.'' *Pittsburgh Press* 12 Aug. 1984: F6.

Philip, Neil. ''Final Accolade.'' *Times Educational Supplement* 5 Apr. 1985: 37.

Pool, Gail. ''Excellent Women.'' *Nation* 4–11 Aug. 1984: 88–90.

''Pym's Number One.'' *Economist* 1 Sept. 1984: 73–74.

Quackenbush, Rich. ''An Excellent Woman.'' *Houston Chronicle Zest* 22 July 1984: 19.

Quigly, Isabel. ''Unprivate Life of 'Prim' Miss Pym.'' *Tablet* 25 Aug 1984: 819–20.

Quill and Quire Sept. 1984: 85.

Reefer, Mary M. ''Barbara Pym Returns with the Same Old Flair.'' *Kansas City* [MO] *Star* 5 Aug. 1984: 8E.

Rowse, A. L. *Financial Times* [London] 1 Dec. 1984: 14.

Rubin, Merle. *Christian Science Monitor* 23 Aug. 1984: 21–22.

Schmitz, Eugenia. *Best Sellers* Sept. 1984: 212.

See, Carolyn. "Plotting Great Escapes for Summer." *Los Angeles Times* 1 July 1984: 9.

Silver, Adele Z. "Barbara Pym—Imprudent Spinster." *The Plain Dealer* [Cleveland] 22 July 1984: 13.

Slackman, Michael. "The Annual *Biography* Evaluative Survey." *Biography* 8 (1985): 288.

Slung, Michele. "Oxford, Jumble Sales and Unhappy Love Affairs." *Newsday* 22 July 1984: 16–17.

Smith, Anne. *New Statesman* 21 Dec. 1984: 44.

Smith, Linell. "A Writer's Growth: Diaries and Letters of Barbara Pym." *Sun* [Baltimore] 8 July 1984: 8L.

Smith, Wendy. *New Republic* 16 July 1984: 41.

Spurling, Hilary. "A Taste of Dust." *Guardian Weekly* 29 July 1984: 22.

Stuttaford, Genevieve. *Publishers Weekly* 4 May 1984: 46.

———. *Publishers Weekly* 26 Apr. 1985: 81.

Toepfer, Susan. "The Passions of Barbara Pym." [New York] *Daily News Leisure* 29 July 1984: 14–15.

Washington Post Book World 30 June 1985: 12.

Waugh, Auberon. "That's Romance with a Rotter!" *Daily Mail* [London] 19 July 1984: 7.

Widmayer, Richard A. *Rocky Mountain Review of Language and Literature* 39 (1985): 77–79.

———. "The Varied Portrait of Barbara Pym: A Review of the Post-1985 Critical Explosion." *Rocky Mountain Review of Language and Literature* 41 (1987): 241–45.

Wilce, Gillian. "Borderland." *New Statesman* 24 Aug. 1984: 23.

Wilson, A. N. "Sock for Posterity." *Literary Review* Sept. 1984: 4–6.

Wyatt, Louise. "A Detailed View of Barbara Pym's Life in Her Own Words." *Free Press* [London] 17 Aug. 1984: 13.

Zelenko, Barbara. *Library Journal* 1 June 1984: 1126.

MISCELLANEA

"Barbara Pym 1913–1980." *Contemporary Literary Criticism: Excerpts from Criticism of the Works of Today's Novelists, Poets, Playwrights, Short Story Writers, Scriptwriters, and Other Creative Writers.* Vol. 37. Ed. Daniel G. Marowski. Detroit: Gale, 1986. 367–380.

Barbara Pym: Out of the Wilderness. Videotape. Belmont, MA: Greybirch Productions, 1984. Interview with Hilary Walton and Hazel Holt; footage of Pym from a 1977 BBC Interview. Write or call Ellen J. Miller, 40 Greybirch Park, Belmont, MA 02178 (617/484–6366).

Bayley, John. "Life-Enhancing World-Views." Review of *Diversity and Depth in Fiction,* by Angus Wilson. *Times Literary Supplement* 16 Sept. 1983: 978. Brief comparison of Pym with Jane Austen.

Binding, Paul. "Barbara Pym." *British Novelists Since 1960: Part Two: H-Z.* Vol. 14 of *Dictionary of Literary Biography.* Ed. Jay L. Halio. Detroit: Gale, 1983. 604–07. Biography and summaries of novels.

Biography. *The Author's and Writer's Who's Who.* 4th ed. Ed. L. G. Pine. London: Burke's Peerage, 1960.

Biography. *The Author's and Writer's Who's Who.* 5th ed. London: Burke's Peerage, 1963. 399.

Biography. *The Author's and Writer's Who's Who.* 6th ed. Darien, CT: Hafner, 1971. 653.

Biography. *The Cambridge Guide to Literature in English.* Ed. Ian Ousby. Cambridge: Cambridge University Press, 1988. 811.

Biography. *Contemporary Authors: A Bio-Bibliographical Guide to*

Current Authors and Their Works. Permanent Series Vol. 1. Ed. Clare D. Kinsman. Detroit: Gale, 1975. 523.

Biography. *Contemporary Authors: A Bio-Bibliographical Guide to Current Writers in Fiction, General Nonfiction, Poetry, Journalism, Drama, Motion Pictures, Television, and Other Fields.* New Revision Series Vol. 34. Ed. James G. Lesniak. Detroit: Gale, 1991. 362–66.

Biography. *Feminist Companion to Literature in English: Women Writers from the Middle Ages to the Present.* Ed. Virginia Blain, Patricia Clements, Isobel Grundy. New Haven: Yale University Press, 1990. 880–81.

Biography. *A Guide to Twentieth Century Literature in English.* Ed. Harry Blamires. London: Methuen, 1983. 227–28.

Biography. *Major Twentieth-Century Writers: A Selection of Sketches from Contemporary Authors.* Ed. Bryan Ryan. Detroit: Gale, 1991. 2430–33.

Biography. *Novels and Novelists: A Guide to the World of Fiction.* Ed. Martin Seymour-Smith. New York: St. Martin's, 1980. 203.

Biography. *The Oxford Companion to English Literature.* 5th ed. Ed. Margaret Drabble. Oxford: Oxford University Press, 1985. 801.

Biography. *Who Was Who 1971–1980.* New York: St. Martin's, 1981. 646.

Biography. *World Authors 1970–1975.* Ed. John Wakeman. New York: H. W. Wilson, 1980. 663–66. Includes a brief sketch by Pym, novel summaries, and critical excerpts.

Biography. *The Writers Directory 1971–1973.* Ed. A. G. Seaton. London; Chicago: St. James, 1971. 356.

Biography. *The Writers Directory 1974–1976.* London: St. James; New York: St. Martin's, 1973. 653–54.

Biography. *The Writers Directory 1976–1978.* Ed. Nancy E. Duin. New York: St. Martin's, 1976. 867.

Biography. *The Writers Directory 1980–1982.* New York: St. Martin's, 1979. 1010.

Brooke-Rose, Christine. "Illiterations." *Breaking the Silence: Women's Experimental Fiction.* Ed. Ellen G. Friedman and Miriam Fuchs. Princeton: Princeton University Press, 1989. 55–71. Brief mention of Pym on p. 56.

Cavaliero, Glen. "Pym, Barbara." *British Women Writers: A Critical Reference Guide.* Ed. Janet Todd. New York: Continuum, 1989. 548–50. Biography and brief discussion of the novels.

Cecil, Lord David. "Barbara Pym." *Journal of the Society of Literature,* Biennial Report, 1980–1981, 25–26. Obituary article.

Cooley, Mason. "Barbara Pym." *Dictionary of Literary Biography Yearbook 1987.* Ed. J. M. Brook. Detroit: Gale, 1988. 275–83. Biography and discussion of themes in the novels, including posthumous publications.

Criticism excerpts. *Contemporary Literary Criticism: Excerpts from Criticism of the Works of Today's Novelists, Poets, Playwrights, and Other Creative Writers.* Vol. 13. Ed. Dedria Bryfonski. Detroit: Gale, 1980. 469–71.

Criticism excerpts. *Contemporary Literary Criticism: Excerpts from Criticism of the Works of Today's Novelists, Poets, Playwrights, and Other Creative Writers.* Vol. 19. Ed. Sharon R. Gunton. Detroit: Gale, 1981. 386–89.

Dipple, Elizabeth. *The Unresolvable Plot: Reading Contemporary Fiction.* New York: Routledge, 1988. Brief reference to Pym on pp. 255–56.

Duncan, Sally. "The Two Lives of Miss Pym." Interview. *Oxford Times* 26 May 1978: 13.

"Indexers in Fiction." *Indexer* 13 (1982): 26. Excerpts from *No Fond Return of Love.*

Kaplan, Carey. Biography. *Encyclopedia of British Women Writers.* Ed. Paul Schlueter and June Schlueter. Hamden, CT: Garland, 1988. 372.

Kenyon, Olga. *Women Novelists Today: A Survey of English Writing in the Seventies and Eighties.* New York: St. Martin's, 1988. Brief reference to Pym on pp. 149–50.

Kirk-Greene, A. H. M. "Barbara Pym 1913–1980." Obituary. *Africa* 50 (1980): 94–95.

La Belle, Jenijoy. *Herself Beheld: The Literature of the Looking Glass.* Ithaca: Cornell UP, 1988. Brief reference to Pym on pp. 4–5.

Larkin, Philip. Biography. *Dictionary of National Biography 1971–1980.* Ed. Lord Blake and C. S. Nicholls. Oxford: Oxford University Press, 1986. 695.

Macheski, Cecilia. ". . . Elizabeth Taylor (the Novelist, of Course) . . . ." *Barbara Pym Newsletter* 3.1 (1988): 5–7. Brief comparison of Pym and Taylor.

Memorial. *Publishers Weekly* 5 Aug. 1983: 16.

"Miss Barbara Pym: Novelist of Distinctive Qualities." Obituary. *Times* [London] 14 Jan 1980: 14.

Monteith, Charles. "Publishing Larkin." *Times Literary Supplement* 21 May 1982: 551–52. Brief discussion of Pym.

"Not-Quite Indexers in Fiction (and Non-Fiction)." *Indexer* 14 (1985): 277–78. Paragraph on *Quartet in Autumn.*

Obituary. *Contemporary Authors: A Bio-Bibliographical Guide to Current Writers in Fiction, General Nonfiction, Poetry, Journalism, Drama, Motion Pictures, Television, and Other Fields.* Vols. 97–100. Ed. Frances C. Locher. Detroit: Gale, 1981. 449.

Obituary. *Publishers Weekly* 14 Mar. 1980: 16.

Olendorf, Donna. Biography. *Contemporary Authors: A Bio-Bibliographical Guide to Current Writers in Fiction, General Nonfiction, Poetry, Journalism, Drama, Motion Pictures, Television, and Other Fields.* New Revision Series. Vol. 13. Ed. Linda Metzger. Detroit: Gale, 1984. 421–24.

"Points from Publishers." *Bookseller* 24 Sept. 1977: 2168. Two paragraphs announcing the "rediscovery."

Polster, Erving. *Every Person's Life Is Worth a Novel*. New York and London: Norton, 1987. Brief discussion of *Excellent Women* on pp. 149–50.

"Reputations Revisited . . . ." *Times Literary Supplement* 21 Jan. 1977: 66–67.

Review excerpts. *Fiction Catalog*. 10th ed. Ed. Juliette Yaakov and Gary L. Bogart. New York: H. W. Wilson, 1981. 431.

Review excerpts. *Fiction Catalog*. 10th ed., 1981 Suppl. Ed. Juliette Yaakov. New York: H. W. Wilson, 1982. 50–51.

Review excerpts. *Fiction Catalog*. 10th ed., 1982 Suppl. Ed. Juliette Yaakov and John Greenfieldt. New York: H. W. Wilson Co., 1983. 49.

Review excerpts. *Fiction Catalog*. 12th ed. Ed. Juliette Yaakov and John Greenfieldt. New York: H. W. Wilson, 1991. 514–16.

Rossen, Janice. *Philip Larkin: His Life's Work*. Iowa City: University of Iowa Press, 1989. xv, xix, 22–23, 52, 62–4, 117–21. Cites Larkin's letters to Pym.

Rubins, Josh. "The Browser." *Harvard Magazine* Jan./Feb. 1979: 64–65. Brief discussion of Pym.

Sadler, Lynn Veach. *Anita Brookner*. English Authors Series 473. Boston: Twayne, 1990. Compares Brookner and Pym.

———. "Anita Brookner's Dons: Literature as the Way for a Woman in *A Start in Life* and *Providence*." *Barbara Pym Newsletter* 4.2 (1989): 1–8. Brief mention of Pym.

———. "Drabbling in Pym's Garden of the Critics." *Barbara Pym Newsletter* 4.2 (1989): 1–8. Compares Drabble and Pym.

Salwak, Dale. "Barbara Pym." *Critical Survey of Long Fiction*. English Language Series. Vol. 6. Ed. Frank N. Magill. Englewood Cliffs, NJ: Salem Press, 1983. 2179–85.

Swinden, Patrick. *The English Novel of History and Society, 1940–1980*. London: Macmillan; New York: St. Martin's, 1984. Brief mention of Pym with quotation from *Excellent Women* on p. 2.

Tirbutt, Susan. "Autumn Sweetness for Barbara Pym." Interview. *Yorkshire Post* 21 Nov. 1977: 6.

Toepfer, Susan. "Ten Pym Novels: An Introduction." [New York] *Daily News Leisure* 29 July 1984: 14.

Tyler, Anne. "Symposium: Books That Gave Me Pleasure." *New York Times Book Review* 5 Dec. 1982: 9. Brief mention.

Updike, John. "Letters." *Saturday Review* Sept./Oct. 1983: 10.

Welty, Eudora. "Symposium: Books That Gave Me Pleasure." *New York Times Book Review* 5 Dec. 1982: 9. Brief mention.

Will. *Times* [London] 5 May 1980: C10.

Wood, Anthony. "Right Back in Fickle Favour." Interview. *Oxford Mail* 2 Dec. 1977: 7.

Zlobina, L. "Barbara Pym: Osennii kvartet." *Novyi Mir: Literaturno Khudozhestvennyi i Obshchestvenno Politicheskii Zhurnal* Jan. 1993: 285.

LIST OF WORKS CITED

Ableman, Paul. "Genteelism." Review of *The Sweet Dove Died. Spectator* 8 July 1978: 26.

Ackley, Katherine Anne. *The Novels of Barbara Pym.* New York: Garland, 1989.

Ackroyd, Peter. "Manufacturing Miss Pym." Review of *A Very Private Eye. Times Literary Supplement* 3 Aug. 1984: 861.

———. "Minor Passions at a Good Address." Review of *The Sweet Dove Died. Sunday Times* [London] 16 July 1978: 41.

Allen, Paula Gunn. "Grandma's Dying Poem." *Skins and Bones: Poems 1979–87.* Albuquerque: West End, 1988. 62–65.

Bachelder, Frances H. "The Importance of Connecting." *The Life and Work of Barbara Pym.* Salwak 185–92.

Bailey, Paul. "The Art of the Ordinary." Review of *A Few Green Leaves. Observer* 27 July 1980: 29.

———. "A Novelist Rediscovered." Review of *Quartet in Autumn, Excellent Women,* and *A Few Green Leaves. Observer* 25 Sept. 1977: 25.

Barr, Charles. "The 'Miracle' of Rediscovery." Review of *An Academic Question,* and *Barbara Pym,* by Robert Emmet Long. *Listener* 31 July 1986: 24.

Bayley, John. "Where, Exactly, Is the Pym World?" *The Life and Work of Barbara Pym.* Salwak 50–57.

Beiswenger, Eleanor. "Teaching Barbara Pym in Britain." *Barbara Pym Newsletter* 4.2 (1989): 8–10.

Bellasis, M. "Ladies and Gentlemen." Review of *Jane and Prudence*. *Tablet* 24 Oct. 1953: 405.

Benet, Diana. "The Language of Christianity in Pym's Novels." *Thought* 59 (1984): 504–13.

———. *Something to Love: Barbara Pym's Novels*. Literary Frontiers Edition 27. Columbia: University of Missouri Press, 1986.

Binding, Paul. "Barbara Pym." *British Novelists Since 1960: Part Two: H-Z. Dictionary of Literary Biography*. Ed. Jay L. Halio. Detroit: Gale, 1983. 604–607.

Bixler, Frances. "Female Narrative in Barbara Pym's *Excellent Women*." *Barbara Pym Newsletter* 5.2 (1991): 2–6.

Boeth, Richard. "Brief Lives." Review of *Quartet in Autumn*. *Newsweek* 23 Oct. 1978: 121, 125.

Bowman, Barbara. "Barbara Pym's Subversive Subtext: Private Irony and Shared Detachment." *Independent Women: The Function of Gender in the Novels of Barbara Pym*. Rossen 82–94.

Bradham, Margaret C. "Barbara Pym's Women." *World Literature Today* 61 (1987): 31–37.

Braine, John. "Truth for Writing's Sake." Review of *A Few Green Leaves*. *Sunday Telegraph* [London] 3 Aug. 1980: 11.

Brothers, Barbara. "Love, Marriage, and Manners in the Novels of Barbara Pym." *Reading and Writing Women's Lives: A Study of the Novel of Manners*. Ed. Bege K. Bowers and Barbara Brothers. Ann Arbor, MI: UMI, 1990. 153–70.

———. "Women Victimized by Fiction: Living and Loving in the Novels of Barbara Pym." *Twentieth-Century Women Novelists*. Ed. Thomas F. Staley. Totowa, NJ: Barnes and Noble, 1982. 61–80.

Broyard, Anatole. "A Funnier Jane Austen." Review of *No Fond Return of Love*. *New York Times* 1 Jan. 1983: 10.

———. "Overflowing Her Situation." Review of *Jane and Prudence*. *New York Times Book Review* 15 Aug. 1982: 27.

Burkhart, Charles. "Barbara Pym and the Africans." *Twentieth-Century Literature* 29 (1983): 45–53. Rpt. as "Miss Pym and the Africans." *The Pleasure of Miss Pym.* Burkhart 60–69.

———. "Glamorous Acolytes: Homosexuality in Pym's World." *Independent Women: The Function of Gender in the Novels of Barbara Pym.* Rossen 95–105.

———. *The Pleasure of Miss Pym.* Austin: University of Texas Press, 1987.

Butler, Marilyn. "Keeping Up with Jane Austen." Review of *An Unsuitable Attachment. London Review of Books* 6–19 May 1982: 16–17.

Bywaters, Barbara Lee. *"Rereading Jane": Jane Austen's Legacy to Twentieth-Century Women Writers.* Diss. Bowling Green State University, 1989. Ann Arbor, MI: UMI, 1990. 9011607.

Campbell, James. "Kitchen Window." Review of *An Unsuitable Attachment. New Statesman* 19 Feb. 1982: 25.

Cantwell, Mary. "Book of the Times." Review of *An Unsuitable Attachment. New York Times* 10 May 1982: C15.

Clapp, Susannah. "Genteel Reminders. Review of *The Sweet Dove Died. Times Literary Supplement* 7 July 1978: 757.

Clemons, Walter. "The Pleasures of Miss Pym." Review of *The Sweet Dove Died. Newsweek* 16 Apr. 1979: 91–92.

Cooley, Mason. *The Comic Art of Barbara Pym.* New York: AMS, 1990.

Cotsell, Michael. *Barbara Pym.* Macmillan Modern Novelists. London: Macmillan; New York: St. Martin's, 1989.

De Paolo, Rosemary. "You Are What You Drink." *Barbara Pym Newsletter* 2.2 (1987): 1–5.

Dinnage, Rosemary. "Comic, Sad, Indefinite." Review of *A Very Private Eye. New York Review of Books* 16 Aug. 1984: 15–16.

"Divided Loyalties." Review of *Excellent Women. Times Literary Supplement* 28 Mar. 1952: 217.

Doan, Laura L. "Introduction." *Old Maids to Radical Spinsters: Unmarried Women in the Twentieth-Century Novel.* Ed. Doan. Urbana: University of Illinois Press, 1991. 1–16.

————. "Pym's Singular Interest: The Self as Spinster." *Old Maids to Radical Spinsters: Unmarried Women in the Twentieth-Century Novel.* Ed. Doan. Urbana: University of Illinois Press, 1991. 139–54.

————. "Text and the Single Man: The Bachelor in Pym's Dual-Voiced Narrative." *Independent Women: The Function of Gender in the Novels of Barbara Pym.* Rossen 63–81.

Dobie, Ann B. "The World of Barbara Pym: Novelist as Anthropologist." *Arizona Quarterly* 44 (1988): 5–18.

Donahue, Deirdre. "The Lost Novel of a Latter-Day Jane Austen." Review of *An Unsuitable Attachment. Washington Post Book World* 20 June 1982: 6.

Dorris, Michael. "Posthumous Pym." Review of *Civil to Strangers and Other Writings. Chicago Tribune* 3 Jan. 1988: sect. 14, 4.

————. Review of *An Academic Question. Los Angeles Times Book Review* 14 Sept. 1986: 6.

————. Review of *Crampton Hodnet. New York Times Book Review* 1 Sept. 1985: 14.

Duchêne, Anne. "Brave Are the Lonely." Review of *Excellent Women, A Glass of Blessings,* and *Quartet in Autumn. Times Literary Supplement* 30 Sept. 1977: 1096.

————. "Handing on Loneliness." Review of *An Unsuitable Attachment. Times Literary Supplement* 26 Feb. 1982: 214.

Duffy, Martha. "Blue Velvet." Review of *Crampton Hodnet. Time* 24 June 1985: 81.

Dyer, Richard. "The Action Runs Beneath the Surface." Review of *Jane and Prudence. Boston Globe* 27 Oct. 1981: 16.

————. "The 'Real' Barbara Pym." Review of *A Very Private Eye. Boston Globe* 3 July 1984: 11.

Epstein, Joseph. "Miss Pym and Mr. Larkin." *Commentary* July 1986: 38–46. Rpt. in *Quadrant* Dec. 1986: 9–17.

Everett, Barbara. "The Pleasures of Poverty." Review of *A Very Private Eye. London Review of Books* 6–19 Sept. 1984: 5–6. Rpt. in *Independent Women: The Function of Gender in the Novels of Barbara Pym.* Rossen 9–20.

Ezell, Margaret J. M. " 'What Shall We Do with Our Old Maids?': Barbara Pym and the 'Woman Question.' " *International Journal of Women's Studies* 7 (1984): 450–65.

Fairbanks, Ellen. Review of *A Glass of Blessings. Ms.* July 1980: 30–31.

"Family Failings." Review of *Jane and Prudence. Times Literary Supplement* 2 Oct. 1953: 625.

Feinstein, Elaine. Review of *A Few Green Leaves. Times* [London] 17 July 1980: D11.

Fenton, James. "The Passionate Spinster Who Found Humour." Review of *A Very Private Eye. Times* [London], 19 July 1984: 10.

———. "A Team of Those Old Oxford Blues." Review of *Crampton Hodnet. Times* [London] 20 June 1985, 11.

Fergus, Jan. "*A Glass of Blessings,* Jane Austen's *Emma* and Barbara Pym's Art of Allusion." *Independent Women: The Function of Gender in the Novels of Barbara Pym.* Rossen 109–36.

Fisichelli, Glynn-Ellen. "The Novelist as Anthropologist—Barbara Pym's Fiction: Fieldwork Done at Home." *Papers on Language and Literature* 24 (1988): 436–45.

Fisichelli, Glynn-Ellen Maria. "*The Trivial Round, the Common Task,*" *Barbara Pym: The Development of a Writer.* Diss. State University of New York at Stony Brook, 1984. Ann Arbor: UMI, 1984. 8416639.

Fitzgerald, Penelope. "A Secret Richness." Review of *A Few Green Leaves. London Review of Books* 20 Nov.–4 Dec. 1980: 19.

Frye, Northrop. *Anatomy of Criticism: Four Essays.* Princeton, NJ: Princeton University Press, 1957. 238.

Fuller, Edmund. "Stylish High Comedy and Astute Perception." Review of *Less Than Angels. Wall Street Journal* 2 Mar. 1981: 16.

Glendinning, Victoria. "The Best High Comedy." Review of *Excellent Women* and *Quartet in Autumn. New York Times Book Review* 24 Dec.1978: 8.

———. "Spontaneous Obsessions, Imposed Restraint." Review of *A Very Private Eye. New York Times Book Review* 8 July 1984: 3.

Godwin, Gail. "Years of Neglect." *The Life and Work of Barbara Pym.* Salwak 193.

Gordon, Joan. "Cozy Heroines: Quotidian Bravery in Barbara Pym's Novels." *Essays in Literature* [Macomb, IL] 16 (1989): 224–33.

Graham, Peter W. "Emma's Three Sisters." *Arizona Quarterly* 43 (1977): 39–52.

Graham, Robert J. "Cumbered with Much Serving: Barbara Pym's 'Excellent Women.' " *Mosaic* 17 (1984): 141–60. Rpt. in *"For Better or Worse": Attitudes Toward Marriage in Literature.* Ed. Evelyn J. Hinz. Winnipeg: University of Manitoba, 1985. 141–60.

———. "The Narrative Sense of Barbara Pym." *The Life and Work of Barbara Pym.* Salwak 142–55.

Griffin, Barbara. "Order and Disruption in *Some Tame Gazelle.*" *Barbara Pym Newsletter* 5.1 (1990): 2–4.

———. "Private Space and Self-Definition in Barbara Pym's *Excellent Women. Essays in Literature* [Macomb, IL] 19 (1992): 132–43.

Groner, Marlene San Miguel. "Barbara Pym's Allusions to Seventeenth-Century Poets." *Cross-Bias: Newsletter of the Friends of Bemerton* 11 (1987): 5–7.

———. *The Novels of Barbara Pym.* Diss. St. John's University, 1988. Ann Arbor, MI: UMI, 1989. 8900580.

Halio, Jay L. "Fiction and Reality." Review of *No Fond Return of Love. Southern Review* 21 (1985): 204–13.

Halperin, John. "Barbara Pym and the War of the Sexes." *The Life and Work of Barbara Pym.* Salwak 88–100.

———. Review of *A Very Private Eye. Modern Fiction Studies* 30 (1984): 780–82.

Harvey, Stephen. Review of *Jane and Prudence. Village Voice* 2 Dec. 1981: 56.

Hazzard, Shirley. "Excellent Women." *The Life and Work of Barbara Pym.* Salwak 3.

Heberlein, Kate Browder. "Barbara Pym and Anthony Trollope: Communities of Imaginative Participation." *Pacific Coast Philology* 19 (1984): 95–100.

———. "Barbara Pym." Review of *A Very Private Eye. Contemporary Literature* 26 (1985): 368–71.

———. *Communities of Imaginative Participation: The Novels of Barbara Pym.* Diss. University of Washington, 1984. Ann Arbor, MI: UMI, 1984. 8419147.

———. "Pym's Carry-Over Characters." *Barbara Pym Newsletter* 1.1 (1986): 1–2.

———. "Thankless Tasks or Labors of Love: Women's Work in Barbara Pym's Novels." *Barbara Pym Newsletter* 2.1 (1987): 1–5.

Heilbrun, Carolyn G. *Writing a Woman's Life.* New York: Norton, 1988.

Henderson, Heather. "Vain Affairs of the Heart." Review of *Crampton Hodnet. Macleans* 24 June 1985: 62.

Hite, Molly. Foreword. *Redefining Autobiography in Twentieth-Century Women's Fiction: An Essay Collection.* Ed. Janice Morgan and Collette T. Hall. New York: Garland, 1991. xiii-xvi.

Holt, Hazel. "The Home Front: Barbara Pym in Oswestry, 1939–41." *Independent Women: The Function of Gender in the Novels of Barbara Pym.* Rossen 50–59.

———. *A Lot to Ask: A Life of Barbara Pym.* London: Macmillan, 1990; New York: Dutton, 1991.

———. "The Novelist in the Field: 1946–74." *The Life and Work of Barbara Pym*. Salwak 22–33.

———. "Philip Larkin and Barbara Pym: Two Quiet People." *Philip Larkin: The Man and His Work*. Ed. Dale Salwak. London: Macmillan; Iowa City: University of Iowa Press, 1989. 59–68.

Hooper, William Bradley. Review of *A Glass of Blessings*. *Booklist* 1 Apr. 1980: 1109.

Iyer, Pico. "Tricks of Self-Consciousness." Review of *No Fond Return of Love*. *Partisan Review* 52 (1985): 286–91.

Jacobs, Bruce Richard. *Elements of Satire in the Novels of Barbara Pym*. Diss. Fordham University, 1988. Ann Arbor, MI: UMI, 1988. 8809473.

Jones, Michelle Lynne. *Laughing Hags: The Comic Vision as Feminist*. Diss. University of Alberta, 1992. Ann Arbor, MI: UMI, 1992. DANN73080.

Kane, Patricia. "A Curious Eye: Barbara Pym's Women." *South Dakota Review* 24 (1986): 50–59.

Kapp, Isa. "Out of the Swim with Barbara Pym." *American Scholar* 52 (1983): 237–42.

Kaufman, Anthony. "The Short Fiction of Barbara Pym." *Twentieth-Century Literature* 32 (1986): 50–77.

Keener, Frederick M. "Barbara Pym Herself and Jane Austen." *Twentieth-Century Literature* 31 (1985): 89–110.

Kemp, Peter. "Oxford Beginnings." Review of *Crampton Hodnet*. *Listener* 27 June 1985: 31.

Knuth, Deborah J. "Teaching Barbara Pym." *Barbara Pym Newsletter* 4.1 (1989): 1–2, 6–8.

Kubal, David. "Fiction Chronicle." Review of *A Glass of Blessings*. *Hudson Review* 33 (1980): 437–48.

———. "Fiction Chronicle." Review of *Less Than Angels*. *Hudson Review* 34 (1981): 456–66.

Larkin, Philip. Foreword. *An Unsuitable Attachment.* By Barbara Pym. London: Macmillan, 1982. 5–10. Rpt. as "The Rejection of Barbara Pym." *The Life and Work of Barbara Pym.* Salwak 171–75.

———. "The World of Barbara Pym." *Times Literary Supplement* 11 Mar. 1977: 260. Rpt. in *Required Writing: Miscellaneous Pieces 1955–1982.* By Larkin. New York: Farrar, 1984. 240–44.

Larson, Edith S. "The Celebration of the Ordinary in Barbara Pym's Novels." *San Jose Studies* 9.2 (1983): 17–22.

Lee, Sun-Hee. *Love, Marriage, and Irony in Barbara Pym's Novels.* Diss. University of North Texas, 1991. Ann Arbor, MI: UMI, 1991. 9128713.

Levin, Bernard. "Middles Marches. . . ." Review of *A Few Green Leaves. Sunday Times* [London] 27 July 1980: 40.

Liddell, Robert. *A Mind at Ease: Barbara Pym and Her Novels.* London: Peter Owen, 1989.

———. "A Success Story." *The Life and Work of Barbara Pym.* Salwak 176–84.

Little, Judy. "Influential Anxieties: Woolf and Pym." *Virginia Woolf Miscellany* 39 (Fall 1992): 5–6.

Lively, Penelope. "Books and Writers: Recent Fiction." Review of *An Unsuitable Attachment. Encounter* Apr. 1982: 76–78.

———. "Unpublished Pym." Review of *Civil to Strangers and Other Writings. Books* Nov. 1987: 21–22.

———. "The World of Barbara Pym." *The Life and Work of Barbara Pym.* Salwak 45–59.

Long, Robert Emmet. *Barbara Pym.* New York: Ungar, 1986.

Lyles, Jean Caffey. "Pym's Cup: Anglicans and Anthropologists." *Christian Century* 21–28 May 1986: 519–22.

Malloy, Constance. "The Quest for a Career." *The Life and Work of Barbara Pym.* Salwak 4–21.

McDonald, Margaret Anne. *Alone Together: Gender and Alienation.* Diss. University of Saskatchewan, 1991. Ann Arbor, MI: UMI, 1991. DANN68227.

Mernit, Susan. "Spinster of the Parish." Review of *A Very Private Eye.* *Women's Review of Books* Jan. 1985: 5.

"The Milieus of Love." Review of *No Fond Return of Love. Times Literary Supplement* 17 Feb. 1961: 108.

Moseley, Merritt. "Barbara Pym's Dark Novels." *Barbara Pym Newsletter* 1.1 (1986): 3–4.

Moseley, Merritt, and Pamela J. Nickless. "Pym's Homosexuals." *Barbara Pym Newsletter* 5.1 (1990): 5–8.

Nardin, Jane. *Barbara Pym.* Twayne's English Author Series 406. Boston: Twayne, 1985.

Naulty, Patricia M. *"I Never Talk of Hunger"*: *Self-Starvation as Women's Language of Protest in Novels by Barbara Pym, Margaret Atwood, and Anne Tyler.* Diss. Ohio State University, 1988. Ann Arbor, MI: UMI, 1989. 8907274.

Oates, Joyce Carol. "Barbara Pym's Novelistic Genius." *The Life and Work of Barbara Pym.* Salwak 43–44.

O'Conner, Patricia T. "Romance Comes to Up Callow." Review of *Civil to Strangers and Other Writings. New York Times Book Review* 17 Jan 1988: sect. 7, 29.

Phelps, Gilbert. "Fellow Writers in a Cotswold Village." *The Life and Work of Barbara Pym.* Salwak 34–39.

Phillips, Robert. *Denton Welch.* Twayne's English Authors Series 163. New York: Twayne, 1974.

———. "Narrow, Splendid Work." Review of *A Few Green Leaves. Commonweal* 8 May 1981: 284–85.

Pilgrim, Anne C. "Teaching the Novels of Barbara Pym and Jane Austen." *Barbara Pym Newsletter* 4.2 (1989): 12.

Pippett, Aileen. "Observers Observed." Review of *Less Than Angels*. *New York Times Book Review* 31 Mar. 1957: 33.

Pym, Barbara. *An Academic Question*. Ed. Hazel Holt. London: Macmillan; New York: Dutton, 1986.

———. *Civil to Strangers and Other Writings*. Ed. Hazel Holt. London: Macmillan, 1987; New York: Dutton, 1988.

———. *Crampton Hodnet*. London: Macmillan; New York: Dutton, 1985.

———. *Excellent Women*. 1952. London: Jonathan Cape; New York: Dutton, 1978.

———. *A Few Green Leaves*. London: Macmillan; New York: Dutton, 1980.

———. *A Glass of Blessings*. 1958. London: Jonathan Cape, 1977; New York: Dutton, 1980.

———. *Jane and Prudence*. 1953. London: Jonathan Cape, 1978; New York: Dutton, 1981.

———. *Less Than Angels*. 1955. London: Jonathan Cape, 1978; New York: Vanguard, 1957; Dutton, 1980.

———. *No Fond Return of Love*. 1961. London: Jonathan Cape, 1979; New York: Dutton, 1982.

———. *Quartet in Autumn*. London: Macmillan, 1977; New York: Dutton, 1978.

———. *Some Tame Gazelle*. 1950. London: Jonathan Cape, 1978; New York: Dutton, 1983.

———. *The Sweet Dove Died*. London: Macmillan, 1978; New York: Dutton, 1979.

———. *An Unsuitable Attachment*. Ed. Hazel Holt. London: Macmillan; New York: Dutton, 1982.

————. *A Very Private Eye: An Autobiography in Diaries and Letters.* Ed. Hazel Holt and Hilary Pym. London: Macmillan; New York: Dutton, 1984.

Pym, Hilary, and Honor Wyatt. *The Barbara Pym Cookbook.* New York: Dutton, 1988.

Radner, Sanford. "Barbara Pym's People." *Western Humanities Review* 39 (1985): 172–77.

Raphael, Isabel. "Cool Pym's Number Seven." Review of *An Academic Question. Times* [London] 31 July 1986: 11.

"Reputations Revisited . . . ." *Times Literary Supplement* 21 Jan. 1977: 66–67.

Review of *An Academic Question. New Yorker* 3 Nov. 1986: 165.

Review of *The Barbara Pym Cookbook,* by Hilary Pym and Honor Wyatt. *New York Times Book Review* 4 Dec. 1988: 86.

Review of *The Barbara Pym Cookbook,* by Hilary Pym and Honor Wyatt. *Publishers Weekly* 16 Sept. 1988: 81.

Review of *Civil to Strangers and Other Writings. Kirkus Reviews* 1 Nov. 1987: 1537.

Review of *Civil to Strangers and Other Writings. New Yorker* 22 Feb. 1988: 117.

Review of *Excellent Women. Church Times* 16 May 1952.

Review of *Less Than Angels. Catholic World* Sept. 1957: 473.

Review of *A Very Private Eye. New Yorker* 16 July 1984: 91–92.

Rosenstein, Harriet. "Have You Discovered Barbara Pym Yet?" Review of *Excellent Women, Quartet in Autumn,* and *The Sweet Dove Died. Ms.* May 1979: 33–35.

Rossen, Janice, ed. *Independent Women: The Function of Gender in the Novels of Barbara Pym.* Brighton, England: Harvester; New York: St. Martin's, 1988.

———. "Love in the Great Libraries: Oxford in the Work of Barbara Pym." *Journal of Modern Literature* 12 (1985): 277–96.

———. "On Not Being Jane Eyre." *Independent Women: The Function of Gender in the Novels of Barbara Pym.* Rossen 137–56.

———. "The Pym Papers." *The Life and Work of Barbara Pym.* Salwak 156–67.

———. *The World of Barbara Pym.* London: Macmillan; New York: St. Martin's, 1987.

Roth, Laura Kathleen Johnson. *Performance Considerations for the Adaptation of Selected Barbara Pym Novels for Chamber Theatre Production.* Diss. University of Texas at Austin, 1989. Ann Arbor, MI: UMI, 1989. 8920829.

Rowse, A. L. "Austen mini?" Review of *Excellent Women* and *A Glass of Blessings. Punch* 19 Oct. 1977: 732–34.

———. "Miss Pym and Miss Austen." *The Life and Work of Barbara Pym.* Salwak 64–71.

Rubenstein, Jill. "Comedy and Consolation in the Novels of Barbara Pym." *Renascence* 42 (1990): 173–83.

———. " 'For the Ovaltine Had Loosened Her Tongue': Failures of Speech in Barbara Pym's *Less Than Angels.*" *Modern Fiction Studies* 32 (1986): 573–80.

Rubin, Merle. "A Cooler, Tougher Woman." Review of *An Academic Question. New York Times Book Review* 7 Sept. 1986: 25.

Saar, Doreen Alvarez. "Irony from a Female Perspective: A Study of the Early Novels of Barbara Pym." *West Virginia University Philological Papers* 33 (1987): 68–75.

———. Review of *The Barbara Pym Cookbook,* by Hilary Pym and Honor Wyatt. *Barbara Pym Newsletter* 4.1 (1989): 9–10.

Sadler, Lynn Veach. "Drabbling in Pym's Garden of the Critics: Asserting One's World." *Barbara Pym Newsletter* 3.1 (1988): 1–4.

――――. "Spinsters, Non-spinsters, and Men in the World of Barbara Pym." *Critique* 26 (1985): 141–54.

Salwak, Dale. *Barbara Pym: A Reference Guide.* Boston: G. K. Hall, 1991.

――――, ed. *The Life and Work of Barbara Pym.* London: Macmillan; Iowa City: University of Iowa Press, 1987.

Satchell, Tim. "From Beyond." Review of *An Academic Question. Books and Bookmen* Aug. 1986: 4.

Schmidt, Daniel W. "Excellent Women and the Code of Suitability." *Barbara Pym Newsletter* 6.1,2 (1992): 7–9.

Schofield, Mary Anne. "Well-Fed or Well-Loved? Patterns of Cooking and Eating in the Novels of Barbara Pym." *University of Windsor Review* 18.2 (1985): 1–8.

Schulz, Muriel. "The Novelist as Anthropologist." *The Life and Work of Barbara Pym.* Salwak 101–19.

Seymour, Miranda. "Spinsters in Their Prime." Review of *Crampton Hodnet. Times Literary Supplement* 28 June 1985: 720.

Shapiro, Laura. Review of *An Academic Question. Newsweek* 10 Nov. 1986: 84.

Sherwood, Rhoda Irene. *"A Special Kind of Double"*: Sisters in British and American Fiction. Diss. University of Wisconsin, 1987. Ann Arbor, MI: UMI, 1987. 8725284.

Shrimpton, Nicholas. "Bucolic Bones." Review of *A Few Green Leaves. New Statesman* 15 Aug. 1980: 17–18.

Singer, June. *Androgyny: Toward a New Theory of Sexuality.* New York: Anchor, 1976.

Slung, Michele. "Barbara Pym: The Quiet Pleasure of Her Company." Review of *Civil to Strangers and Other Writings. Washington Post Book World* 17 Jan. 1988: 3, 13.

Smith, Robert. "How Pleasant to Know Miss Pym." *Ariel: A Review of*

International English Literature 2.4 (1971): 63–68. Rpt. in *The Life and Work of Barbara Pym*. Salwak 58–63.

———. "Remembering Barbara Pym." *Independent Women: The Function of Gender in the Novels of Barbara Pym*. Rossen 159–63.

Snow, Lotus. "Literary Allusions in the Novels." *The Life and Work of Barbara Pym*. Salwak 120–41. Rpt. as " 'Some Sweet Smattering of Culture': Literary Allusions in the Novels." *One Little Room an Everywhere: The Novels of Barbara Pym*. Snow 31–54.

———. *One Little Room an Everywhere: The Novels of Barbara Pym*. Orono, ME: Puckerbrush, 1987.

Stanley, Isabel Ashe Bonnyman. *The Anglican Clergy in the Novels of Barbara Pym*. Diss. University of Tennessee, 1991. Ann Arbor, MI: UMI, 1991. 9121756.

Stetz, Margaret Diane. "*Quartet in Autumn:* New Light on Barbara Pym as a Modernist." *Arizona Quarterly* 41 (1985): 24–37.

Stovel, Bruce. "Subjective to Objective: A Career Pattern in Jane Austen, George Eliot, and Contemporary Women Novelists." *Ariel* 18 (1987): 55–61.

Strauss-Noll, Mary. "Love and Marriage in the Novels." *The Life and Work of Barbara Pym*. Salwak 72–87.

Strouse, Jean. "Elegant Surgery." Review of *Less Than Angels*. *Newsweek* 19 Jan. 1981: 84.

Stuttaford, Genevieve. Review of *An Academic Question*. *Publishers Weekly* 11 July 1986: 54.

Taliafero, Frances. Review of *Some Tame Gazelle*. *Harpers* Aug. 1983: 74–75.

Till, Roger. "Coincidence in a Bookshop." *Independent Women: The Function of Gender in the Novels of Barbara Pym*. Rossen 164–68.

Tomalin, Claire. "Wife Support System." Review of *Civil to Strangers and Other Writings*. *Observer* 15 Nov. 1987: 26.

Toulson, Shirley. Review of *The Sweet Dove Died. British Book News* Oct. 1978: 843.

"Trouble Brewing." Review of *Less Than Angels. Times Literary Supplement* 18 Nov. 1955: 685.

Tyler, Anne. Foreword. *Excellent Women, Jane and Prudence, An Unsuitable Attachment.* By Barbara Pym. New York: Harper and Row, 1984. v-xviii.

————. Review of *No Fond Return of Love. New York Times Book Review* 13 Feb. 1983: 1, 22.

Updike, John. "Lem and Pym." Review of *Excellent Women* and *Quartet in Autumn. New Yorker* 26 Feb. 1979: 116–20. Rpt. in *Hugging the Shore: Essays and Criticism.* By Updike. New York: Knopf, 1983. 516–25.

Vogel, Christine B. "A Sip of Pym's Number One." Review of *Some Tame Gazelle. Washington Post Book World* 21 Aug. 1983: 1, 14.

Wade, Rosalind. "Quarterly Fiction Review." Review of *Excellent Women, Glass of Blessings,* and *Quartet in Autumn. Contemporary Review* 232 (1978): 45–46.

Wall, Stephen. "Being Splendid." Review of *Civil to Strangers; The Pleasure of Miss Pym,* by Charles Burkhart; *The World of Barbara Pym,* by Janice Rossen; and *The Life and Work of Barbara Pym,* ed. Dale Salwak. *London Review of Books* 3 Mar. 1988: 10–11.

Waugh, Harriet. "Promoting the Pym Industry." Review of *An Academic Question. Illustrated London News* Oct. 1986: 80–81.

Waxman, Barbara Frey. "Barbara Pym's Retired Women: Intoxicating Choices and Spinsterly Love." *From the Hearth to the Open Road: A Feminist Study of Aging in Contemporary Literature.* New York: Greenwood, 1990. 105–19.

"Ways of Women." Review of *A Glass of Blessings. Times Literary Supplement* 23 May 1958: 281.

Weld, Annette. *Barbara Pym and the Novel of Manners.* London: Macmillan; New York: St. Martin's, 1992.

Weld, Annette Forker. *Barbara Pym and the Novel of Manners.* Diss. University of Rochester, 1989. Ann Arbor, MI: UMI, 1989. 8926064.

White, Antonia. "New Novels." Review of *Some Tame Gazelle. New Statesman and Nation* 1 July 1950: 21–22.

Whitney, Carol Wilkinson. " 'Women Are So Terrifying These Days': Fear Between the Sexes in the World of Barbara Pym." *Essays in Literature* 16 (1989): 71–84.

Wickenden, Dan. "Fun Among Anthropologists." Review of *Less Than Angels. New York Herald Tribune Book Review* 5 May 1957: 3.

Widmayer, Richard A. Review of *A Very Private Eye. Rocky Mountain Review of Language and Literature* 39 (1985): 77–79.

Wilson, A. N. "Thinking of Being Them." Review of *A Few Green Leaves. Times Literary Supplement* 18 July 1980: 799. Rpt. in "Barbara Pym." *Pen Friends from Porlock.* By Wilson. London: Hamish Hamilton, 1988. 112–20.

Winnett, Susan. "Coming Unstrung: Women, Men, Narrative, and Principles of Pleasure." *PMLA* 105 (1990): 505–18.

"Women of Character." Review of *Some Tame Gazelle. Times Literary Supplement* 7 July 1950: 417.

Woolf, Virginia. *Moments of Being.* Ed. Jeanne Schulkind. 2nd ed. Orlando, FL: Harcourt Brace Jovanovich, 1976.

Wyatt-Brown, Anne M. *Barbara Pym: A Critical Biography.* Columbia: University of Missouri Press, 1992.

———. "Ellipsis, Eccentricity and Evasion in the Diaries of Barbara Pym." *Independent Women: The Function of Gender in the Novels of Barbara Pym.* Rossen 21–49.

Wymard, Eleanor B. "Barbara Pym on Organized Religion: A Case of Folly." *Month* Aug./Sept. 1987: 318.

———. "Characters in Search of Order and Ceremony: Secular Faith of Barbara Pym." *Commonweal* 13 Jan. 1984: 19–21.

ABOUT THE AUTHOR

ORPHIA JANE ALLEN (Ph.D., University of Oklahoma, Norman, OK; B.A. and M.A., New Mexico State University, Las Cruces, NM) is Associate Professor of English and Director of Graduate Studies in the English Department at New Mexico State University. She teaches courses in women's studies, women's autobiographical writing, professional writing, and publications management. Her professional publications include articles in *Genre, Modern Fiction Studies, Latin American Literary Review,* and the *Doris Lessing Newsletter.*